Be a Blessing

Be a Blessing

The Theology of Work in the
Narrative of Genesis

Elizabeth Ellen Ostring

WITH A FOREWORD BY
Richard M. Davidson

Doctoral dissertation presented
under the auspices of Avondale
College of Higher Education

Cooranbong, Australia

WIPF & STOCK · Eugene, Oregon

BE A BLESSING
The Theology of Work in the Narrative of Genesis

Copyright © 2016 Elizabeth Ellen Ostring. All rights reserved. Except for brief quotations in critical publications or reviews, no part of this book may be reproduced in any manner without prior written permission from the publisher. Write: Permissions, Wipf and Stock Publishers, 199 W. 8th Ave., Suite 3, Eugene, OR 97401.

Wipf & Stock
An Imprint of Wipf and Stock Publishers
199 W. 8th Ave., Suite 3
Eugene, OR 97401

www.wipfandstock.com

PAPERBACK ISBN: 978-1-4982-7870-6
HARDCOVER ISBN: 978-1-4982-7872-0

Scripture quotations unless otherwise marked are from The Holy Bible, English Standard Version (ESV), copyright© 2001 by Crossway Bibles. A publishing ministry of Good News Bibles. Used by permission. All rights reserved.

Scripture Quotations marked NKJV are from the New King James version. Copyright© 1982 by Thomas Nelson, Inc. Used by permission. All right reserved.

Manufactured in the U.S.A.

This book is dedicated to my beloved husband,
Sven Anders Roland Ostring

Contents

List of Tables | viii
Foreword by Richard M. Davidson | ix
Acknowledgments | xi
Introduction | xiii

1 Research Methods | 1
2 Social History Background of Theologies of Work | 13
3 Biblical Foundations for Contemporary Theologies of Work | 37
4 General Concepts from Genesis Literature | 55
5 God's Labor of Love: Creation and the Fall, Genesis 1:1—3:24 | 60
6 Doing It Our Way: The Primordial Curses, Genesis 3:14—11:26 | 93
7 Blessing: The Patriarchal Narrative Signature Tune | 125
8 The Literary Structure of Genesis | 141
9 The Call and Life of Abraham, Genesis 12:1—25:10 | 162
10 Jacob the Worker, Genesis 25:19—50:14 | 192
11 The Epiphany of Joseph, Genesis 37:1—50:26 | 222
12 Conclusions | 242

Bibliography | 253

Tables

1 Elohim's Work, Genesis 1:1—2:4a | 63
2 Yahweh Elohim's Work, Genesis 2:4b–25 | 67
3 Yahweh Elohim's Work, Genesis 3:1–24 | 90
4 Schematic Presentation of All Primordial Curses, Genesis 3–11 | 122
5 Blessing | 135
6 Genesis Begins and Ends with a Work of God | 151
7 Abraham's Work | 174
8 Sarah's Work (with Hagar) | 184
9 The Oldest Servant's Work | 188
10 Isaac's Work | 193
11 Rebekah's Varied Work | 197
12 Jacob's Work | 200
13 Commercial Transactions in the Jacob Narrative | 204
14 Laban's Work | 210
15 Rachel and Leah's Work (with Bilhah and Zilpah) | 212
16 Judah's Work (with Tamar) | 218
17 Joseph's Work | 226

Foreword

It gives me great pleasure to write the foreword to this study by Elizabeth Ostring on the theology of human work. Ostring's research clearly makes an original contribution to theological learning. To my knowledge, no one else has examined in depth the book of Genesis to discover the biblical theology of human work that emerges from this foundational text, and no one has done such a thorough evaluation of the co-creationist theology of human work based upon biblical data. This work is highly original. The originality is not confined to the biblical theology of work, but also encompasses original analysis of the literary structure of Genesis and provides many new insights into the narrative flow of the book.

In my view, Dr. Ostring has made an outstanding contribution to biblical studies in setting forth a solid biblical theology of human work based upon the foundational book of Genesis. She has forcefully argued that human work is not only one major theme of Genesis among others, but that understanding human endeavor in relation to God's work is central to the whole message of the book of Genesis.

In general, I have found this study to represent a very high level of scholarship and excellent quality of content. While I occasionally might have argued for a slightly different emphasis of the narratives, overall there is very good exegetical-theological substantiation of the conclusions presented.

This monograph reveals a remarkable breadth of theoretical and substantive knowledge of the research topic, including the background of understanding in the flow of church history, the current debate in theological and biblical circles, and the understanding of the biblical text and the principles of narratology. Secondary literature is used responsibly and adequately.

The study is well organized, with clear headings revealing the sequence and development of arguments. The writing is clear and scholarly, without being stuffy or obtuse. There is a clear and methodical line of thinking, and a sustained and cohesive line of argument throughout. The work carries the reader along from beginning to end, with well-structured and clearly demarcated sections and easy-to-follow and well-reasoned argumentation.

Ostring makes very good use of the principles of narrative analysis in analyzing the narratives of Genesis. She consistently applies these principles throughout her research, citing authorities on the narratives of Genesis to support her conclusions. Overall, I found her analytical techniques consistent with the research topic.

The author covers much ground in the review of literature, and in the tracing of this biblical theme throughout Genesis, and yet presents this material in a clear and convincing manner for the most part. At times the material is presented in schematic fashion, but such is inevitable as she covers such a large amount of ground in one monograph. There is an excellent component of analysis of the data and clear communication of the results of the research.

A concluding section of this book places the study in the larger context of understanding the nature and significance of human work for a Christian. Ostring's conclusions, based upon solid biblical evidence, are programmatic for a radical reassessment of the meaning of human work in various modern Christian organizations. Implications of this study for the practice of human endeavor are indeed far-reaching and highly significant.

Ostring's background as a medical practitioner and long-time missionary as well as biblical theologian gives her "fresh eyes" to look at the issue of human work from a wider life-perspective than biblical scholars without such background could have done. I salute Dr. Ostring for an incisive and insightful study on a topic of crucial contemporary relevance, and also express appreciation to Steven Thompson and Laurence Turner for their expert guidance in supervising the doctoral research upon which this monograph is based.

—Richard M. Davidson
Andrews University

Acknowledgments

I would like to acknowledge with gratitude the many thousands of patients, friends, and family who contributed to my awareness of the significance of work in human lives. These persons' presence in my life has been God's special blessing to me.

"Thank you" seems bland words that do not begin to express my appreciation for the support of my supervisor Dr. Steven Thompson. With great patience and courtesy he has gently tutored someone completely unlearned in his discipline, given me tools to work with, and I hope he will feel rewarded for his effort. He inspired me to study Hebrew and to write with precision. My associate supervisor in London, Dr. Laurence Turner, challenged my conventional thinking and nudged me to discover new approaches. I am also very grateful for the unexpected scholarship given me by Avondale College of Higher Education that encouraged the continuation of this study.

It would be impossible to record all those who have helped me, but especially significant are: Pr. Alistair Mackenzie, of Laidlaw College in Christchurch, who shared unstintingly his own research; Michelle Downs, Lynelle Waring, Roberta Matai, my children Sven and Marilyn, Genevieve and Eewei (especially Sven and Eewei), who all patiently helped with the word processing aspects of the study; and my receptionist Yvonne van Eerden whose help went far beyond the call of duty. The immeasurable support of my husband, Dr. Roland Ostring, could only be from love. And for supplying me with all of the above, a measure of health, and particularly safety during very the difficult times of the Christchurch earthquakes, I thank God from the bottom of my heart.

Introduction

AFTER DECADES OF WORKING with people involved in all activities of life, my question, "What contribution could or did Christian theology offer every day human work?" seemed to be answered historically by varying concepts related mainly to changes in social philosophy, and currently by Christian theologies perceived as fraught with inadequacy.

Calvin Redekop observed, "Work can be almost infinitely defined. The most elemental definition refers to the energy exerted to achieve a desired goal."[1] The definition of work accepted in this study is: "Work is purposeful, goal-directed human activity requiring effort, either physical or mental, whether self-directed or externally directed." This agrees with the *New Catholic Encyclopedia* definition: "Work is human activity designed to accomplish something needed and valued in civilized life."[2] Although twenty-first century society tends to limit work to employment, this is not satisfactory because it excludes important contributions people make in household duties, the care of children, the sick, the elderly, preparation of nutritious food, and many other socially important activities.

Statement of Study

Using a narrative literary approach all of Genesis is explored, and the theology of work that emerges from this close examination is developed. This is compared with current Christian theologies of work, especially that known as co-creationism. The justification for basing a biblical theology of work on Genesis is provided by Bill Arnold who wrote, "Genesis is above all a theological book. Its theological propositions and convictions are foundational

1. Redekop, "Promise of Work," 2.
2. *New Catholic Encyclopedia*, vol. 14, s.v. "Work," 1015.

for the rest of the Bible."[3] The "rest of the Bible" means Genesis is the first and foundational book for both the Jewish and Christian Bibles. Kenneth Mathews endorsed this view, "Genesis stands second to none in its importance for proclaiming 'the whole will of God' (Acts 20:27) . . . Can we possibly understand Law and Gospel without Genesis? Do we have Matthew and Luke's historical Gospel without their Genesis? Does not Paul's Galatians and Romans rely on Adam and Abraham?"[4] Significantly, Ecclesiastes, which plainly deals with human work, is "probably the biblical book that refers or alludes most to Genesis."[5]

Genesis Interest in Work

Genesis commences with a magnificent portrayal of the work of God, and human work is introduced in the Edenic phase of the narrative. Examining the entire Genesis narrative determines whether or not there were significant changes in the work situation of humanity after expulsion from the Garden of Eden, in the primordial or patriarchal age. Genesis, it will be shown, presents two approaches to human work. It is noted that human work, both the original tilling of the soil and the reproduction of humanity, seems to be highlighted by the curses applied to the ground and in the pain of childbirth, although the curse was not the introduction of either of these activities. The role of work in the first three chapters in Genesis provides the basis for critiquing the co-creationist theology of work. The primordial narrative provides material for evaluating human work following the expulsion from Eden. The patriarchal narratives in the remainder of Genesis provide the basis to illuminate appropriate approaches to work when the people of God are waiting for him to act.

Work and Blessing

The Tower narrative of Genesis 11 was recognized by von Rad[6] and others as the significant culmination of the primordial narrative, and forms the backdrop to the call of Abram. It is argued that the work situation instigated by God in the creation narratives and to be performed under God's blessing is not sustained in the curse-dominated primordial narrative, which cul-

---

3. Arnold, *Genesis*, 18–19.
4. Mathews, *Genesis 1–11:26*, 22–23.
5. Doukhan, *Ecclesiastes: All is Vanity*, 14.
6. Rad, *Genesis: A Commentary*, 134.

minates in the Tower pericope. The call of Abram in Genesis 12 suggests a different approach to ordinary, every-day work from that of the Tower builders, a return to the creation mandate of blessing.

The work implications of the call of Abraham from the self-focused Tower of Babel work ethic to one that reiterates and reinstates God's creation intentions of blessing and relationship are explored. The call of Abraham emphasizes that he and his offspring are to bless, are commanded to bless, "all the families of earth" (Gen 12:3), but they can accomplish blessing only through relationship with God, the source of blessing. The patriarchal narratives show humans struggle to work with and wait for God, and demonstrate that human efforts to accelerate divinely promised blessing tend to result in delayed blessing and relational distress. The concluding Joseph novella offers insights regarding human achievement. The notable success he achieved and the blessing he shared with his family and adopted country is repeatedly attributed as entirely due to the blessing of God. Thus, the culminating Joseph narrative offers significant insights into both the opportunities for, and limits to, human work, and brings the theology of work in the Genesis narrative to a cohesive conclusion.

Work and Worship

Several recent theologies of work[7] make a strong connection between human work and worship. This connection between work and worship is also demonstrated in the passages all Christians recognize as the guide for daily living: the Ten Commandments (Exod 20:1–17; Deut 5:6–21). By making a connection between work and the blessing promised to and commanded from Abram by God, the study makes a stronger connection between work and worship than simply the human need for rest. The Genesis portrayal of worship is not creedal or cultic, but is encapsulated in the phrase "walking with God" (Gen 5:22, 6:9, 17:1), a term that implies regular connection with God rather than an intermittent worship "act."

Chiastic Structure of Genesis

It is argued that the complete book of Genesis has the classic Torah form of narrative, that is, the conclusion reflects the opening,[8] known as inclu-

---

7. For example Kaiser, *Theology of Work*, 457ff.; Pope John Paul II, "Laborem Exercens," sections 24–27; Stott, *New Issues Facing Christians*, 189; Jensen, *Responsive Labor*, 108; Keller, *Every Good Endeavor*, 233–41.

8. Cassuto, *Commentary on Genesis (Part Two)*, 190.

sion. This reveals Genesis has an overall chiastic structure that illuminates what was expected of Adam, and reiterated to Abram and his immediate descendants. This structure links the various pericopes to the theme of work and blessing and has implications for contemporary work, and for developing a theology of work from the Genesis narrative. The chiastic structure highlights the work of God and the need for humanity to recognize their dependence on him and therefore be willing to renounce claim to their own achievements. The prologue shows God's work is done in an atmosphere of relationship and blessing. The theme of work is accompanied by a significant theme of curse in the primordial narratives and of blessing in the patriarchal. The curses of the primordial narrative portray the negative results of human work unaided by divine guidance. They provide the warrant to argue against the concept that all human work can be regarded as fulfilling the dominion given by God. They also offer the insight needed to illuminate the divine objections being made. The theology that emerges from Genesis is described as a blessed relationship theology of work, with the focus on a good relationship with God, and the privilege of co-operating with him to achieve the divinely intended good.

The Genesis Theology of Work Compared

The Genesis theology is compared with developments in Christian theologies of human work. The co-creationist theology is used as representative of contemporary theologies of work, and the primary base for comparison, which forms the second component of the thesis. Lee Hardy observed that the official Roman Catholic theology of work, co-creation, coincides with current mainline Protestant positions at every major point.[9] Whereas at the Reformation there was a divide between the Roman Catholic and Protestant theologies of work, this was narrowed by the 1891 encyclical *Rerum Novarum* of Pope Leo XIII,[10] and virtually closed by deliberations in Vatican II, 1962–65. Timothy Keller has recently endorsed Hardy's assessment that there is essential agreement between Roman Catholic and Protestant theologies of work.[11] The co-creationist theology of work is portrayed against the background of social thinking in which it has emerged and been refined. Therefore as an integral third part of the study, a history of Christian theologies of work is presented. This shows the tendency for theologies of work to be influenced more by social philosophies than biblical input.

9. Hardy, *Fabric of This World*, 68, 76.
10. Pope Leo XIII, "Rerum Novarum."
11. Keller, *Every Good Endeavor*, 257.

INTRODUCTION xvii

Summary of Current Theologies of Work

In 1974, Gideon Goosen made a summary, still valid, of the various theologies of work identified over the last fifty or sixty years. He showed that current theologies of work have three fundamental avenues of approach.[12]

The Penitential Theology of Work

The penitential theology of work is the traditional mediaeval Christian view, based on the concept that to work in the "sweat of your face" was the punishment given by God for original sin (Gen 3:19). Although contemporary theologians discredit this theology because they recognize that work was given to humanity prior to the fall (Gen 2:15), its long history means this theology is still accepted by many Christians. Exponents of the penitential view include Thomas Aquinas, St. Benedict, and Augustine.[13] They made much of Christ's words of commendation to Mary who sat at Jesus' feet listening, and his apparently negative advice to Martha and her serving.

The [Co-]creationist Theology of Work

The [co-]creationist theology of work is currently the official position of the Roman Catholic Church.[14] According to Pope John Paul II, this view is based on the biblical mandate to have dominion over the earth and bring it into subjection (Gen 1:26–28), and to cultivate and care for it (Gen 2:15).[15] Goosen elaborated, "Man's work is . . . seen as cooperation with God in the *continuing act of creation* and dominating matter. Man is free to shape and determine creation which has been entrusted to him, and in the exercise of this *sovereignty over creation he is truly the 'image' of God*," emphasis supplied. Goosen, although sympathetic to co-creationism, recognized that the "exciting view of the [co-]creationist" has to be tempered by the reality of imperfection, and some work (he suggests as examples those of a repair mechanic or street sweeper) does not fit easily into the co-creationist view.[16]

---

12. Goosen, *Theology of Work*, 65.
13. See Aquinas, *Summa Theologiae*; St Benedict, *Rule of St Benedict*.
14. Goosen used the term "creationist," but for the sake of consistency in this thesis [co-] has been added.
15. John Paul II, *Laborem Exercens*, section 4
16. Goosen, *Theology of Work*, 68–69.

The Eschatological Theology of Work

Goosen considered that this theology asks, "In what way can human activities be a preparation for what is to come?" and whether human work will have any value after death. It has gained support from Protestant theologians over the last 50 years, notably Miroslav Volf.[17] Goosen suggested the eschatological theology of work "has the Second Coming of Christ as its starting point, and the new heaven and earth as its culmination."[18] This transforming work is essentially the same as that envisioned in co-creation. Co-creationism tends to an a-millennial view of the Second Coming, whereas the eschatological theology has a post-millennial, with human work under the direction of the Holy Spirit bringing about the utopian conditions that will allow Christ to return.

Significance of Study

This study offers a theology of work that responds to the difficulties perceived in the current theologies of work and therefore is of value for all Christians. The "Faith at Work" movement indicates there is grassroots interest in a practical theology of work.[19] The theology of work herein presented is practical, and it does not presuppose an amillennial or postmillennial eschatology, as do the current theologies work. Furthermore, the concept of working in blessing enables work and worship to be integrated into a meaningful whole in the lives of God's people.

---

17. See for example Volf, *Work in the Spirit*; Cosden, *Theology of Work*.
18. Goosen, *Theology of Work*, 69.
19. Miller, *God at Work*.

1

Research Methods

AN ECLECTIC APPROACH WAS used in this study, as no single method allowed full development of the material. Gerhard Hasel identified ten methods for studying the biblical theology of the Old Testament,[1] and John Reumann called the field "kaleidoscopic."[2] James Mead offered a simplified three-pronged approach to biblical theology, consisting of content (sub-classified as systematic/doctrinal, cross-section/central/theme topics, and story/narrative), shape, and perspective.[3] Within Mead's scheme this study focuses on content.

Mead stated the "narrative/story method [of biblical theology] studies the current form itself [that is, accepts the canon as final form] and identifies the theological content in that form. Biblical theology thus becomes a narrative theology, with its method being informed by literary criticism of the 'story' rather than by historical criticism of the origin and form of its sources."[4] Mead pointed out the essential concepts of biblical theology pertinent for this study, noting it means "exploring the many contexts of the Bible, such as its history and culture, its languages and literary forms, the perspectives of its authors, the arrangement of its writing, and the interpretation of individual passages and books . . . these contexts relate in some way to questions about the theological meaning or message of the Bible."[5] Thus, although this inquiry studies the topic of work in Genesis, drawing on language and literary forms, the perspective of its author, the arrangement of its writing, and the interpretation of individual passages, it ultimately attempts to find the foundational theological concept of human

1. Hasel, *Old Testament Theology*, 38–114.
2. Reumann, "Introduction: Whither Biblical Theology," in *Promise and Practice*, 4.
3. Mead, *Biblical Theology*, 124.
4. Ibid., 135.
5. Ibid., 1.

work informing the material. Mead asked, "Is biblical theology concerned only with the describing of theological concepts within the Bible, or is it also concerned with articulating theological views that become authoritative standards (i.e., norms) for today?"[6] To discover the biblical norm for work in the foundational Genesis narrative, and then to use this to evaluate current theologies ("authoritative standards") of work is the primary aim of this study.

However, first dealt with in the study is the appraisal of the various theologies of work and their social history background during the two-thousand-year history of Christianity, with special attention to the last fifty years.

Social History Background of Theologies of Work

While not the primary focus of this study, the history of theologies of work and the social situations under which they developed is an important backdrop to it. This is integrated into the study to build an understanding of the social and cultural currents impacting the reception of the Genesis texts and their use in the development of current Christian theologies of work.[7] It is asserted that Christian theologies of work have tended to reflect the social milieu of the theologians formulating them. For example, the original Christian theology of work revealed the Jewish background of the first Christians, but this changed to the penitential theology of work when Greek thinking dominated the church. A wide variety of sources were utilized for this aspect of the study; three key sources were William Platcher,[8] Niall Ferguson,[9] and Richard Tawney.[10]

The Genesis Narrative

Genesis is described as narrative, indicating it is more than bare facts. In narrative, "the way in which an episode is related is as important as the events related."[11] A story "must be more than an enumeration of events in

6. Ibid., 7.
7. Koselleck, *Futures Past*, 73.
8. Placher, *Callings*.
9. Ferguson, *Ascent of Money*.
10. Tawney, *Religion and the Rise*.
11. Marguerat and Bourquin, *How to Read Bible Stories*, 22.

serial order; it must organize them into an intelligible whole, of a sort that we can always ask what is the 'thought' of this story."[12] Thus, it is not just the information shared in Genesis, but the arrangement of its material that offers insight into its ideas. Brevard Childs observed that the literary approach to biblical study was one of the most important developments in recent decades, although he expressed concern about "reading the Bible not as sacred literature but as a 'classic' devoid of authoritative role."[13] He noted that Meir Sternberg, a pioneer in the literary approach to biblical material, observed, "Were the [biblical] narratives written or read as fiction, then God would turn from the lord of history into a creature of the imagination with the most disastrous results."[14] These concerns are significant, but do not exclude the value of a literary approach, as shown by V. Phillips Long.[15]

Robert Alter's Contribution

Robert Alter, an expert on literary narrative, pioneered a literary approach to Genesis, although he did not recognize it as divinely inspired.[16] He criticized translations of Genesis for not giving a true presentation of the "semantic nuances and lively orchestration of literary effects of the Hebrew."[17] This he attributed to "a shaky sense of English" in modern translations, and for the King James Version, a "shaky sense of Hebrew."[18] Alter insisted on appreciating that the actual literary structure of Genesis is essential to understand its ideas and teaching.

Alter observed some special aspects of biblical narrative that are utilized in this study. First is the importance of dialogue. Alter stated: "direct speech is made the chief instrument for revealing . . ."[19] and "[t]he biblical scene . . . is composed almost entirely as a verbal intercourse, with the assumption that what is significant about a character, at least for a particular narrative juncture, can be manifested almost entirely in the character's

---

12. Ricoeur, *From Text to Action*, 3.
13. Childs, *Biblical Theology*, 20.
14. Sternberg, *Poetics of Biblical Narrative*, 32.
15. See the argument in the following: Long, *Art of Biblical History*; Long, "Historiography of the OT."
16. Alter, *Art of Biblical Narrative*, 24.
17. Alter, *Genesis: Translation and Commentary*, ix.
18. Ibid.
19. Ibid., 66–87.

speech."[20] Another important biblical narrative technique is repetition.[21] This includes not only repeated phrases, sentences and speeches, small variations in which that are important and revealing, but also such things as the *leitwort*, motif, theme, sequence of actions, and type-scene.[22]

Biblical Narrative as Theology

Examination of the narratives of Genesis forms the unique contribution of this study towards the development of a theology of work, so the tools of narratival theology are utilized. Marvin Pate's group showed that narrative is a serviceable tool for developing theology. Pate and his co-authors observed, "Biblical theology . . . first seeks to reconstruct the individual theologies of the writings of the Bible. The accent in such a discipline is on the particular contribution to theology of the book or books in question,"[23] which observation is pertinent to the present study. John Goldingay has produced a three-volume work of "narrative theology" describing the story of the Old Testament.[24] He stated, "Old Testament faith expresses itself initially in narrative. The main bulk of the Old Testament is a narrative account of Israel's story and God's involvement in it . . . theological reflection on its gospel needs to work with its narrative form."[25]

Laurence Turner applied a narrative approach to the study of Genesis, and noted that "Narratives in general have several ways of alerting readers to what is likely to transpire in the story as it unfolds, or how to make sense out of what they have just read, and Genesis itself uses several such conventions. For example, it prefaces some individual stories with headlines which give advance warning about the significance or meaning of the ensuing narrative, as in 22:1: 'After these things God tested Abraham.'"[26] Turner further noted, "Each of the four major narrative blocks which comprise the book (i.e., the primeval history and the stories of Abraham, Jacob, and Jacob's family) is prefaced by statements which either explicitly state what will happen, or suggest to the reader what the major elements of the plot are likely to be."[27]

20. Ibid., 70.
21. Ibid., 88.
22. Ibid., 95–96.
23. Pate et al., *Story of Israel*, 12.
24. Goldingay, *Old Testament Theology*, 3 vols.
25. Goldingay, *OT Theology: Israel's Gospel*, 28.
26. Turner, *Announcements of Plot*, 13.
27. Ibid.

Tod Linafelt pertinently observed Biblical literature has a "drastic economy of style" that makes it seem primitive when compared with other ancient world literature such as the *Iliad* and the *Odyssey*, and yet this is its distinctive literary style.[28] The meaning may not be accessible from a surface reading, and the terseness of the narrative forces the reader to negotiate many possible ways of imagining the characters' lives.[29]

Paul House thought that narrative approaches to theology might help postmodern readers understand the Bible in fresh ways.[30] He endorsed Long's assertions that some types of literary criticism can be applied to Old Testament narratives without questioning these texts' accuracy or authority,[31] a positive response to Childs' concerns regarding biblical authority, and he believed narrative analysis produces theological data that involves readers in the biblical story in an effective way.[32]

The implication of these assertions is that biblical narrative has value not only for the original readers, but also for contemporary ones. Goldingay noted that "Old Testament theology" could mean simply the thought world and faith held by the authors of the Old Testament, which would carry no implication for contemporary belief. But he alleged that Old Testament theology is actually an attempt not only to describe the faith of these Old Testament authors, but also to reflect on it, which suggests it has implications for contemporary living.[33] Thus, as illustration, whilst the nineteenth century philosophical theories of Marx and Engels may or may not be accepted as relevant for contemporary society, the nineteenth century Charles Dickens' narrative *Oliver Twist* still provides reflection relevant for contemporary situations of exploitation, child employment, and poverty.

Goldingay suggested there are two ways of helping people understand another person. One is a narrative of their life and achievements, and the other a description of their character and beliefs. He suggested one approach is not better than the other, but each achieves something the other cannot.[34] But, importantly, he noted that all "descriptions" (that is, the regulations of Torah, pronouncements of prophets, praises and prayers of the Psalms, and

---

28. Linafelt, "Prolegomena to Meaning," 65–71.
29. Ibid., 74.
30. House, "Examining the Narratives," 229.
31. See the argument: Long, *Art of Biblical History*; also Long, "Historiography of the OT," 145–75.
32. House, "Examining the Narratives," 230.
33. Goldingay, *OT Theology: Israel's Gospel*, 16–17.
34. Goldingay, *OT Theology: Israel's Faith*, 15.

more) of the Bible are set in the context of narrative.[35] M. Jay Wells noted that by using "figural presentation" (what I would prefer to call illustration), the "authors of biblical texts are not merely recording events" but are reflecting on them so as to use past events in a way that instructs future situations, with implication for contemporary application.[36]

However, to avoid inappropriate interpretation, the importance of recognizing to whom the text was originally directed is appreciated. "A text is essentially a message from an author to its first readers, which the author hopes would be understood and acted upon."[37] Thus while Genesis is now seen as a book about creation, the fall and the call of the patriarchs, it was positioned in the Hebrew Bible as the first book of the law, the *Torah*,[38] which implies it both had and has a fundamental teaching aspect.

Unfortunately, "in [biblical] narrative it is often unclear whether the writer is making an ethical comment at all: he may be describing an action because it happened, or because it was a link in a chain of events which lead to something significant."[39] The narrator in most biblical narrative is apparently omniscient, which for Sternberg indicated divine inspiration,[40] but for Robert Alter merely fiction.[41] Sternberg recognized that although the narrator's comments on the story may be important, they do not present the full view of the author, and the complete story needs to be examined.[42] Two examples of this would be "the Lord saw that the wickedness of man was great in the earth" (Gen 6:5), which needs to be seen in the context of the whole flood narrative; or the single-word comment that "Sarai *ill-treated* her [Hagar]" (Gen 16:6), which must be considered in the context of Sarai's desire to produce a son.[43] The narrative often presents several points of view in a single pericope, allowing the reader to sympathize with each person's outlook and avoid simple black and white judgments, for example the views of Isaac, Esau, Rebekah, and Jacob in the blessing scenes of Genesis 27.[44]

---

35. Goldingay, *OT Theology: Israel's Life*, 45.
36. Wells, "Figural Representation," 113–14.
37. Wenham, *Story as Torah*, 1.
38. Ibid., 2.
39. Ibid., 1–2.
40. Sternberg, *Poetics of Biblical Narrative*, 25–35.
41. Alter, *Art of Biblical Narrative*, 24.
42. Wenham, *Story as Torah*, 11.
43. Ibid., 14.
44. Ibid., 15.

An important aspect of narrative theology, therefore, is that individual stories must be seen in the context of complete books,[45] and a global approach to Genesis is the overall methodology of this study. Wenham noted that whereas Christian theologians have focused on chapters 1–11 of Genesis, and Jewish on chapters 12–50, the whole of Genesis needs to be considered. He suggested reading Genesis 1–11 as an introductory exposition that allows exposition of the remainder of the book,[46] noting that the patriarchal stories are nearly five times as long as the preceding primeval history, and this shows clearly where the author's[47] interest lies.[48]

Genesis begins by announcing a work of God, "In the beginning God created the heavens and the earth" (Gen 1:1), which indicates the possibility of a theme of work in the whole book. Ian Hart asserted this announcement indicates work is a major theme of Genesis,[49] and invited the reader to consider how all the stories relate to this concept.

Reception History

Another tool utilized in this study is reception history. "The reception history of the Bible comprises every single act or word of interpretation of that book (or books) over the course of three millennia."[50] Reception history thus examines the whole range of interpretations of biblical passages, and can be defined as a scholarly exercise consisting of selecting and collating the huge wealth of reception material in accordance with the particular interest of the researcher concerned. This study utilizes recognized scholarly essays, theologies, and papers (both Christian and Jewish) written on the Genesis narrative over the centuries, with a focus on those of the last fifty years. John Riches suggested a valuable reason for utilizing reception history is that it draws one into the debate about the meaning of a text by seeing what others have recognized.[51] The vast quantity of Genesis material is recognized, as well as the limited amount dealing with work.

---

45. Ibid., 17.
46. Ibid., 18–19.
47. Use of the term "author" rather than "redactor" is justified under the section dealing with difficulties of the study, specifically the Documentary Hypothesis. The term "redactor" suggests little intentional input, whereas the Genesis narrative shows both careful editing and arrangement of the material.
48. Wenham, *Story as Torah*, 37.
49. Hart, "Genesis 1:1—2:3 as a Prologue."
50. Roberts, "Introduction to the Oxford Handbook," 1.
51. Riches, "Why Write a Reception-Historical Commentary," 324.

Timothy Beal suggested that the impact of reception history on biblical studies is comparable to source criticism.[52] Donald A. Hagner observed that Luz's reception historical method may have revolutionary implications in the quest for a single objective meaning, namely, the original intention of the author, and believes this could be lost. Hagner was concerned that "new meanings" of a text could be placed on the same level as original meanings.[53] The value of Hagner's concern about the foundational nature of the original meaning of the text is appreciated, but the study simply attempts to recover the meaning of the text in its final form. The use of the whole Genesis text as a suitable basis for developing a theology of work has not been previously acknowledged, and therefore reception history in the context of the study is limited to a general use of textual material, and not one specific to a theology of work. It is recognized that the "Reception history of the Bible is not just a repository of readings . . . it is the record of a lived history, of the life of communities for whom theses texts provided direction and a sense of meaning . . ."[54]

Difficulties of the Study of the Theology of Work in Genesis

The purpose of the study is to develop a biblical theology of work that emerges from the Genesis narrative, and utilize this to evaluate current theologies of work. The goal is to ascertain whether Genesis material deals with the difficulties encountered in the co-creation theology of work, recognizing the foundational status of Genesis forms the warrant for this study. But there are several challenges to a study of the Genesis narrative and the evaluation of theologies of work, which include:

The Sheer Volume of Genesis Material

Mathews, whilst endorsing the value of Genesis studies, also noted a significant problem, "The scholarly literature concerning Genesis could be appropriately named 'Legion.'"[55] This makes a reception history of the material

---

52. Beal, "Reception History and Beyond," 359.

53. Hagner, Review of *Matthew 8–20*, 766–69, quoted in Roberts, "Introduction to the Oxford Handbook," 4.

54. Riches, "Reception History as a Challenge," 185.

55. Mathews, 22–23.

somewhat daunting. I must agree with Mathews' observation, as well as adding to it.

Theories of the Sources and Composition of Genesis

With the introduction of the Graf-Wellhausen Documentary Hypothesis and its increasing acceptance during the twentieth century, the "sources" of the Pentateuch are said to be J, E, P and D. Genesis is regarded as the product of a redactor writing late in Jewish history. This not only challenges the foundational nature of Genesis theology, but means reading it as a unity can be questioned. However, as early as 1934, Benno Jacob, and later in 1944, Umberto Cassuto, challenged this view.[56] Since then, there has been a chorus of scholarly voices arguing that Genesis has been in its final form long before there was any Christian use of it, and that most likely it is the carefully written product of an early rather than late single Jewish author, utilizing pre-existing information.

Wenham noted: "Recent scholarship has shown a marked preference for a simpler source-critical analysis of Genesis . . . Furthermore the general parallel between Gen 1–11 and the Sumerian flood story and the particular Babylonian parallels with the flood story suggest that the thematic unity of this biblical material antedates J or P. Most of the narratives in Genesis are so vivid and well told that it seems high-handed to deny their substantial unity and split them up into various much less fetching parts."[57] Mathews also provided a useful survey of the issues relating to this question,[58] and throughout his two-volume Genesis commentary presented evidence for, and made reference to, the unity of the Genesis narrative.[59] Turner observed that the documentary hypothesis is like eating a cake in order to reconstruct the recipe and assess the origins and quality of its ingredients, rather than simply savoring the cake as a finished product. He "admits to more than a mild skepticism."[60]

So whilst there may not be unanimity on this subject, there is now good support for recognizing Genesis as the product of a single author providing foundational thought for Jewish and Christian theology. The

---

56. Wenham, *Genesis 1–15*, xxvii.
57. Ibid., xxxvii.
58. Mathews, *Genesis 1—11:26*, 63, 68–85.
59. Ibid.
60. Turner, *Genesis*, 11–12.

position is taken that the text of Genesis, as it appears in the canon, is in its "final form," and the evolution of the text will not be addressed.

Apparent Limits to the Contribution of Scripture to a Theology of Work

It is recognized that there is some uneasiness with biblical ideas on the theology of work because of obvious differences in the work situations of the biblical narratives and contemporary life. Alistair Mackenzie suggested that Alan Richardson's widely acknowledged *The Biblical Doctrine of Work* is not strictly a theology of work because his study confined itself to a discussion of biblical material alone.[61] Volf claimed there is not enough material in the entire Bible to formulate a theology of work, and that biblical culture was so far removed from modern cultures as to make conclusions drawn inapplicable to modern work situations.[62] This approach was also adhered to by many Anglican ethical thinkers, such as J. H. Oldham, William Temple, Denys Munby, Ronald Preston, John Atherton, and Peter Sedgwick, who emphasize that one cannot move directly from primary Christian principles and biblical material to detailed guidelines for modern living.[63] This claim may be even more valid with study of a single book. But since the co-creationist theology of work utilizes Genesis material, and the foundational nature of Genesis for formulating Christian theology in general is recognized, focusing on Genesis for its theology of work seems justified.

The specific concerns regarding biblical working situations should be recognized. However, it is asserted that the problems in modern working situations are not as far removed from the ancient patriarchal conditions as is generally thought. It will be shown that the various working activities of the patriarchs in particular can readily be given correspondence to modern work activities.

The study also responds to David Hollenbach, SJ, who, writing soon after the publication of *Laborens Exercens* and its exposition of co-creationism, described it as a "religious vision of work."[64] However, Hollenbach observed the selectivity of the Genesis material used in the encyclical[65] and

---

61. Mackenzie, "Faith at Work," 38.
62. Volf, *Work in the Spirit*, 77.
63. Moore, "Theology of Work," 520–26.
64. Hollenbach, "Human Work," 75.
65. Ibid., 69.

stated he would value a theology based on a more complete reading of Genesis than that found in *Laborens Exercens*.[66]

These concerns about a biblical theology of work may reflect current uneasiness generally with the adequacy of biblical theology alone to provide guidelines for contemporary humans, but they also suggest a departure from the original Protestant theological stance of *sola scriptura*. Whilst concerns about the use of biblical material for forming theological and ethical guidelines for modern living should be recognized, for centuries Christians have successfully applied the principles of the teachings of the Bible to the changing circumstances of their lives.

James Dunn suggested a biblical theology must take into account both Jewish and Christian understanding of the Old Testament as well as Christian understanding of the New,[67] and Scott Hafemann proposed that biblical theology is the Bible's understanding of the character of God and his purposes.[68] This suggests that biblical theology requires a broad and in-depth understanding of the material presented, rather than the use of proof texts. Although Brevard Childs pointed out, pertinently for this study, that in attempting to find themes in the Bible it is possible to distort the whole,[69] this is an issue for all literature.

Opportunity of the Study

Despite the challenges, it is useful to study how ordinary work was portrayed in Genesis, the text given primacy in both the Jewish and Christian canon. There is little previous work in this area, yet the contemporary doctrine of co-creationism is based on limited Genesis material.[70] Miroslav Volf's theology of work specifically discarded a "protological," that is Genesis, theology of work,[71] giving further cause to examine the Genesis text.

Apart from the obvious fact that work dominates human lives, the need to develop appropriate theologies of work is highlighted by recognizing that the approach to work is linked to the issues of both rest and worship.[72] This linkage, as well as the dominant place work holds in human lives, means that understanding the issues of ordinary everyday work is of

66. Ibid., 75.
67. Dunn, "Problem of Biblical Theology," 172–83.
68. Hafemann, "Covenant Relationship," 20.
69. Childs, *Biblical Theology*, 15.
70. John Paul II, *Laborem Exercens*.
71. Volf, *Work in the Spirit*, 101.
72. John Paul II, *Dies Domini*.

great importance, not only for an academic understanding of the Genesis narratives and the rest of the Pentateuch, but for all Christians awaiting the promised Kingdom of God.

2

Social History Background of Theologies of Work

THE HISTORY OF THEOLOGIES of work suggests that contemporary social philosophies have consistently been the major force shaping these various theologies, including recent developments. Whilst biblical material is utilized to support current Christian thinking on the theology of everyday work, a biblical study on the topic has rarely been undertaken, exceptions being those by Alan Richardson,[1] Göran Agrell,[2] and R. Paul Stevens.[3]

Early Influence of the Jewish Philosophy of Work

The original social influence on Christian attitudes to work was Jewish. Jesus Christ, himself a Jew, was a skilled manual worker: "Is not this the carpenter?" (Mark 6:3). The Jewish apostle Paul felt no need to apologize for his work as a tent maker, but instead was proud of it, regarding it as an example for others (Acts 18:3; 2 Thess 3:7–10). Ordinary work was the norm for rabbis, who received no remuneration for their teaching, but each was expected to acquire a trade to support himself by honest toil.[4] Paul was very clear in his prescription to those who became Christians: "If anyone will not work, neither shall he eat" (2 Thess 3:10). The Jewish apostle James spoke for workers cheated of their rightful wages, reminding wealthy landowners that the cries of these people reached God in heaven (James 5:1–6). Despite the Greco-Roman cultural tendency to denigrate ordinary everyday work,

1. Richardson, *Biblical Doctrine of Work*.
2. Agrell, *Work, Toil and Sustenance*.
3. Stevens, *Work Matters: Lessons from Scripture*.
4. Richardson, *Biblical Doctrine of Work*, 21.

the Christian approach was to appreciate workers, and by implication, their work.

In the earliest surviving church manual, the *Didache*, advice was given regarding would-be settlers. "But if he wishes to settle with you, being a craftsman, let him work for and eat his bread. But if he has no craft, according to your wisdom provide how he shall live as a Christian among you, but not in idleness."[5] Clearly, the early Christian was expected to work.

Twentieth-century Jewish theologian Abraham Joshua Heschel noted, "Just as we are commanded to keep Sabbath, we are commanded to labor. The duty to work for six days is just as much a part of God's covenant with man as to abstain from work on the seventh day."[6] Jacob Neusner, another twentieth century Jewish theologian, stated, "[It is] of the greatest importance . . . that the Hebrew word for 'work' is *abodah*, the same word used for 'divine service,' 'liturgy,' or the labor of the priests in the Temple making offerings to God."[7] Neusner declared Jews regard work as natural, what humans are created to do, and that "unemployment," that is, having nothing of worth to do, is unimaginable. He considered Jews find their model for work in the account of creation, where God worked for six days and rested on the seventh. Both Neusner and Heschel asserted that it is just as much a duty to work for six days as it is to rest on the seventh.[8] They considered having to work at unpleasant jobs results from the curse placed on the land after the "fall of humanity from God's grace."[9]

Recognizing the Jewish roots of Christianity, it is no surprise that Tertullian, writing his *Apology* in the early third century, asserted that ordinary work, manual or intellectual, was regarded by Christians as a normal aspect of their lives.[10] He confirmed that Christians at that time were involved in all occupations, except those having to do with idol-making, acting in pagan theatres, astrology, and the sponsoring of gladiatorial combats.[11] Thus the original Christian theology of work was essentially the Jewish theology of work, that is, the theology of work as found in the Torah.

---

5. Lightfoot, *Apostolic Fathers*, 233–34.
6. Heschel, *The Sabbath*, 28.
7. Neusner, "Work in Formative Judaism," 2829.
8. Ibid., 2830.
9. Ibid., 2831.
10. Tertullian, "Apology," as cited in Kaiser, E., *Theology of Work*, 89–90.
11. Ibid., 106ff.

Influence of Greek and Roman Philosophies of Work

By the end of the first century, the social influence in the Christian church was no longer primarily Jewish. The church now comprised mainly of Hellenized Jews in the diaspora, and non-Jews.[12] Christian theology on ordinary work came to reflect classic Greek philosophy and Roman household social thinking.

Hesiod, an early Greek author writing in the eighth century BCE, encouraged work for its material benefits, but claimed the gods had created humans to do their work as punishment for stealing fire. The gods sent Pandora "the gift," and when she unstopped her jar she let out all the harsh toils and grievous sicknesses that have plagued humanity ever since.[13] Early Greek thinking was influenced by Mesopotamian philosophy and cosmology, which also taught humans were created by the gods to do their work.[14]

One exception to this Greek and Roman tendency to disparage work was the attitude to farmers. Kenneth Dover observed, "In Greek literature, the man who is proud to call himself a 'worker' is the farmer; it was always respectable to be a good farmer who raised the value of his land by hard work, intelligence and frugality."[15] Homer, also writing in the eighth century BCE, affirmed this perspective in his description of the shield of Achilles. After chilling descriptions of conflict-ridden cities, he portrayed attractive pastoral scenes of workers reaping corn, and young men and women harvesting grapes to the sound of music.[16] This, of course, was the attitude of upper class citizens; we have no picture of what Greek slaves and peasants thought of their work. However, the numerous small business entrepreneurs of Greco-Roman cities tended to pride themselves in their work, and to identify themselves by their occupations, even though the upper classes regarded them as common and servile.[17]

Approximately four hundred years before Christianity, Plato (427–347 BCE), whose teachings strongly influenced first Greek, then Roman and Christian thinking, taught that the human soul was eternal, and worth more than the material body that imprisoned it, the classic body-soul dualism.[18] Thus the pursuit of knowledge to nourish the soul was the only proper work

---

12. Stark, *Rise of Christianity*, 49–71.
13. Hesiod, *Works and Days*, 38–39.
14. See, for example, West, *East Face of the Helicon*; Dalley, *Myths from Mesopotamia*.
15. Dover, *Greek Popular Morality*, 173.
16. Homer, *The Iliad*, 322.
17. Stambaugh and Balch, *NT in its Social Environment*, 117.
18. Trigg, *Ideas of Human Nature*, 11.

for humans. Physical work to sustain the needs of the inferior body was a necessity relegated to slaves who had no choice. Aristotle (384–322 BCE), Plato's pupil, taught that the man who worked for a livelihood would not have the time to attain virtue. The Romans Cato (234–139 BCE) and Cicero (106–43 BCE) distinguished between the mundane cares of living by manual labor, and the "liberal," primarily political, pursuits of gentlemen.[19]

The Penitential Theology of Work and Monasticism

Greek philosophy that denigrated physical work but honored intellectual activity encouraged the development of the penitential theology of work that dominated the mediaeval Christian community for a thousand years. Exponents of this theology include Augustine (writing in the late fourth and early fifth centuries CE),[20] St. Benedict (writing about one hundred years later),[21] and Thomas Aquinas (in the thirteenth century).[22] The penitential theology of work considered work the punishment for original sin. Biblical support for this appeared available in the third chapter of Genesis that describes the curses pronounced after the Fall. This theology considered that Adam's curse was the sentence to eat his bread in the sweat of his brow (Gen 3:17–19), and Eve's to bring forth children in pain. Whilst post-apostolic and mediaeval Christian theologians ascribed work a spiritual and ascetic value that gave it an advanced status over that given by the Greek philosophers, they regarded the active working life as inferior to the contemplative.[23] Volf noted that both Greeks and "traditional" Christians depreciated work.[24]

Laity Versus Clergy

Christian thinking on work was influenced by the dramatic social change of status Christians experienced when the Emperor Constantine was converted in 312 CE. "People who in their youth had faced death for being

19. Stambaugh and Balch, *NT in its Social Environment*, 116–17.

20. Augustine's thoughts on work are presented in general form in his works, *Confessions*, 405–14; *City of God*.

21. Benedict, *Rule of St Benedict*, 43–45, 54–55, 76–78, 86–87, quoted in Placher, *Callings*, 128ff.

22. Aquinas, *Summa Theologiae*, 1926–27, 1931–34, 1941–42, 1954–55, quoted in Placher, *Callings*, 154–75.

23. See below for Kaiser's assessment of Jerome's teaching on work.

24. Volf, *Work in the Spirit*, 138.

Christians came to middle age in a time when it could be socially advantageous to join the church."[25] People were now baptized into the church by parental, not individual, choice, and the distinction between truly committed Christians and those who were simply members of a "Christian" society came to lose its clarity. This had major implications for attitudes towards everyday work. What in apostolic times had been one concept, the "people called" (*laos klēros*) of God, became, under the influence of Greek thinking on the superiority of intellectual work over manual labor, two quite distinct Christian groups, the "called clergy" (*klēros*) and the people, or laity (*laos*).[26] The laity were ordinary humans who, because of apparent lack of special calling, did the everyday necessary bodily survival work. The *klēros/clergy* were those especially called by God into elevated intellectual and spiritual work to nourish the soul, people who lived in monasteries set apart from routine existence. Thus, whereas the Jewish attitude to ordinary work placed it on a level with religious activity, under the influence of Greek philosophy the Christian community now regarded work as separate from religious experience.

This significant change in thinking is demonstrated by the writings of theologians during this period. Placher observed that Augustine, writing at the end of the fourth century, was, like most of the early church theologians, influenced by Plato's thinking.[27] Yet it is to Augustine that Father Edwin Kaiser, a Roman Catholic theologian who developed his *Theology of Work* as background material for Vatican II, credits developing what might be called the first organized Christian theology of work,[28] where much was made of Christ's words of commendation to Mary who sat at Jesus' feet listening, and his apparently negative advice to Martha's preoccupation with serving.

Kaiser reports that in the early fifth century, Jerome taught "work has three-fold value: it makes the worker self-supporting, enables him to give to the needy, and helps him to form his life in holiness,"[29] the classic penitential view of work. It gave work spiritual value in developing virtue, but its physical value was downplayed to mere survival.

Later in this same century, Benedict of Nursia developed his Rule of Benedict that became the Benedictine order.[30] Benedict accepted Jerome's ideas, and manual labor ("to obtain greater charity and commendation")

25. Placher, *Callings*, 31.
26. Preece, "Callings," 12.
27. Placher, *Callings*, 83.
28. Kaiser, E., *Theology of Work*, 108–19.
29. Ibid., 105.
30. Placher, *Callings*, 128; Benedict, *Rule of St Benedict*.

was included in his plan for monastic daily life. No one was exempt from it, although Benedict was somewhat ambivalent about this: "No one is excused from kitchen duty unless he is ill or he is engaged in a task of greater import, for he can thus obtain greater charity and commendation."[31] Presumably if kitchen duty was not to anyone's taste, then either an illness or a task of "greater import" must be found! One thing that Benedict's Rule strongly condemned was idleness.[32]

Thomas Aquinas, writing his *Summa Theologia* one thousand years later, continued Augustine's Greek-influenced thinking, and presented eight reasons from Aristotle, whom he calls "The Philosopher," as to why the contemplative life was superior to the active. He capped his argument with a ninth biblical reason: our Lord says Mary has chosen the best part.[33]

Influence of Renaissance Philosophy on Reformation Theology

Jürgen Moltmann suggested that the Renaissance that began in the late Middle Ages offered mediaeval Christianity a new picture of God: God is Almighty, and the human made in God's image must strive for power and domination in the earth.[34] From this came the idea that just as God achieves great things, so must humans. Renaissance philosophy thus contributed to an increasingly appreciated value of the individual person, shown by the accomplishments of gifted persons in that age of impressive artistic expression, and later of exploration and discovery. This suggests that the concept of human dominance over the created order, a foundational idea in the development of the doctrine of co-creation, began with the emergence of the Renaissance.

The Renaissance also saw dramatic changes in banking and financial management that were reflected in changed theological ideas on money management that dramatically impacted human work.[35] Whereas the acceptance of usury from a fellow believer had been strictly prohibited both in classical Judaism, (see for example Exod 22:25; Lev 25:36–37; Deut 23:19;

---

31. Benedict, *Rule of St Benedict*, 43–45, 54–55, 76–78, 86–87, quoted in Placher, *Callings*, 130.
32. Benedict, "Rule of St Benedict," 131.
33. Aquinas, *Summa Theologiae*, quoted in Placher, *Callings*, 156–57.
34. Moltmann, *God in Creation*, 26–27.
35. Ferguson, *Ascent of Money*, 4, 42–49.

Neh 5:7), and in mediaeval times by Roman Catholicism,[36] the spectacular success of the banking family of Medici changed this attitude.[37]

Ferguson has shown that the roots of the modern capitalistic approach to work extend deeply into mediaeval developments in the Italian money-lending banking system, perfected by the Roman Catholic Medici family.[38] In 1517, when Luther was nailing his theses to the door of the church in Wittenberg, Catholic conquistadors in the New World, following the wake of Columbus, were hard at work making conquests and discoveries that led to an unprecedented amount of wealth pouring into Europe. The avalanche of precious metals that entered Spain and then the rest of Europe at this time triggered the first documented evidence of inflation not caused by small local disasters such as crop failure and war.[39]

Thus events beyond the Reformation were moving inexorably towards a different economic world from the established mediaeval pattern, and the social situation was ripe for a dramatic change in theological concepts of work. These changes began as early as the fourteenth and fifteenth centuries, with the writings of the mystics Eckhardt and Tauler, who taught that perfection, or *visio Dei*, was possible to the humblest laborer as well as to the cloistered monk.[40] But it was the Reformation that gave impetus to major changes in theological thinking on work.

Luther: A New Look at Work

Luther, who transformed Christian thinking on soteriology with his thesis that salvation was by individual faith in the grace of Christ alone, also transformed Christian attitudes to everyday work.[41] He held that persons could be called by God to work in secular occupations just as surely as they could be called into spiritual occupations in a monastery.

Luther tried to construct his system of doctrine using scripture alone, and his ideas on work emerged from his theology concerning faith and works.[42] He noted the previously unrecognized significance of Gen 2:15, "The Lord God took the man and put him in the Garden of Eden to work it and keep it," commenting, "man was created not for leisure but for work,

36. Tawney, *Religion and the Rise*, 46–53.
37. Ferguson, *Ascent of Money*, 42–48.
38. Ibid.
39. Ibid., 27.
40. Richardson, *Biblical Doctrine of Work*, 38.
41. Hart, "Teaching: Martin Luther," 36.
42. Ibid., 39.

even in the state of innocence."[43] Luther had much to say about ordinary everyday work in his voluminous *Works*, possibly recognizing that the doctrine of righteousness by faith may be construed by some to impact negatively on human effort in daily living.[44] Luther believed ordinary work was the primary way for humans to serve fellow humans.[45] One of his favorite illustrations was the shepherds, who, though called to witness remarkable events associated with the birth of Christ, returned to their work guarding sheep.[46] This interest in secular callings was primarily a protest against a "double standard" that limited calling exclusively to a person being called into a monastery.[47]

Luther, however, aware of peasant uprisings of his time, seems to have been conscious of the social and political implications of his doctrines that elevated individuality, and was desirous to maintain the political and social status quo.[48] Thus when he translated the Bible into German vernacular, he translated the word *klēsis* (Greek for calling) in 1 Corinthians 7:20 as *Beruf*,[49] the ordinary German word for occupation. Luther was well educated, and it is unlikely that he simply made a poor translation. First Corinthians 7:17 gives context to verse 20, and implies that occupation was at least part of what Paul had in mind when he wrote that Christians should accept the life situation in which they found themselves. Hart defends Luther's translation, basing his defense on the various Greek translations of the scriptures available to Luther.[50]

Luther, sensitive to social situations, was concerned by the rising commercialism of his day.[51] His famous attacks on indulgences were triggered by the fact that Tetzell, the papal agent collecting them, was accompanied by a representative of the German banking firm of Fuggers who took no less than half of the profits.[52] But although Luther was eager to reform the religious practices of his time, he was keen not to trigger a social or financial revolution. He accorded everyday work equality with ecclesiastic, but did

---

43. Ibid., 38.
44. Placher, *Callings*, 207.
45. Hart, "Teaching: Martin Luther," 41.
46. Luther, "Gospel for the Early Christmas Service," 37.
47. Richardson, *Biblical Doctrine of Work*, 38.
48. Tawney, *Religion and the Rise*, 80–81. See also Churchill, *History of the English-Speaking*, 5.
49. Holl, "History of the Word Vocation," 126–54.
50. Hart, "Teaching: Martin Luther," 43–44.
51. Tawney, *Religion and the Rise*, 79–82.
52. Ibid., 72.

not elevate it beyond this. His concept of Christian work was one of service. However, the concept of serving, of preserving the world, has not met with modern enthusiasm.[53]

Calvin: Sympathetic to Commerce

Calvin, contemporary with but in contrast to Luther, was sympathetic to the rising commercialism of his day.[54] He theologically extended the field of secular activity when he accepted the legitimacy of the appropriate use of usury, which had been hotly disputed throughout mediaeval times.[55] "What reason is there," he wrote to a correspondent, "why income from business should not be larger than that from landowning?"[56] Donald Heiges, twentieth century Lutheran theologian, noted "Luther was suspicious of, and opposed to, the rising commercialism of his day, while Calvin recognized the burgeoning world of commerce as an area of legitimate activity for Christians."[57] Thus it was Calvin who theologically sanctioned the modern economic world.

However, Calvin retained a significant connection with mediaeval concepts of work by setting out his thoughts on the Christian life under the title of "self-denial."[58] Like Luther, Calvin, contrary to the prevailing theological opinion of the time, recognized that Gen 2:15 indicated work was not the result of the fall of humanity into sinfulness, but was part of the original ontology of the race.[59]

Calvin alleged humanity lost dominion over this world because of the fall, but their dominion was restored by Christ's sacrificial death.[60] This idea contributed to the development of the Protestant work ethic. Hart commented that on this point Calvin is furthest away from the position of Luther,[61] but that Calvin, like Luther, equated everyday work with calling.[62] However, whereas Luther taught that a "calling" was fixed, Calvin

53. Volf, *Work in the Spirit*, 101.
54. Tawney, *Religion and the Rise*, 92–93.
55. Ibid., 39–54; and see Hart, "Teaching: John Calvin," 132.
56. Calvin, quoted by Troeltsch, *Soziallehren der Christlichen*, 707, in Tawney, *Religion and the Rise*, 93.
57. Heiges, *Christian's Calling*, 60.
58. Hart, "Teaching: John Calvin," 121.
59. Calvin, *Genesis*, 35–36.
60. Hart, "Teaching: John Calvin," 123.
61. Ibid.
62. Ibid.

considered it was possible to learn another trade.[63] Timothy Keller noted the important distinctive characteristics of the two main lines of Reformation thinking: "the Calvinists saw it [human work] as a way of continuing God's creative work of building a God-honoring culture. Lutherans saw it as a vehicle for God's providential work of caring for his creation."[64]

Calvinism, Puritans, and the Protestant Work Ethic

The frugal life encouraged by Calvinistic Reformed Protestant Christianity, combined with dedicated industriousness, tended to the acquisition of surplus funds. Given the long-standing Christian recognition of the importance of charitable causes, legitimacy was provided for investing surplus funds in business ventures for later use in good causes. Hart noted a significant change: whereas both Calvin and Luther saw daily work as a service to humanity, Puritans saw it as a service to God, that even the rich should work.[65] Francis Bacon exemplified this thinking. As a Reformed believer, he felt "'called to work.' His view of work as a *creation mandate* [emphasis supplied] undergirded his vision of science for the 'glory of the Creator and the relief of man's estate.'"[66]

Hart refuted Weber's theory[67] that Puritan teaching led to a psychological compulsion to hard work and thus the "Protestant work ethic."[68] Although Puritans' views about calling were similar to those of Luther and Calvin, and Puritans were cautious about changing jobs, they offered advice about how to choose a job, implying choice as well as providence were significant in obtaining the most appropriate work.[69] However, the concept of choice in lifework led to ideas about the importance of lifework, and gradually to an increasing emphasis on making a financially advantageous choice, giving permission for work to take center stage in a person's life.

---

63. Ibid., 125.
64. Keller, *Every Good Endeavor*, 196–97.
65. Hart, "Teaching of the Puritans," 196–97.
66. Holmes, *Building the Christian Academy*, 73.
67. Weber, *Protestant Ethic*.
68. Hart, "Teaching of the Puritans," 209.
69. Ibid., 197–202.

Calvinists and the Transformation of Society

Calvinists considered their work was to transform society, exemplified by the address Puritan minister Thomas Case gave the English House of Commons in 1641: "Reformation must be universal. Reform all places, all persons, and all callings; reform the benches of judgment, the inferior magistrate . . . Reform the universities, reform the cities, reform the countries, reform the inferior schools of learning, reform the Sabbath, reform the ordinances, the worship of God . . . you have more work to do than I can speak."[70]

Leland Ryken noted Puritans regarded work as the best use of time, and "leisure" was a frivolous use of time.[71] Ryken considered, "the doctrine of creation renders impossible any dichotomy between the earthly and the sacred" and he considered the fourth commandment commanded humans to work as God worked.[72]

Vocation: Focus on Work

Just when the Reformation was on the brink of developing a theology that could have brought together a better understanding of the relationship between the spiritual and physical realms, the pendulum began to swing; the goal of physical blessing (particularly financial) took precedence over spiritual needs. Eventually "the call," the vocation, became synonymous with career and employment. Mackenzie suggested, "while Luther is most concerned to emphasize that there is no connection between vocation and salvation, the reformed tradition begins to form a connection."[73]

The "call" of work, i.e., vocation, was eventually seen as remunerated employment, overshadowing the call of salvation, and mirroring the social situation where work, especially employment, became more central to life than ecclesiastical institutions. This is clearly expressed by Thomas Carlyle. He altered the old monastic rule, *ora et labora* (pray and work), to *laborare est orare* (working is praying), and wrote "work is the latest Gospel in this world"[74] because it helps people find their true selves and elevates them "from the low places of this Earth, very literally, into divine Heavens."[75]

70. Hardy, *Fabric of This World*, 66–67.
71. Ryken, *Work and Leisure*, 110.
72. Ibid., 122.
73. Mackenzie, "Faith at Work," 17.
74. Volf, *Work in the Spirit*, 126.
75. Ibid.

Influence of Work Ideologies: Capitalism and Communism

The late eighteenth and nineteenth centuries saw intensely competing social ideologies regarding human work, leading to changes in theological thinking on this subject.

Capitalism: Economics of Self-Interest

Mingling social and theological ideas became more complex with the development of the Industrial Revolution. Weber's[76] argument that the Protestant work ethic, specifically the Puritan work ethic, was the basis for capitalism has been criticized, but there is no doubt that Puritan attitudes to work contributed to the acceptance of a capitalistic way of life. Heiges observed Calvinistic tradition indicated a person's status as elect and part of God's own people was confirmed by their being blessed and prospering in their work.[77] Jensen noted an important distinction: while Calvin understood self-interest to be the fundamental obstacle to the good life, capitalism makes it the means to abundance.[78] Eventually the concept of service, to either humanity or God, was lost, and the acquisition of surplus funds for personal benefit through individual hard work became the focus.

Tawney suggested, "Individualism in religion led insensibly, if not quite logically, to an individualist morality, and an individualist morality to a disparagement of the significance of the social fabric as compared with personal character."[79] He asserted, "Few tricks of the unsophisticated intellect are more curious than the naïve psychology of the business man who ascribes his achievements to his own unaided efforts . . . That individualist complex owes part of its self-assurance to the suggestion of Puritan moralists, that practical success is at once the sign and the reward of ethical superiority."[80] The reward, the blessing, became the goal. Unfortunately the quip, "He is a self-made man and he worships his creator," became all too true.

---

76. Weber, *Protestant Ethic*.
77. Heiges, *Christian's Calling*, 58.
78. Jensen, *Responsive Labor*, 116.
79. Tawney, *Religion and the Rise*, 211.
80. Ibid.

Adam Smith

The individualistic Scottish theoretician Adam Smith (trained to be a clergyman in the reformed tradition[81]), founder of modern economics, suggested in 1776 that the greatest impetus to personal effort was competition with other individuals. He pled powerfully for free trade with the American colonies. His treatise *The Wealth of Nations* is a potent description of the work and business motivations of modern humanity. His key idea for creating wealth was work productivity improved by specialization, what he called "the division of labor." He believed this was the only way to increase the productivity of workers.[82] This concept of a division of labor fitted the Protestant understanding of an individual call to a specific type of work.

Goldingay and Innes considered Adam Smith reversed the Reformation link between work and self-denial in favor of a direct link between work and self-interest, changing the theological justification for work. "The purpose of work is no longer that of lovingly producing goods for my neighbor. The value of work has become tied to the income it generates and severed from the worthiness of the product or service. As a consequence, work which brings in no income, such as voluntary work or the bringing up of children, is 'zero rated.'"[83]

Alienation of Work

What Karl Marx in the nineteenth century called the alienation of work,[84] and today is called loss of job satisfaction, was recognized by Adam Smith,[85] but he made little effort to suggest any remedy. In Smith's time there was little theological reflection on the issues confronting workers. Smith's sympathy for the American colonies and his book's date of publication made his treatise enthusiastically accepted in the newly formed United States.[86] Some of his ideas seem decidedly odd now, for example he classified service workers (such as physicians, musicians, and soldiers) as "unproductive"

---

81. Wight, "Introduction," vi.
82. Smith, *Wealth of Nations*, 3, 220.
83. Goldingay and Innes, *God at Work*, 16.
84. Marx, "Estranged Labor," 110.
85. Smith, *Wealth of Nations*, 734.
86. Wight, "Introduction," vii.

because they produced nothing tangible,[87] but his works are experiencing a revival of interest, in part due to the collapse of communism.[88]

Social Misery and Early Capitalism

The Industrial Revolution of the eighteenth and nineteenth centuries, spawned and accepted by capitalistic thinking, resulted in working conditions that challenged all previous philosophical and theological thinking on the subject of work. It produced social misery for the working classes on a vast scale. "A society that reverences the attainment of riches as the supreme felicity will naturally be disposed to regard the poor as damned in the next world, if only to justify making their life a hell in this."[89] "The self-sufficiency of the traditional household gave way to dependence on wage labour . . . The locus of economic work moved from the household to the factory."[90]

These dramatic social changes led to significant developments in philosophical and theological thinking concerning human work. Tawney's comments suggest some perceived that Christianity itself contributed to the workers' situation, causing people to turn away from it to find answers elsewhere; certainly, for many years there was no significant Christian response to the workers' dilemma.[91]

Marxism: Antecedents and Precepts

But if there was little Christian response to workers' needs, others in the eighteenth and nineteenth centuries were thinking about their situation. Voltaire, pen-name for Frenchman Francois-Marie Arouet, an anti-church deist, is regarded by many as the philosophic forerunner of the French Revolution that encouraged the power of the worker above that of the landowner or financier.[92] Rousseau, a Calvinist from Geneva, challenged the capitalistic idea of individual ownership: "The first man who, having fenced in a piece of land, said 'This is mine,' and found people naïve enough to believe him, that man was the true founder of civil society. From how

---

87. Ibid., x.
88. Ibid.
89. Tawney, *Religion and the Rise*, 222.
90. Mackenzie, "Faith at Work," 23.
91. That Christians were thinking about the issues is indicated by the encyclical of Leo XIII, the writings of Rauschenbusch, *Christianity and the Social Crisis*, and Sheldon, *In His Steps*, but their responses were slow.
92. Davidson, I., *Voltaire: A Life*.

many crimes, wars, and murders, from how many horrors and misfortunes might not any one have saved mankind, by pulling up the stakes, or filling up the ditch, and crying to his fellows: Beware of listening to this impostor; you are undone if you once forget that the fruits of the earth belong to us all, and the earth itself to nobody."[93] German philosopher Hegel developed his ideas on "dialectical idealism," supporting constant social change, which had widespread influence,[94] notably on Karl Marx, who greatly influenced thinking on work.

Marxism and Christianity Contrasted

The theories of Karl Marx and Friedrich Engels demonstrate a reaction against Christianity. Engels' family espoused Pietism, and Marx's parents converted from Judaism to Christianity.[95] Marx was baptized, and his senior gymnasium thesis was titled, "Religion: The Glue That Binds Society Together."[96] It is interesting to speculate the course of history if Christianity at that time had offered a credible theology of work. Marx collaborated with wealthy German industrialist, Engels, both of whom moved to Britain and developed their theories on work in the political safety of that country.[97] Engels, without whose financial support Marx would hardly have survived, stated bluntly and clearly: "Both Christianity and the workers' association preach forthcoming salvation from bondage and misery; Christianity places this salvation in a life beyond, after death, in heaven; socialism places it in this world, in a transformation of society."[98] This denigrated Christianity to "pie in the sky, bye and bye." A theology of work is thus closely associated with a social philosophy of life. Ultimately, Marx's philosophy of work for the temporal good came to influence contemporary theologies of work, such as that of Volf.[99]

---

93. Rousseau, *Discourse and Other*, 111ff.
94. Hegel, *Elements of the Philosophy*.
95. Cannadine, *Undivided Past*, 97.
96. Ibid.
97. Wheen, *Karl Marx*.
98. Engels, "On the History," 209.
99. Volf, *Work in the Spirit*, 55–65, 170–72.

Christian Responses to Marxist Thinking

As noted, there were isolated Protestant responses to the challenge of Marxist theory, and one important Roman Catholic reply. In 1891, Pope Leo XIII produced his encyclical *Rerum Novarum* that was very sympathetic to the importance and needs of ordinary workers and their work.[100] Among many notable observations, Pope Leo stated: "[F]or man, created in God's image, received a mandate to subject to himself the earth and all that it contains and to govern the world with justice and holiness."[101]

This elevated ordinary human work to a position closer to Reformation Protestant theology than to the mediaeval penitential theology of work. The social situation was again impacting the Christian theology of work. Significantly, Pope Leo's thoughts became the basis for the co-creationist theology of work[102] (explained further below) in the late twentieth century.

Post World War II Social Developments

The social changes caused by the industrial revolution were dwarfed in the twentieth century by two world wars, the explosion of atomic power, the implementation of Marxist theory on a multinational scale, the massive influx of women into the paid workforce, and the colossal burgeoning of technology of all types, including an information technology almost beyond understanding. This blurred even the definition of work. Once work meant hard physical toil, and leisure was the opportunity to debate philosophy and discuss politics. Now, work meant employment. Volf's observation is critical: "The reduction of vocation to employment, coupled with the belief that vocation is the primary service ordinary people render God, contributed to the modern fateful elevation of work to the status of religion."[103]

Post World War II Economic Boom

After World War II there was a massive economic boom and an era of general optimism concerning the possibilities of human achievement. The purpose of work was to achieve. Again this social situation influenced new theological thinking on the meaning of work. Graeme Smith observed that

---

100. Leo XIII, "Rerum Novarum."
101. Ibid.
102. John Paul II, *Laborem Exercens*, section 1.
103. Volf, *Work in the Spirit*, 109.

it was not until 1948 that the term "theology of work" was used, and there has been an increasing interest in this topic since.[104] The era was noted for its general pride in technological advancement and achievement, its increasing standards of living (at least in first-world countries), and especially the fierce ideological battles between communism and capitalism.[105]

Perceived Need for Updated Theology of Work after World War II

In the immediate post-war period, Christian views on work were seen as out-dated and out of step with mainstream Western society. Both Protestant and Roman Catholic theologians responded to this challenge. Anglican Alan Richardson published his study *The Biblical Doctrine of Work* in 1952.[106] The title is significant because since its publication the use of the Bible as a source of relevant material for the study of human work has been challenged.[107] Many theologians regard the working conditions of biblical times as so different from modern that they offer little insight into the complexities of contemporary challenges. This reflects what was seen as the failure of "biblically based" Reformation Christianity to respond to the needs of workers during the Industrial Revolution.[108]

J. H. Oldham and the World Council of Churches

At its inaugural meeting in 1948, the World Council of Churches heard presentations regarding workers' needs from Anglican lay theologian J. H. Oldham.[109] The council delivered its report, *Christian Faith and Daily Work*, from its second assembly in 1954.[110] The ground-breaking composition of Oldham, *Work in Modern Society* (1950)[111] should, according to Graeme Smith, be regarded as the first formal theology of work.[112] In this

104. Smith, G. W., "Theology of Work in the Postwar," 15.
105. Ibid., 16.
106. Richardson, *Biblical Doctrine of Work*.
107. Mackenzie, "Faith at Work," 38; Volf, *Work in the Spirit*, 77; Moore, "Theology of Work."
108. See allegations in Tawney, *Religion and the Rise*.
109. Clements, *Faith on the Frontier*.
110. Mackenzie, "Faith at Work," 32.
111. Oldham, *Work in Modern Society*.
112. Smith, G. W., "Theology of Work in the Postwar," ch. 2.

study, Oldham suggested that rather than looking to the Bible and its pre-industrial society for a theology of work, we should look there instead for what it means to be a person in relation to God. He asked the question that considerably influenced future thinking on theologies of work: "If man's responsibilities toward the world are larger than earlier generations supposed them to be, may they not contain new possibilities of man's co-operation with God in making the world?"[113] This reflects post World War II social optimism regarding the possibilities of work and technology, and is the first intimation of the doctrine known as co-creationism.

M. D. Chenu, E. Kaiser, and Vatican II

Roman Catholic Vatican II, 1962–65, included this new thinking on work with studies from M. D. Chenu[114] and Edwin Kaiser[115] being presented. These discussions ultimately resulted in the formal development of the doctrine of co-creationism.[116] This doctrine gives a very optimistic and high value to human work. Built on the foundation of Pope Leo XIII's encyclical in 1891, its first clear articulation was by Pope Paul VI in *Gaudium et Spes* in 1965.

Pope John Paul II and Co-creationism

Pope Paul VI's 1965 encyclical was followed by the widely acclaimed *Laborens Exercens* of Pope John Paul II in 1981. In this encyclical, Pope John Paul II described the doctrine of co-creation thus: "that *man*, created in the image of God, *shares by his work in the activity of the Creator*,"[117] emphasis original. These developments in Roman Catholic theology were understood by Keller to mean that "today there is no longer a great divide between Catholic social teaching on the importance of work and that of the Protestant Reformation."[118]

Both Roman Catholics and Protestants have praised Pope John Paul's encyclical. The doctrine of co-creationism satisfactorily combines several scientific and social philosophies with biblical material. Its assumption that

---

113. Oldham, *Work in Modern Society*, 34.
114. Chenu, *Theology of Work*.
115. Kaiser, E., *Theology of Work*.
116. See ibid.; Paul VI, "Gaudium et Spes."
117. John Paul II, *Laborem Exercens*, section 25.
118. Keller, *Every Good Endeavor*, 257.

the original physical creation was not fully completed by God meshes well with current scientific evolutionary theory. It is complementary to Marxist as well as capitalist concepts that work is central to human life and through it humanity achieves personal self-actualization, and develops its own superior world by working on the existing raw materials of nature to transform the world. It recognizes a human responsibility towards nature that can assist in developing an appropriate ecological approach. And it implies that those best able to do all of these would be those with a mandate from God to build up his kingdom on earth, those who are his vicars on earth.

Protestant responses to *Laborens Exercens* have been generally positive. However, there has been a tendency to downgrade the "protological," that is the Genesis base of Pope John Paul's encyclical. Volf's theology sees the activity of humans, guided by the Holy Spirit, as ushering in the New Creation.[119]

Several post World War II Protestant theologians have not been enthusiastic about the doctrine of co-creationism. Richardson was generally positive about work but said, "Our secular occupations are to be regarded not as ends in themselves but as means to the service of the Kingdom of God."[120] Karl Barth strongly rejected co-creationism. "It would be highly arrogant and materially more than doubtful to maintain that God's work is improved or adorned by human labour . . . It is pure assumption to suppose that this human activity is secretly identical with action in which God Himself asserts and magnifies His glory . . . Work is the typical earthly and creaturely act, which distinguishes man as the center of the earthly creation. This is dignity. In no sense is it heavenly or divine. When it tries to be, it can only be demonic."[121] Graeme Smith was critical of co-creationism but did not reject it outright.[122]

Stanley Hauerwas described co-creation as a "remarkably bad idea," and suggested that by attributing such a high status to human work we risk idolatry.[123] He noted that Pope John Paul II suggested that although sin may have affected work it did not change its essential nature, and he was very concerned about that assumption.[124]

---

119. Volf, *Work in the Spirit*, 88–122.
120. Richardson, *Biblical Doctrine of Work*, 37.
121. Barth, *Doctrine of Creation*, 520–21.
122. Smith, G. W., "Theology of Work in the Postwar," 92–94.
123. Hauerwas, "Work as Co-Creationism," 42–58.
124. Ibid., 47.

Brian Brock suggested the emphasis of eschatology over protology could lead to unhealthy "activist and progressivist programs."[125] Anglican theologian John Stott, commenting on Volf's concepts asked, "Can humans really co-operate with God in the eschatological transformation of the world? Is not the Kingdom of God, both in its present reality and future perfection, a gift from God, rather than a human achievement?"[126] He admitted he was very "uneasy."[127]

Other Post World War II Theologies of Work

There are three other valuable post World War II contributions to the development of a theology of work.

R. Paul Stevens and Gordon Preece

R. Paul Stevens contributed to the current search for a theology of work with his concept of "three vocations," a human, a Christian, and a personal.[128] Much of Stevens' concern has been with the centuries old, but inappropriate, *klēros/laos* divide. Stevens has produced a large volume of useful marketplace ethical as well as biblically supported material. One of his recent works, *Work Matters: Lessons from Scripture*, provides a valuable overview of biblical material. His theology of work appears to be a nuanced New Creation theology that is in line with Volf's theology, and as such will not be presented separately. However, his useful practical insights make his contributions useful in the marketplace.

Gordon Preece expanded Stevens' ideas to suggest that the human vocation to care for the world was commissioned by God the Father to all people at creation, a Christian vocation given by Christ to go into all the world to preach the gospel, and a personal vocation was given Christians to apply to their own lives the great Commission of love through the power of the Holy Spirit.[129] Stevens' concept of an original "human" vocation, and Preece's recognition of the creation commission to care for the world endorse the value of a Genesis study for a theology of work.

---

125. Brock, Review of *Theology of Work* and *Heavenly Good*, 93–94.
126. Stott, *New Issues Facing Christians*, 196.
127. Ibid.
128. Stevens, *The Other Six Days*.
129. Preece, "Threefold Call: Trinitarian Character."

Jacques Ellul

One consistently negative voice in the generally increased contemporary appreciation of the value of human work is that of French sociologist and theological thinker Jacques Ellul.[130] Nowhere in his writing does Ellul share the optimism and enthusiasm for modern technology and human endeavor that characterizes those who offer a high theological value for human work. Ellul is overall seriously pessimistic. Furthermore, Hart considered Ellul's concepts impacted negatively on work ethics in Christian South East Asian communities where they contrast strikingly with Confucianism's positive attitude to work.[131] Ellul's ideas on human work were influenced by his experiences as a leader of the French resistance during World War II.[132]

Graeme Smith proposed: "The theologies of work in this study, [1990] with the exception of Ellul, do not discuss the Bible in the context of the general history of work."[133] Since Ellul is very negative about work, this suggests that either the Bible is negative about human work, which neither Richardson nor Agrell found, or if the Bible is relegated to a subordinate role, human work is elevated to a position more important than warranted.

Twenty-first Century: Secularism and Leisure-focused Society

The twenty-first century is being labeled the "post-Christian" era, and the social emphasis is relentlessly on both work and leisure. Despite the promise that mechanization and automation of work would provide more leisure, people perceive that they are working harder and longer than ever. This century has thus seen the theological interest in work continue, but with a special focus on the need to rest. There has been no change in either the Roman Catholic teachings of co-creationism, or the Protestant New Creation theology, although there have been several new Protestant voices. These include works of practical application such as William Heatley's *The Gift of Work*[134] and Timothy Keller's *Every Good Endeavor*,[135] the serious

---

130. Ellul published extensively on the topic. As an example, see Ellul, *Technological Society*.

131. Personal communication from Alistair Mackenzie, Oct. 2010, who provided Ian Hart's, "Theology of Every Day Work," unpublished PhD thesis.

132. Ellul, *Technological Society*, ix.

133. Smith, G. W., "Theology of Work in the Postwar," 137.

134. Heatley, *Gift of Work*.

135. Keller, *Every Good Endeavor*.

theological considerations of Darrell Cosden,[136] Armand Larive,[137] and David Jensen,[138] as well as related theologies such as Terence Fretheim's *God and World in the Old Testament: A Relational Theology of Creation*.[139]

Leisure, Rest, and Work

Ryken responded to modern needs for leisure when he suggested work and leisure are on a continuum scale, work having an obligatory quality and leisure the quality of freedom.[140] He proposed that regarding work simply as a source of income robs it of intrinsic value, and the good question "What good does this work accomplish?" has been replaced by "How much does it pay?"[141] Ryken's questions capture the current social focus on accomplishment and achievement. Ryken concluded his study with the reminder that the biblical institution of the Sabbath endorses rest and leisure.[142]

Jensen noted: "for many of us, work now has become synonymous with identity: I 'am' a teacher, an engineer, a truck driver, and we log enough hours per day on the job to justify that identity."[143] Jensen considered the need to rediscover a relationship with the earth, other people, and the Creator as so urgent that he considered re-institutionalizing Sunday blue laws, but decided this would be a desperate move.[144] Cosden closed his "reworked doctoral monograph"[145] on the theology of work with: "Theologically the sabbath is the crown of God's creation. All work, therefore, is to be permeated with the ethos of the sabbath."[146]

---

136. Cosden, *Theology of Work*.
137. Larive, *After Sunday*.
138. Jensen, *Responsive Labor*.
139. Fretheim, *God and World in the OT*.
140. Ryken, *Work and Leisure*, 20–21.
141. Ibid., 23–24.
142. Ibid., 182ff.
143. Jensen, *Responsive Labor*, 108.
144. Ibid.
145. Cosden, *Theology of Work*, xvi.
146. Ibid., 184.

Biblical Basis for Theologies of Work

As noted, the early Christian theology of work was essentially Jewish, based on the biblical creation narratives. These narratives recognize the interdependence of the physical and spiritual aspects of humanity.

The penitential theology of work of the mediaeval church reflected Greco-Roman social reality and Greek dualism. It had a limited biblical base in the story of the human Fall and the curses pronounced as a result of this (Gen 3:16–19), which was thought to indicate that work was punishment for sin. Jesus' apparently negative advice to his friend Martha and his affirmation of Mary's contemplative listening (Luke 10:38–42) was considered confirmation that physical work was inferior to intellectual work.

Luther's Reformation theology of work had its scriptural base in the creation account with its divinely given human responsibility to work and care for the garden (Gen 2:15), the concept of call as demonstrated in the life of Abraham and the first disciples, and Paul's advice that workers should keep their station (1 Cor 7:17–24). Some biblical material was rejected, or ignored, at the time of the Reformation, allowing acceptance of usury from a fellow-believer which had been strictly prohibited both in historical Judaism (see Exod 22:25; Lev 25:36–37; Deut 23:19; Neh 5:7), and in mediaeval times by Roman Catholicism.[147] The spectacular success of the Renaissance Medici family bank changed this attitude.[148] This suggests biblical material was used, or in some situations not used, to support current social attitudes, rather than biblical material being used to shape theology.

Recently, biblical material has been intentionally rejected in the quest for a theology of work. Oldham's reluctance to engage biblical material is typical of many contemporary scholars working in this area. However, there have been a few exceptions to this trend away from the use of biblical material: Alan Richardson's detailed study of biblical concepts on work;[149] Pope John Paul II grounded his theology of co-creationism in biblical material;[150] Gören Agrell noted an ambivalent attitude to work in the Bible, but proposed, "All these variations in the view of work are related to different ways of looking at eschatology."[151]

---

147. Tawney, *Religion and the Rise*, 46–53.
148. Ferguson, *Ascent of Money*, 42–48.
149. Richardson, *Biblical Doctrine of Work*.
150. Hauerwas, "Work as Co-Creationism," 43.
151. Agrell, *Work, Toil and Sustenance*, 151.

Summary

Over the last two thousand years, Christian theologies of work have been undergoing considerable change. The mediaeval church's penitential theology of work was challenged at the time of the reformation by Luther's understanding of the calling of "vocation" of every Christian, whether to the monastery or the farm. But since Vatican II there has been significant convergence of Roman Catholic and Protestant theologies of work. The driving factor for these changes has been both sociological and theological, but the biblical component of contemporary theologies appears to have become diluted.

3

Biblical Foundations for Contemporary Theologies of Work

THIS CHAPTER PRESENTS THE concepts of co-creation and the New Creation theology of work, and reactions to them. Reasons why the author considers the doctrine of co-creation to be inadequate are given, and why the New Creation theology of work does not answer the issues raised.

Hollenbach considers Co-creationism has Inadequate Genesis Base

Roman Catholic theologian David Hollenbach provided the warrant for this study. Although generally sympathetic towards co-creation, when commenting on Pope John Paul's encyclical he noted, "*Laborem Exercens* does not present the whole biblical perspective on the potentialities and limits of human creativity in work... there is a certain selectivity in the way *Laborem Exercens* reads the book of Genesis."[1] He would like "a theology which is based on a more complete reading of Genesis than that found in *Laborens Exercens*," but concluded co-creationism is a "religious vision of work."[2] Although a selective reading of Genesis may not be inappropriate, it should not distort the overall meaning of the text.

---

1. Hollenbach, "Human Work," 69.
2. Ibid., 75.

The Doctrine of Co-creationism

Pope Leo XIII's *Rerum Novarum* of 1891,[3] which responded to the dramatic changes brought about by the Industrial Revolution, changed Roman Catholic teaching on work, leading to co-creationism becoming the church's official doctrine. The encyclical was sympathetic to the needs and problems of ordinary workers, bringing the Roman Catholic view of work close to that of Reformation Protestantism: the work of all humans is of equal value, whether in the monastery, the workshop, or the farm.[4] Co-creationism was formally enunciated from the deliberations of Vatican II, notably the 1965 thoughts of Pope Paul VI in *Gaudium et Spes*.[5] Its most widely appreciated expression is the 1981 encyclical of Pope John Paul II, *Laborens Exercens*.

Definition

Pope John Paul II described the doctrine of co-creation thus: "that *man, created in the image of God, shares by his work in the activity of the Creator* [emphases original] and that, within the limits of his own human capabilities, man in a sense continues to develop that activity, and perfects it as he advances further and further in the discovery of the resources and values contained in the whole of creation. We find this truth at the very beginning of Sacred Scripture, in the Book of Genesis, where the creation activity itself is presented in the form of 'work' done by God during 'six days' (Gen 2:2)."[6]

History

Co-creation was first intimated in Jewish theology, where rabbis taught that God did not finish creation in the first six days but accepted the collaboration of humanity to build the tabernacle and thus complete what he had planned.[7]

---

3. Leo XIII, "Rerum Novarum."
4. Keller, *Every Good Endeavor*, 257.
5. Paul VI, "Gaudium et Spes."
6. John Paul II, *Laborem Exercens*, section 24.
7. Alexander, "Pre-Emptive Exegesis," 230–45.

M. D. Chenu and Edwin Kaiser were invited experts for Vatican II (1962–65),[8] when the Roman Catholic Church examined the doctrine of co-creationism, and Pope Paul VI issued his 1965 encyclical *Gaudium et Spes—Pastoral Constitution on the Church in the Modern World*. "[W]hen men and women provide for themselves and their families in such a way as to be of service to the community as well, *they can rightly look upon their work as a prolongation of the work of the Creator* [emphasis supplied], a service to their fellowmen, and their personal contribution to the fulfilment in history of the divine plan. Human achievements are not to be seen as opposing God's power and purposes, but as a sign of God's greatness and the flowering of His own mysterious design."[9] "[F]or man, created in God's image, received a mandate to subject to himself the earth and all that it contains and to govern the world with justice and holiness . . . This mandate concerns even the most ordinary everyday activities . . . men and women . . . can justly consider by their labour they are unfolding the Creator's work and contributing by their personal industry to the realization in history of the divine plan . . . Therefore let there be no false opposition between professional and social activities on the one part and religious life on the other. *The Christian who neglects his temporal duties neglects his duties toward his neighbour and even God and jeopardizes his eternal salvation* [emphasis supplied]."[10]

Pope Paul emphasized humanity's rulership of the world, and maintained that by ordinary secular work humans achieve God's original creative strategy for the planet. He indicated these activities are as important as religious activities, and emphasized the value of human work in achieving divine goals. He was consistent with historical Roman Catholic teaching on the importance of human effort in achieving eternal salvation. Although the Reformation insights of Luther and Calvin gave ordinary work a strong value, the suggestion that humans are unfolding the Creator's work and neglecting temporal duties jeopardizes salvation goes beyond this.

Pope John Paul II's *Laborens Exercens* extended the thoughts of *Gaudium et Spes* and endorsed co-creationism. Pope John Paul II experienced the outworking of Marxist theory in his native Poland, and would have had an interest in work and workers. This Marxist background may explain the central role John Paul II ascribed to work in human existence, although both capitalism and Marxism suggest work is central to human existence and wellbeing. The introduction to *Laborens Exercens* states, "Only man is

8. *Encyclopedia of Catholicism*, "Chenu, M. D."
9. Paul VI, "Gaudium et Spes."
10. Ibid.

capable of work, and only man works."[11] The encyclical maintains a wide definition of work, but seems primarily to identify work with employment.

John Paul II clearly identified technology as an aid in the process of co-creating and transforming the world, and was optimistic about the results of human activities. "The development of industry and the various sectors connected with it, even the most modern electronics technology, especially in the fields of miniaturization, communications and telecommunications and so forth, shows how vast is the role of technology, that ally of work that human thought has produced . . . [T]echnology is undoubtedly man's ally. It facilitates his work, perfects, accelerates and augments it."[12]

Oliver Williams explained "The key theme . . . is that the person is actually sharing in the work of creation by labor" and "'the development of the Kingdom of God' entails not only the transformation of the world by human labor (the *objective* dimension of work), but also, and more importantly, the transformation of the person (the *subjective* dimension of work) . . . The challenge is one of discerning the best way of fashioning an environment attuned to fostering the growth of individual character and creativity," emphases original.[13]

Biblical Basis for Co-creationism

Unlike Oldham, who thought there was insufficient biblical material to develop a theology of work, John Paul II was desirous to ground his theological perspective of work in biblical material. He utilized a wide selection of biblical material, but his fundamental concepts were developed from the Genesis creation narrative. Hauerwas, generally critical of *Laborens Exercens*, observed, "Pope John Paul II attempts to ground his perspective directly in scripture . . . He employs an extensive discussion of scriptures, *in particular the creation account in the first three chapters of Genesis*, [emphasis supplied] to establish a theological perspective on work. He explicitly says, 'the Church's social teaching finds its source in sacred scripture, beginning with the Book of *Genesis* and especially in the Gospel and the writings of the apostles.'"[14]

John Paul's key concept was that when God created humanity he gave them dominion over all the earth and the rest of his creation (Gen 1:26–28). "Man is the image of God partly through the mandate received from his

---

11. John Paul II, *Laborem Exercens*, Introduction.
12. Ibid., section 2.
13. Houck and Williams, *Co-Creation and Capitalism*, 7.
14. Hauerwas, "Work as Co-Creationism," 43.

Creator to subdue, to dominate, the earth."[15] "The expression 'subdue the earth' has an immense range. It means all the resources that the earth (and indirectly the visible world) contains and which through the conscious activity of man, can be discovered and used for his ends. And these words, placed at the beginning of the Bible, *never cease to be relevant* [emphasis supplied]."[16] Hollenbach indicated this dominion involves continuing the creative activity of God and which is part of the *imago Dei*.[17]

John Paul II found endorsement of co-creation in the life of Jesus Christ. "The truth that by means of work man participates in the activity of God himself, his Creator, was given particular prominence by Jesus Christ . . . 'Is not this the carpenter?' (Mark 6:2–3)."[18] He noted the books of the Old Testament contain many references to work and human professions (order his): the doctor, the pharmacist, the craftsman or artist, the blacksmith, the potter, the farmer, the scholar, the sailor, the builder, the musician, the shepherd and the fisherman,[19] recognized Jesus' frequent references to work in his parables, and that Christ's teachings on work were echoed in the life and teachings of Paul who labored at his trade and taught "If anyone will not work, let him not eat" (2 Thess 3:10).[20]

The doctrine of co-creation gives work an elevated theological position. It inspires because, as John Paul II emphasized, work is important because man is important: "*the primary basis of the value of work is man himself*, who is its subject . . . [H]owever true it may be that man is destined for work and called to it, in the first place work is 'for man' and not man 'for work' . . . [I]t is always man who is *the purpose of the work*."[21] "This description of creation, which we find in the very first chapter of the Book of Genesis, is also *in a sense the first 'gospel of work.'* For it shows what the dignity of work consists of: it teaches that man ought to imitate God, his Creator, in working, because man alone has the unique characteristic of likeness to God."[22]

---

15. John Paul II, *Laborem Exercens*, section 4.
16. Ibid.
17. Hollenbach, "Human Work," 63.
18. John Paul II, *Laborem Exercens*, section 26.
19. Ibid.
20. Ibid.
21. Ibid., section 6.
22. Ibid., section 25.

Work and Rest

John Paul also connected work and worship: "Man ought to imitate God both in working and also in resting, since God himself wished to present his own creative activity under the form of work and rest. This activity by God in the world always continues, as the words of Christ attest: 'My Father is working still . . .' (Jn 5:17); he works with creative power in sustaining in existence the world that he called into being from nothing, and he works with salvific power in the hearts of those whom from the beginning he destined for 'rest' (Heb 4:1, 9–10) in union with himself in his 'Father's house' (Jn 14:2). Therefore man's work too not only requires a rest every 'seventh day' (Dt 5:12–14; Ex 20:8–12), but also cannot consist in the mere exercise of human strength in external action; it must leave room for man to prepare himself, by becoming more and more what in the will of God he ought to be, for the *'rest' that the Lord reserves for his servants and friends* (Matt 25:21)." "Awareness that man's work is a participation of God's activity ought to permeate, as the Council teaches, even *'the most ordinary everyday activities.* For, while providing the substance of life for themselves and their families, men and women are performing their activities in a way which appropriately benefits society. They can justly consider that by their labor they are unfolding the Creator's work, consulting the advantages of their brothers and sisters, and are contributing by their personal industry to the realization in history of the divine plan' . . . The knowledge that by means of work man shares in the work of creation constitutes the most profound motive for undertaking it in various sectors."[23]

Thus John Paul II, in his discussion of work, linked work and rest, concepts that are associated in the creation narrative. He followed up his thoughts on work with a powerful encyclical on Sunday worship.[24] The emphasis is on the importance of humanity itself. He suggested this is the vital point to remember in situations where the results of human work are deemed more important than the human performer.

Work as Part of Redemption

John Paul II saw everyday work as collaboration with Christ in the redemption of humanity, the ultimate way of subduing the earth. "By enduring the toil of work in union with Christ crucified for us, man in a way collaborates with the Son of God for the redemption of humanity. He shows himself

---

23. Ibid.
24. John Paul II, *Dies Domini*.

a true disciple of Christ by carrying the cross in his turn every day in the activity that he is called upon to perform."[25] He considered the resurrection of Christ as the decisive proof of his elevation to Lordship over all creation, and his receiving all authority in heaven and earth, and asked, "If it is true that the many forms of toil that go with man's work are a small part of the Cross of Christ, what is the relationship of this new good to *the Resurrection of Christ?* . . . Earthly progress must be carefully distinguished from the growth of Christ's kingdom. Nevertheless, to the extent that the former can contribute to the better ordering of human society, it is of vital concern to the kingdom of God."[26]

Evaluations of Co-creationism

The doctrine of co-creationism has received positive reception from Christian theologians, both Roman Catholic and Protestant, but not universal acceptance. In the modified form of work being transformational and instrumental to help bring in the longed-for eschatological New Creation, it is attractive to Protestant theologians.

Edwin Kaiser

Kaiser, who prepared his theology for Schema 14 of Vatican II, but before publication of *Laborens Exercens*, clearly endorsed co-creationism: "Through the union of man with the world there is the mutual development of man and cosmos through work and the resources, values and forces of nature. These collaborate with man and function as his instruments, the tools of his mind and will, of his spirit . . . The height of creation is attained in this free operation of the spirit in correspondence with the vast teleology of a most complicated and intricate universe . . . Thus history is lifted from the heavy chain of determinate causes; man becomes the master of fate . . . [W]e cannot fail to realize something of the *almost divine dignity* of work . . . In a very true sense we may say that the universe is unfinished because man the worker creates new values as he expands in spirit and integrates an expanding universe . . . By work man draws the whole universe to himself, to the inner source of his being."[27] Kaiser was eloquent about a humanity

---

25. John Paul II, *Laborem Exercens*, section 27.
26. Ibid.
27. Kaiser, E., *Theology of Work*, 234–37.

that through work becomes master of its own fate, and thus attained "almost divine" status.

David Hollenbach

Hollenbach, writing soon after the publication of *Laborens Exercens*, was generally supportive of the doctrine, but, as noted, observed the selectivity in the use made of Genesis in *Laborem Exercens*.[28] He wanted to see a theology based on a "more complete reading of Genesis," but concluded that co-creationism is a "religious vision of work."[29]

Michael Novak

Novak approvingly noted "The Pope has highlighted the crucial role played by invention and discovery in the human vocation to 'subdue the earth.' . . . The Creator in Pope John Paul II's vision has hidden within creation untold riches, resources, and possibilities which it is the vocation of humans to discover and to realize for the common good of all. He, therefore, places great emphasis upon invention and discovery."[30]

Alan Richardson

Richardson (writing when Oldham was presenting ideas supportive of co-creation) rejected co-creationism. He stated "the work of creation . . . in the Bible is attributed to God alone,"[31] and "the Bible does not encourage the suggestion that man's work is creative in the same sense as God's."[32] "[T]hough man thus shares in God's dominion over the creation, nothing is said about his sharing in God's creativity."[33] Richardson was generally positive about work but said, "Our secular occupations are to be regarded not as ends in themselves but as means to the service of the Kingdom of God. They have Christian value only in so far as they can be made means to the end of the Gospel."[34]

28. Hollenbach, "Human Work," 69.
29. Ibid., 75.
30. Novak, "Creation Theology," 17, 28.
31. Richardson, *Biblical Doctrine of Work*, 13.
32. Ibid., 17.
33. Ibid., 18.
34. Ibid., 37.

Karl Barth

Barth (writing after Vatican II but before the publication of *Laborens Exercens*) strongly rejected co-creationism. "It would be highly arrogant and materially more than doubtful to maintain that God's work is improved or adorned by human labour."[35] Barth was doubtless influenced by his experiences of Third Reich Germany during his times of working there, and perhaps knowledge of the motto above the gates of Dachau concentration camp, *Arbeit macht frei*, "work makes free."[36] By personal experience he could challenge John Paul II's idea that humans "can justly consider by their labour they are unfolding the Creator's work and contributing by their personal industry to the realization in history of the divine plan."

Claus Westermann

Westermann objected to the notion of *creatio continua*, preferring the concept of blessing to that of on-going creation.[37] The term *creatio continua* refers to God's continuing creative activity throughout the history of the universe.[38]

Terence Fretheim

Fretheim saw creation not as a single event but as God's ongoing involvement with the world and its creatures, that is, *creatio continua*, although he was aware of Westermann's objections.[39] He considered "creation also includes that activity of creatures (human and nonhuman) in and through which God works to create in ever new ways."[40] Thus he differed from John Paul II's assertion that only humans work. Fretheim did not see the New Creation as a return to the original beginning, for otherwise, he says, everything that has happened in between would be of no consequence.[41] "God has freely chosen to be dependent upon both human and nonhuman in the

---

35. Barth, *Doctrine of Creation*, 520–21.
36. Preece, *Changing Work Values*, 174.
37. Westermann, *Genesis 1–11*, 175.
38. Ward, K., "Creatio Continua," *Encyclopedia of Science and Religion*.
39. Fretheim, *God and World in the OT*, xii, 4.
40. Ibid., 4.
41. Ibid., 9.

furtherance of God's purposes in the world."[42] These concepts seem supportive of co-creationism.

John Stott

Stott noted the importance John Paul II ascribes to work, but he challenged the view that work is the important distinguishing characteristic of humanity, and suggested it is the ability to worship that makes humans "most human."[43] He refuted the claim of *Laborens Exercens* that work is essential for humanness. "It would be an exaggeration to affirm that work is actually indispensable to our humanness, for the climax of Genesis 1 is not the creation of man, male and female, to subdue the earth, but the institution of the sabbath. We human beings are at our most human not so much when we work, as when we lay aside our work in order to worship . . . Here lies the fundamental difference between Marxism and Christianity. In the end a human being is not *homo faber* but *homo adorans*."[44]

Stanley Hauerwas

As noted, Hauerwas strongly disapproved of the doctrine of co-creationism. He described co-creationism as a "remarkably bad idea," and stated his belief that humanity was made to be a representative of God on earth, and that a representative is not a co-creator.[45] Hauerwas suggested that by attributing such a high status to human work we risk idolatry.[46] He was concerned about John Paul's II assumption that sin may have affected work but it has not changed its essential nature.[47]

Concerns Regarding Co-creationism

Although the doctrine of co-creationism meshes with current psychological and social theory,[48] and is sympathetic to workers, there are some unanswered questions. These concerns are:

42. Ibid., 270.
43. Stott, *New Issues Facing Christians*, 189.
44. Ibid.
45. Hauerwas, "Work as Co-Creationism," 42–58.
46. Ibid., 47–49.
47. Ibid.
48. Blustein, *Psychology of Working*, 114–52.

Can God's Appraisal be Trusted?

The implication that God's declaration that the world he created was very good and finished was in fact not true seems in accord with the serpent's allegations in the Garden of Eden. What God declares cannot be trusted, and the world is not the way he said it was when he created it. Furthermore, the concept that humans are to finish and perfect this defective world also seems in accord with the serpent's allegations, which implied that God did not provide humans with the essential knowledge to carry out their assigned role of caring for the garden, but the serpent would provide for that deficiency if the couple would just disobey and eat the forbidden fruit. Thus, the doctrine of co-creation intimates that humans have indeed been given the knowledge of the gods, and are able to bring to perfection God's imperfectly created world. Once the world is brought to perfection, God will be able to return to it.

Does Human Toil help achieve Redemption?

Another concern is John Paul II's suggestion that "by enduring the toil of work in union with Christ crucified with us, man in a way collaborates with the Son of God for the redemption of humanity."[49] Can it be said that the "toil" that resulted from the disobedience of humanity (Gen 3:1–19), and which appears from the Genesis narrative to have changed the essential nature of work (see further), be significant in collaborating in the redemption of humanity? Whilst the disciples of Jesus have clearly been given a mandate to be witnesses of the redemptive actions of Jesus Christ, can it be said that by our ordinary work we carry the cross of Christ in redemption of the world? Further, does the undeniable lordship of Jesus Christ offer any proof that humans have the right to dominate the earth, and lord over it?

Is Work the Fundamental Dimension of Human Existence?

Of concern is the assertion: "The Church finds *in the very first pages of the book of Genesis* the source of her conviction that work is the fundamental dimension of human existence on earth. Man is the image of God partly through the mandate received from his Creator to subdue, to dominate, the earth. In carrying out this mandate, man, every human being, reflects the

---

49. John Paul II, *Laborem Exercens*, section 27.

very action of the Creator of the universe."[50] Is work really the fundamental dimension of human existence?

Has all Human Work been Beneficial?

Can it be a settled point that *all* human effort to better the circumstances of their lives, both collective and individual, has been in accordance with God's will? Doubtless many inventions and discoveries have been beneficial, but it must be asked, have all inventions been beneficial? Have all discoveries been utilized in accordance with the will of the Creator God? The implication that these discoveries and inventions must be "for the common good of all" brings in the possibility that something beyond invention and discovery needs to be in operation.

Has the Original Gift of Dominion remained Unchanged?

Did humans, when they disobeyed in the Garden of Eden, lose anything from their original mandate to have dominion and subdue the earth? It is noted that the "mandate" to have dominion and subdue the earth was part of the blessing God gave humanity in its original, freshly created, perfect state (Gen 1:28), and this must be coupled with the expanded instruction to serve and to care for and guard the earth (Gen 2:15). Since there were curses pronounced on the serpent and the ground after humans chose to disobey, and since the effects of those curses were clearly directed towards human working conditions, can it be assumed that the words of blessing, to have dominion and to subdue the earth, "never cease to be relevant"[51] in exactly the same way as for humanity freshly created in their original perfection?

Are the Resources of Earth Primarily for Humans?

Can it be argued that to subdue the earth means that it was created primarily for its resources to be used to meet the demands of "human ends"? Although humanity was made in the image of God and clearly given dominion in

---

50. Ibid., section 4.
51. Ibid.

their original state (Gen 1:26–28), can it be assumed today that this means "to subdue, to dominate, the earth"?[52]

Not all Work fits the Doctrine

It is of particular concern that the co-creation theology of work is not applicable to all work. Goosen recognized that the "exciting view of the [co]-creationist" does not fit some work, his examples being a repair mechanic or street sweeper.[53]

Transformational Theology of Work

The transformational theology of work is a contemporary Protestant approach to work. Calvinists considered their work should be used to transform society, as exemplified by the address given by Puritan minister Thomas Case to the English House of Commons in 1641, noted earlier. The purpose of this transformation is to bring in conditions that will allow God to act and thus usher in the New Creation promised in Revelation.

Transformational theology was examined to ascertain whether it provided answers to the questions raised regarding co-creationism. However, Keller recently endorsed the conclusion of Lee Hardy: "in tracing the development of the Protestant concept of vocation from Luther's reaction to the medieval monastic ideal, it is easy to give the impression that the official Catholic position on work crystallized at some point in the high Middle Ages and has dutifully been collecting dust ever since. But that is not the case. In the course of modern Catholic social teaching, beginning with Pope Leo XIII's encyclical *Rerum Novarum* in 1891, we can detect a distinct 'reformed shift' in Catholic estimation of the meaning and place of work in human life . . . the official Catholic theology of work [now] virtually coincides with the traditional Protestant position at every major point."[54] "[T]oday there is no longer a great divide between Catholic social teaching on the importance of work and that of the Protestant Reformation."[55] If these theologies are essentially the same, which the following also suggests, the questions remain unanswered.

---

52. Ibid.
53. Goosen, *Theology of Work*, 68–69.
54. Hardy, *Fabric of This World*, 67.
55. Keller, *Every Good Endeavor*, 257.

Miroslav Volf and Work in the Spirit

Volf, in his seminal book *Work in the Spirit: Towards a Theology of Work*, emphasized the importance of the Holy Spirit in achieving any eternal value of human work. He was critical of Luther's vocational theology of work which he regarded as too confining and static for modern situations.[56] He considered the Christian acceptance of the industrial revolution resulted from equating "the call" with employment. Volf believed Luther's teaching could be used to justify demeaning and alienating work, and that it was a rigid concept encouraging satisfaction with the status quo rather than allowing people to move freely by choice from job to job.[57]

Although he described *Laborens Exercens* "as one of the most remarkable ecclesiastical documents on the question of work ever written,"[58] Volf was critical of what he called its "protological framework" (by which he meant a theology of work developed from a creation perspective). He admitted "we cannot construe a theology of work apart from the doctrine of creation" but considered the "new creation" is "not a mere restoration of the first creation."[59] Volf seems committed to the Puritan transformational dimension of human work that will bring in the New Creation. For him, humans add something worthwhile to the original creation of God by their transformational work activity, and thus effectively act as co-creators.

Volf preferred the concept of working in various "charismata" given to humanity by the Holy Spirit to that of a fixed vocation from God, perhaps influenced by early experience in communist Yugoslavia. In communist regimes work is assigned, often with little opportunity for worker choice, or recognition of interests. The freedom of being guided by the Holy Spirit to work in many different activities, and especially in areas of giftedness, rather than assigned "calling," would be very attractive.

Volf offered four reasons for his preference for "an eschatological theology of work to a protological." First, he believed the eschatological nature of Christianity made it impossible to see work in the creation context, which he saw as purely maintenance. This denigration of maintenance work seems rather incongruous in a world where the maintenance of highly developed technologies is essential. Second, Volf suggested that although a theology of work cannot be constructed apart from creation, the New Creation is *not a mere restoration of the first creation*. The New Creation comes about,

---

56. Volf, *Work in the Spirit*, 103–10.
57. Ibid., 105–9.
58. Ibid., 5.
59. Ibid., 101.

according to Volf, as a transformation of the first. This also seems to allege that the Genesis pronouncement of a very good and completed created world was actually not what God declared it to be. Third, he claimed "protological" theologies of work are inadequate to interpret modern work because they suggest human work is co-operation with God in *preserving* the world, whereas he (like John Paul II) saw powerful modern technologies as *transforming* the world. Fourth, Volf believed protological theologies of work such as Luther's justify the status quo and a mere preservation of the world.[60]

Thus, whilst Volf emphasized the importance of the role of the Holy Spirit in achieving the eternal value of human work, and never used the term co-creationism, he considered humans as adding something worthwhile to the original creation of God, and therefore, in their transformational work activity they effectively act as co-creators with God in bringing in the New Creation. His theology of work does not challenge the concept of co-creationism, and most importantly does not offer answers to the questions raised.

Darrell Cosden

Cosden searched to find a "satisfactory ontology and teleology" of work.[61] He acknowledged being significantly influenced by Marx. He declared he was not adopting Marx's particulars regarding the ontology of work, but did not reject them, and admitted there "will be similarities between my unfolding construct and his."[62] He seemed to endorse Friedrich Engels' assessment that "both Christianity and the workers' association preach forthcoming salvation from bondage and misery."[63] It is therefore in the transformation of society by human effort that Marx, Volf, Cosden, and John Paul II connect.

Cosden declared, "*we have a God-given mandate to extensively shape and re-shape the world through our work* [emphasis supplied]. As we do this, of course, we shape ourselves time and again—*and ultimately shape our future as well. Yet, we never work alone. Even when we try to do it without him, God is always there as well . . . Ordinary work in this world is a joint project between the master and his apprentices* [emphasis supplied]."[64] Cosden's

60. Ibid., 101–2.
61. Cosden, *Theology of Work*.
62. Ibid., 16–17.
63. Engels, "On the History," 209.
64. Cosden, *Heavenly Good of Earthly Work*, 98–99.

understanding of the New Jerusalem vision of John's Revelation "suggests that God is pleased to gather up, transform and include not just his 'pure' creation, but also the genuine additions to the created reality that we have brought about through creation-transforming actions."[65]

It is noteworthy that Cosden described what God has done as a "pure" creation. However, it seems somewhat arrogant to suggest that humans can add to that purity. There is an implicit understanding in Cosden's theology that human work not only adds, but also is essential to the eschatologically transforming work of bringing in God's New Creation, and therefore is a co-creation. In an unpublished summary of his thoughts, Cosden recognized a reformed theological position, somewhat modified from co-creation, "that any proposed theology of work, to be both comprehensive and compelling, will need to show how our ordinary work is integrally related to our salvation, and thus to the new creation, but not the cause or condition of it."[66] But this does not elucidate the problems encountered in the doctrine of co-creationism.

Cosden concluded his formal study with "what this concept of work's essential nature primarily guarantees is resistance to any reductionistic ethical prescriptions related to work" and "practically a work ethic may initially need to legitimatize a host of economic activities and structures necessary for the provision of resources for basic life support for the greatest number of people. In doing so it may even legitimatise certain kinds of work which under less extreme circumstances would be deemed unethical."[67]

Brian Brock's Critique of Cosden

Brian Brock had serious concerns about this conclusion. "An ontology that legitimates the unethical is a relatively exotic beast requiring much more explanation than Cosden supplies."[68] Brock considered "work is a context where we show our fidelity to God by obedience to his commands and stewardship of his gifts." He said our work should be seen as "anticipatory rather than participatory" relative to the New Creation, and suggested understanding this will protect from the dangers of misguided utopian visions.

---

65. Ibid., 75.
66. Personal communication via Alistair Mackenzie regarding Cosden's views.
67. Cosden, *Theology of Work*, 180–81.
68. Brock, Review of *Theology of Work* and *Heavenly Good*.

John Stott's Assessment

Stott expressed concerns about both the co-creation and transformational theologies of work: "Is not the Kingdom of God, both in its present reality and future perfection, a gift from God, rather than a human achievement?"[69]

Impact of Eschatology on Theologies of Work

Although Volf did not refer to the work of Swedish theologian Gören Agrell, he recognized the connection between eschatology and theologies of work. He accepted "two basic positions on the eschatological future of the world. Some [have] stressed radical discontinuity between the present and future orders, believing in the complete destruction of the present world at the end of the ages and creation of a fully new world. Others postulated continuity between the two, believing that the present world will be transformed into the new heaven and new earth."[70] Agrell's assessment of his detailed study of Biblical material involving the concept of work was that overall there was an ambivalent attitude to work in the Bible, but that in New Testament writings at least, "variations in the view of work are related to different ways of looking at eschatology."[71]

Richard Langer, however, criticized Volf's emotive contrast between the two basic positions on eschatology. Langer suggested that to compare a "radical discontinuity" with an unmodified "continuity" brings emotive connotations to the discussion.[72] Volf believed that unless there is continuity between the creation and new creation there is no eschatological significance in the work of humanity,[73] and seemed to assume the only reason for Christians to work must be that truly good work has an everlasting existence. "[B]elief in eschatological annihilation . . . is not consonant with the belief in the goodness of creation: what God will annihilate must either be so bad that it is not possible to be redeemed or so insignificant that it is not worth being redeemed. It is hard to believe in the intrinsic value and goodness of something that God will completely annihilate. And without a theologically grounded belief in the intrinsic value and goodness

---

69. Stott, *New Issues Facing Christians*, 196.
70. Volf, *Work in the Spirit*, 89.
71. Agrell, *Work, Toil and Sustenance*, 151.
72. Langer, "Niggle's Leaf and Holland's Opus," 100–117.
73. Volf, *Work in the Spirit*, 90.

of creation, positive cultural involvement hangs theologically in the air."[74] It is of note that the Genesis account does portray the "annihilation" of the antediluvian world God had created, Genesis chapters 6–9, so this argument seems without biblical foundation.

David W. Miller[75] and David Bosch[76] agreed that Christian mission is in essence about transformation, and the understanding of this is manifested in millennialist theology. Miller considered mainstream Protestantism had embraced postmillennialism, with an emphasis on transforming society, but premillennialists have emphasized saving the individual soul.[77] However, the doctrine of postmillennialism has largely been abandoned for that of amillennialism, which sees the millennium as the period between the first and second advents of Jesus.[78] As noted, both the doctrines of co-creation and the transformational theology of work are related to either an amillennial or postmillennial eschatology, and neither addresses the specifics of a theology of work that would be appropriate for a premillennial eschatology.

Summary

The doctrine of co-creation utilizes portions of the Genesis narrative in its formulation, although this use is recognized as selective. The transformational theology of work has an eschatological focus, but recognizes the importance of "protological" concepts. Although there is considerable agreement between these two doctrines, the differences and concerns expressed suggest a re-evaluation of the Genesis material to develop the theology of work that emerges from it would be useful.

---

74. Ibid., 90–91.
75. Miller, D., *God at Work*, 24–25.
76. Bosch, *Transforming Mission*, xv.
77. Miller, D., *God at Work*.
78. See Stefanovic, *Revelation of Jesus Christ*, 562–63; Riddlebarger, *Case for Amillennialism*; Walvoord, "Amillennialism from Augustine to Modern Times."

4

General Concepts from Genesis Literature

Preliminary examination of the voluminous exegetical Genesis literature provided several valuable ideas that contributed to the study, although it was apparent there is a very limited focus on the topic of work in this vast literature. Many have recognized the foundational nature of Genesis material. "The extension of God's action to the whole of humankind, to its sin and revolt in the latter part of the Old Testament (e.g., Deutero-Isaiah) stands in immediate relationship with what the primeval story says about sin as part of the human condition. And the whole of Apocalyptic Literature is intelligible only in this context."[1] Mathews, as noted, recognized the foundational value of Genesis for the development of Christian theology.[2] David Cotter asserted that the early chapters of Genesis are the most influential parts of the Old Testament in the development of Christian theology.[3] Fretheim observed the Bible canon places Genesis first, thus dealing with creation before redemption, which he considered was of immeasurable value in understanding all that follows.[4]

However, not everyone has seen Genesis material as foundational. Brueggemann[5] and von Rad[6] claimed that no biblical prophet, psalmist, or narrator made identifiable reference to the Eden story, Genesis 2–3. But T. Stordalen observed there are several references to the Eden Garden in

---

1. Westermann, *Genesis 1–11*, 67.
2. Mathews, *Genesis 1—11:26*, 22.
3. Cotter, *Genesis*, 20.
4. Fretheim, *God and World in the OT*, xiv.
5. Brueggemann, *Genesis: Biblical Commentary*, 41.
6. Rad, *Genesis: A Commentary*, 74.

biblical literature, and rejection of the passage is partly due to documentary source considerations.[7]

The Unifying Framework

Recent exegetes[8] have commented that Genesis is built on a framework of "*tôlēdôt*" sections. This *tôlēdôt* framework supports the whole of Genesis, and suggests that the book is conceptually a unified whole. This indicates that to develop a doctrine of work from Genesis it would be worthwhile to study the whole book.

Interest in Work / Occupation of Characters

The Work of God

Beginning with the activity of God, the author of Genesis takes considerable interest in the activity and occupations of the characters described. The next chapter enumerates the large number of verbs employed to describe God's work of creation.[9] Genesis begins with work, emphasized by God celebrating his work with blessing and sanctifying a day of rest.[10]

The Work of Humans

Hart argued that the prologue of Genesis (Gen 1:1—2:3) indicates work is a significant theme for the whole book.[11] "The creation narrative of Genesis 1:1—2:3 is characterized by three fundamental ideas which are linked to each other by the theme of man's work: creation in six days, man as the image of God, and the Sabbath. This theme is sustained in the main body of

---

7. Stordalen, *Echoes of Eden*, 22.
8. For example, Turner; Cotter; Mathews.
9. Thompson and Ostring, "God's Labor of Love."
10. Rest reflects the most common translation of Gen 2:3. See later for recognition that šābat more properly means cease. However, both the *Hebrew and Aramaic Lexicon of the Old Testament* (p. 1407) and the *Dictionary of Classical Hebrew* (vol. 8, p. 254) define šābat as meaning both "rest" and "cease."
11. Hart, "Genesis 1:1—2:3 as a Prologue."

the book of Genesis, as one could expect with material which was intended to serve as a careful prologue to the rest of the book."[12]

Cosden did not base his theology of work on Genesis but he suggested the "first eleven" chapters of the book could be viewed as a "play about work, an interactive drama."[13] He suggested the structure of the primordial narrative emphasizes that human activity, and not only God's, will be the theme of the drama.[14]

Westermann contended that the patriarchal narratives have relevance for modern understanding. Commenting on chapter 41, Joseph's release from prison and recognition by Pharaoh, he wrote: "This is a peculiarly modern chapter . . . stating clearly that in certain situations the gift of blessing must be supplemented by a well-thought-out policy which can be administered only by a central authority."[15]

Work an Unrecognized Theme of Genesis

Although Westermann recognized human achievement as a significant theme in the primeval story (the other themes being creation, and crime and punishment), he also noted that this theme is the "section of the primeval story to which exegesis has scarcely given any attention or significance."[16] He claimed "the three groups [of theme] described above belong only to the primeval story, and there is no sign of them in the patriarchal cycle, even though the story of Sodom and Gomorrah has something of crime and punishment about it."[17] Although this absence in the patriarchal narrative can be challenged, it is significant that Westermann recognized the wider work/occupation interest of the Genesis author. Westermann noted the first remark after describing the births of Cain and Abel concerns their occupations, and said: "the purpose of this must be particularly significant."[18]

Hart and Cosden recognized the theme of work in the primeval narrative, but Hart added "the importance of the theme of 'work' in the carefully written prologue" prepares the reader for the further development of this theme in the body of the book.[19] He suggested there is an allusion to fruit-

---

12. Ibid., 315.
13. Cosden, *Heavenly Good of Earthly Work*, 81–86.
14. Ibid., 86.
15. Westermann, *Genesis 37–50*, 98.
16. Westermann, *Genesis 1–11*, 18, 51.
17. Ibid., 19.
18. Ibid., 293.
19. Hart, "Genesis 1:1—2:3 as a Prologue," 336.

ful labor in the frequent use (fifty-nine times according to Hart) of the word "land" in the Abraham cycle. Hart suggested the contemporary reader tends to impute a nationalistic tone to these references to "land," but he proposed in the context of Genesis "land" simply means food and work.[20] Hart noted the Genesis narrative ends with the lengthy Joseph cycle detailing Joseph's work for his father, the Egyptian Potiphar, in the prison, and famously as an official for the Pharaoh.[21] The theme of work is especially prominent in the Jacob cycle, where the patriarch works for both wives and livestock.

Bruce Waltke[22] and C. John Collins[23] offered insights about human work in their studies of Genesis material, without noting it as a significant theme. But an extensive search indicates that few other commentators have recognized work as a significant theme of the entire Genesis narrative.

Westermann's suggestion that there has been little attention given to the theme of achievement in Genesis encourages the focus of this thesis. Further, his suggestion that this does not continue into the patriarchal narrative suggests the possibility of a different focus from achievement in the patriarchal narratives.

The Theme of Blessing

Many commentators have noted the theme of blessing in Genesis, which Scullion poetically called the "signature tune" of the patriarchal story.[24] Westermann observed, "The patriarchal community draws its life from blessing; it is due to God's blessing that children are born and grow up, that work is crowned with productive growth and expansion, that watering places are found and preserved, that the labour of the herdsman is fruitful."[25] This suggests the importance of blessing and its converse when building a theology of work from the Genesis narrative.

Summary

Genesis is recognized as foundational in developing all Christian theology. Although the theme of work in Genesis has not been widely recognized, the

---

20. Ibid.
21. Ibid.
22. Waltke, *Genesis: A Commentary*.
23. Collins, *Genesis 1–4*.
24. Scullion, *Genesis: A Commentary*, 102.
25. Westermann, *Genesis 12–36*, 575.

work activity of its characters is clearly described. Genesis begins with the creative work of God, and this is followed by descriptions of human work. Two characteristics of the Genesis narrative that suggest it should be studied as a whole are the *tôlēdôt* framework on which it is built, and the general theme of blessing.

5

God's Labor of Love: Creation and the Fall, Genesis 1:1—3:24

THE FIRST TWO PERICOPES of Genesis indicate work is a highly positive entity initiated by God himself, and intended as a gift for humanity.[1] "The very first chapter of scripture is about work,"[2] God's work, performed in an atmosphere of blessing (Gen 1:22, 26) and pronounced by God as very good and finished. It concludes in a day of blessing (Gen 2:1–3). However, that God worked, and declared his work good, was a shocking concept for ancients, who considered work was for slaves and women, and a free man's life was characterized by leisure.[3]

Mathews noted that the creation account is theocentric, not creature centric.[4] Clearly, God initiated work. "[T]he structure of the account shows us that our author has presented God as if he were a craftsman going about his workweek."[5] The prologue highlights the pleasing nature of God's creative work by repeatedly using the Hebrew word *tôb*, good (Gen 1:4, 10, 12, 18, 21, 25, 31). The Great Worker, God, in pleased satisfaction surveys the results of his effort, and describes it as good, *tôb*. "To affirm that creation is 'good,' then, is to affirm that God takes delight in it."[6] God's pleasure finally overflows and he describes his work as very good (Gen 1:31). This satisfaction is suggested after the creation of humanity (Gen 2:7), and Kidner effectively portrays God's pleasure in the final work of creating *hā- ʾādām*: "Breathed is warmly personal, with the face to face intimacy of a kiss and the

---

1. Waltke, *Genesis: A Commentary*, 87.
2. Goldingay and Innes, *God at Work*, 3.
3. Lohfink, *Great Themes from the OT*, 203–7.
4. Mathews, *Genesis 1—11:26*, 113.
5. Collins, *Genesis 1-4*, 77.
6. Ibid., 70.

significance that this was giving as well as making; and self giving at that."[7] The blessings bestowed on the products of God's work, including humans, reinforce the idea of divine satisfaction (Gen 1:22, 28). This atmosphere of blessedness and wellbeing culminates in the seventh day of celebration that is blessed in its entirety. This presentation of God's activity suggests that to work, to accomplish something, is good, indeed very good.

God Shares the Work Experience

Since God is portrayed as finding work so good, it is not surprising he shared this positive experience with the creatures made in his own image. The gift of work is intimated as soon as God made humanity: "Let them have dominion over the fish of the sea and over the birds of the heavens and over the livestock and over all the earth and over every creeping thing that creeps on the earth . . . Be fruitful and multiply and fill the earth and subdue it . . ." (Gen 1:26, 28). "Genesis 1–2 implies that humanity's chief and highest end is to work for God in the world,"[8] although Stott considered worship was the pinnacle of human activity.[9] Significantly, as will be shown, the pericope of Genesis 4 indicates God gave priority to worship over human achievement.

Work: A Major Theme of Genesis

Hart argued that this focus on work in the prologue (Gen 1:1—2:3) signifies the important theme of work in Genesis.[10] Collins recognized that "many ethicists have spoken of 'creation ordinances,'" which he regarded as falling under three categories: the family, religion, and labor.[11] Thus the first three chapters of the Genesis narrative that describe God's own work, his original intentions for human work, and the tragic disruption of those intentions, lays the foundation on which to study the theme of work in the rest of the Genesis narrative.

---

7. Kidner, *Genesis*, 60.
8. Goldingay, *OT Theology: Israel's Gospel*, 110.
9. Stott, *New Issues Facing Christians*, 189.
10. Hart, "Genesis 1:1—2:3 as a Prologue," 315.
11. Collins, *Genesis 1–4*, 130.

First Creation Pericope: God Works

The prologue employs a large number of verbs describing God's creative process, and highlights the divine–human relationship. Westermann recognized this,[12] and Steven Thompson has enumerated them (see Table 1). While Thompson suggested there may be discussion about some of the verbs, or their subject, the picture is undeniably one of significant activity and intimate involvement. "God's sustained creative initiative in this section of the creation account is summarized by employing the Hebrew [noun] *məlā'kâ*, 'work,' three times in 2:2–3. God completed (*kālâ*) his work on the seventh day, he then rested (*šābat*),[13] and blessed and consecrated the seventh day, because in it he rested from all his work. This pericope employs twenty-two different verbs a total of sixty-nine times to expand the actions of God under the twin general terms *bārā'*, 'create,' and *məlā'kâ*, 'work.'"[14]

In the first Creation pericope (Gen 1:1—2:3) there is a predominance of speaking and pronouncement verbs. God is portrayed effortlessly speaking into existence whatever he chooses, although the verb *'āśâ*, simply "made," does not clarify how much effort is involved. The pericope clearly portrays God's power and infinite ability to achieve whatever he plans.

---

12. Westermann, *Genesis 1–11*, 86.
13. See later discussion of the full meaning of *šābat*.
14. Thompson and Ostring, "God's Labor of Love."

Table 1. Elohim's Work According to Creation Pericope 1, Genesis 1:1-2:4a

Verb	Gloss	Occurrences	Total
bārā' * qal/niph	"Elohim created"	1:1, 21, 27, 27, 27; 2:3 (all qal) 2:4a (niphal)	6 1
'āmar # qal	"Elohim said" (introducing speech)	1:3, 6, 9, 11, 14, 20, 24, 26, 28, 29	10
hāyâ qal	"Let happen!" (intent) ["It happened" (result)]	1:3, 6, 6, 14, 14, 15, 29 (jussive) [1:3, 6, 6, 7, 9, 11, 15, 24, 30=9]	7
rā'â * qal	"Elohim saw ... was good"	1:4, 10, 12, 18, 21, 25, 31	7
bdl * hiphil	"Elohim divided"	1:4, 6, 7, 14	4
qāra' * qal	"Elohim named"	1:5, 5, 8, 10, 10	5
'āśâ * # qal	"Elohim made" "Let us make!" (intent)	1:7, 16, 25, 31; 2:2, 2, 3, 4a 1:26 (cohortative)	8 1
qwh # niphal	"Be(come) gathered!"	1:9 (jussive)	1
r'h # niphal	"Let appear!" (intent)	1:9 (jussive)	1
dša' # hiphil	"Let sprout/shoot forth!"	1:11 (jussive)	1
nātan * qal	"Elohim placed/set"	1:17, 29	2
šāraṣ # qal	"Let teem with!"	1:20 (jussive)	1
brk * piel	"Elohim blessed"	1:22, 28; 2:3	3
ytz' # hiphil	"Let bring forth!"	1:24 (jussive)	1
rādâ # qal	"(Let) dominate!"	1:26 (jussive), 28 (imperative)	2
pārâ # qal	"Be fruitful!"	1:28 (imperative)	1
rābâ # qal	"Increase!"	1:28 (imperative)	1
mālē' # qal	"Fill!"	1:28 (imperative)	1
kābaš # qal	"Subdue/master!"	1:28 (imperative)	1
kl' * piel	"Elohim completed"	2:2	1
šābat * qal	"Elohim ceased/rested"	2:2, 3	2
qdš * piel	"Elohim consecrated"	2:3	1
22	TOTAL VERBS	TOTAL OCCURRENCES	69

Verbs of Elohim's *actions* are marked with *. Verbs of Elohim's *speech/speaking* are marked with #

Sabbath: God's Blessed and Finished Work

God repeatedly declared his work to be good, and at the end of the first creation pericope pronounced it very good, and blessed it. The blessing involved both future relationships (be fruitful and multiply) and present rest.

God celebrated the success of his accomplishments by taking and blessing a day to cease work (Gen 2:1–3). It is significant that the seventh day was blessed because God had finished the creative work he had set out to accomplish; the value of the seventh day was that the work was finished and could be clearly seen in all its completed goodness. Westermann observed: "In order to understand properly the meaning of the sanctification and blessing of the seventh day, it is most important not to isolate it, but to see it as a conclusion of the whole. Special attention is given to the seventh day; it is holy and blessed precisely as the conclusion of the work of the previous six days, and can only be understood in relation to them."[15] Thus the seventh day emphasizes the good, blessed, and finished quality of the creative work of God. It also suggests that blessing itself involves the concept of completion, wholeness.

The Sabbath emphasizes that this world is the work of God, and God alone. Moltmann stated, "The completion of creation through the peace of the Sabbath distinguishes the world as creation from the view of the world as Nature. It is the Sabbath which blesses, sanctifies and reveals the world as God's creation."[16] Waltke noted that the Sabbath is the first thing in the Torah to which God imparts his holiness,[17] and Turner observed that nothing else God created was made holy.[18] The creation of Sabbath indicates God's plan to offer blessing to the world and its inhabitants. Goldingay said, "The Sabbath confronts the culture. It still does . . . God did not work a seven day week."[19] Further, the Sabbath rest that God instituted suggests human work should culminate in the type of rest and blessing that God's did. The first creation pericope ends with the institution of the Sabbath and emphasizes God's transcendence,[20] yet his pleasure in, and relationship to, the created order.

---

15. Westermann, *Genesis 1–11*, 170.
16. Moltmann, *God in Creation*, 6.
17. Waltke, *Genesis: A Commentary*, 68.
18. Turner, *Back to the Present*, 14.
19. Goldingay and Innes, *God at Work*, 11.
20. Turner, *Genesis*, 35–36.

Divine-Human Relationship intimated in Institution of the Sabbath

Hart observed that the use of the word məlā'kâ in Gen 2:2–3 is unusual, as it is the ordinary word for human work. In its 155 occurrences in the Old Testament, only these three in Gen 2:1–3 and one other (Jer 50:25, denoting God's work of judgment), refer to the work of God. Hart suggested the most probable reason for this was a deliberate intention to emphasize some correspondence between God's work and human work.[21] This suggests a working relationship between humans and the Creator. The observation also implies that God had definite plans about human work, and how this should be done. However, the word bārā' found in this pericope, and throughout the Bible, is applied only to the creative work of God.[22]

Sigve Tonstad pointed out that the word "rest" is an inadequate translation.[23] Cassuto cautioned against attributing to God a need to rest. He preferred to translate šābat as "abstained."[24] Rather than the passivity suggested in "rest," Tonstad suggested either "desisted" or "ceased" could also be used. This implies that the "rest" of the seventh day indicates God had arrived where he wanted to be.[25] He had reached the satisfied conclusion of his work. The importance of this idea had been recognized by Barth: "[the characteristic of God revealed] in the rest of the seventh day is his love," and "the reason why he refrains from further activity on the seventh day is that he has found the object of his love and has no need for any further works."[26] Love, of course, occurs only in relationship.

Second Creation Pericope: God's Active Involvement

Although the apparent ease of the creative work of God depicted in the first creation pericope is in dramatic contrast to the struggles depicted in the Babylonian creation narratives,[27] the text gives evidence that God's creative activity involved pleasant, intimate interaction with his creation, and the

21. Hart, "Genesis 1:1—2:3 as a Prologue," 316.
22. Thompson and Ostring, "God's Labor of Love."
23. Tonstad, *Lost Meaning of the Seventh Day*, 32.
24. Cassuto, *Commentary on Genesis: Adam to Noah*, 63.
25. Tonstad, *Lost Meaning of the Seventh Day*, 32.
26. Barth, *Doctrine of Creation*, 215.
27. Westermann, *Genesis 1–11*, 81; Laurence Turner personal communication, 2011; see also material in Hesiod, *Works and Days*; and Dalley, *Myths from Mesopotamia*.

hint of effort. The second creation pericope pictures the Creator God as handling and moulding the dirt and dust when he creates *hā-'ādām* (Gen 2:7). God himself indicated that the "goodness" of the created world is not a detached cerebral goodness merely aesthetically experienced, but one to be physically handled and enjoyed. God is presented as handling the dirt himself before he asks *hā-'ādām* to work the soil of the created garden, to *'ābad* and *šāmar* (Gen 2:15).[28] The prologue therefore suggests that the intended work of humans made in the image of God may require energy, but this work will be satisfying and will result in blessing and relatedness. Kidner's recognition that breathing the breath of life into *hā-'ādām* was like giving a kiss[29] captures the friendly aspect of God's creative activity.

The second creation pericope of Gen 2:4–25 includes both active and intimately involved categories of verbs. Turner noted that whereas the first creation pericope ends with the institution of the Sabbath that emphasizes God's transcendence, the second ends in marriage, emphasizing relationship.[30]

The second creation pericope employs seventeen verbs twenty-six times to describe God's creative work (see Table 2). The verbs in this pericope imply ease, but importantly also activity and relationship. In verse 7 "he breathes," and verses 21 and 22 "he closed up" and "built up." The word *bārā'* does not occur in this section, indicating a different emphasis more in accord with the work humans would be asked to do. This section contains the ambiguous *'āśâ*, but there are also more clearly active verbs such as *yāṣa* (God as potter), *nāṭa* (God as gardener), *ṣmḥ* (God as planter), *npl* (God as anaesthetist), *sāgar* (God as surgeon), and *bānâ* (God as builder).[31] These verbs indicate that although God did not struggle to make the world, as in Babylonian creation narratives,[32] he clearly expended energy, and was intimately involved with his creation.

---

28. *'ābad* and *šāmar*, to serve and to guard, although with many deeper nuances, is a key phrase explored further in the thesis. It was also used to denote the work of the priests (Num 3:7), linking the term to worship.

29. Kidner, *Genesis*, 60.

30. Turner, *Genesis*, 35–36.

31. These verbs present rich images for work, as noted in the table, but will not be explored in depth because of limitations of space.

32. Westermann, *Genesis 1–11*, 81; see also Dalley, *Myths from Mesopotamia*.

Table 2. Yahweh Elohim's Work According to Creation Pericope 2, Genesis 2:4b-25

Verb	Gloss	Occurrences	Total
'*āśâ* * qal	"Y. El. made" "I will make" (intent)	2:4b 2:18	1 1
mṭr * hiphil	"Y. El. caused to rain"	2:5	1
yāṣar * qal	"Y. El. formed"	2:7, 8, 19	3
nāpaḥ * qal	"Y. El. breathed"	2:7	1
hāyâ qal	"and it happened" (result)	2:7	1
nāṭa * qal	"Y. El. planted"	2:8	1
śîm * qal	"Y. El. placed"	2:8	1
ṣmḥ * hiphil	"Y. El. caused to grow"	2:9	1
lāqaḥ * qal	"Y. El. took"	2:15, 21, 22	3
nwḥ * hiphil	"Y. El. settled"	2:15	1
ṣwh # piel	"Y. El. commanded"	2:16	1
'*āmar* # qal	"Y. El. said"	2:16, 18	2
'*ākal* # qal	"You may/must eat" "You may/must not eat"	2:16 (infinitive absolute) 2:16, 17	1 2
bw' * hiphil	"Y. El. brought"	2:19, 22	2
npl * hiphil	"Y. El. induced [sleep]"	2:21	1
sāgar * qal	"Y. El. closed up"	2:21	1
bānâ * qal	"Y. El. built up"	2:22	1
17	TOTAL VERBS	TOTAL OCCURRENCES	26

*Verbs of Yahweh Elohim's *actions* are marked with *

Verbs of Yahweh Elohim's *speech/speaking* are marked with

The total number of verbs employed in Genesis chapters 1 and 2 to narrate divine creative activity is thus thirty-nine, occurring a total of ninety-five times.[33] This is an impressive recital of God's creative effort, and serves as a tribute to, and acclamation of, the positive and satisfying aspects of his work. But while the verbs in pericope 2 are tightly focused

33. Thompson and Ostring, "God's Labor of Love."

on the creation of humanity and a suitable human diet, they link to features of pericope 1, especially to God's work of creating other creatures, and of providing suitable domains for both them and humans.

The Relational Nature of Human Work

The first creation account of Genesis 1 displays the scope, power, ease, and the finished quality of God's work. Correspondingly it describes the scope of human work under the broad term *rādâ*, dominion. The general broad descriptor of human work is "to have dominion," which the first pericope partially explains as "be fruitful and multiply" and "subdue the earth."[34] Whilst there are studies on the concept of "subdue the earth" in relation to human work,[35] the important intimate aspect denoted by "be fruitful and multiply" should also be acknowledged.

The second pericope (Gen 2:4–25), indicates in more detail the effort God expended in developing the beings made in his own image (Gen 1:27) with whom he could relate. God intimately relates, although in different ways, to both the man and the woman as he takes a rib from one to *bānâ*, "build up," the other. This human couple, who have been made in a manner of intimate relationship, were intended to relate to each other (Gen 2:18, 21–24) and to the natural world around them (Gen 2:15, 19, 20).

Thus the relational aspect of both God's and human work is the focus of the second creation pericope. This pericope describes human work in four relational dimensions. First, *'ābad*, is to serve, or cultivate, the garden (noting *'ōbēd 'ădāmâ*, literally "worker of the ground," is the Hebrew expression for "farmer" in Gen 4:2; Zech 13:5; Prov 12:11, 28:19[36]), and second, *šāmar*, meaning to guard, or take care of, the garden. This care of the garden implies not only relationship with the soil, but also with what makes a garden, that is, the plants. Third, *hā-'ādām* was asked to name, *qārā'* the animals. Finally, the man and woman are to relate so intimately with each other that they become one (Gen 2:4, 15, 19, 20, 22–24).

This emphasis on relationship suggests that in this second, more detailed account of the creation of *hā-'ādām*, God has at least partially demonstrated what he purposed by giving humanity "dominion." The concept of relationship with the earth, plants, and the other creatures was central for

---

34. "Subdue the earth" will be discussed more later.

35. See for example John Paul II, *Laborens Exercens*; Ravid, "Kebash: Marital Commandment," 66–70; Williams, "'Fill the Earth,'" 51–65; Harrison, "Fill the Earth," 3–24.

36. Ringgren entry "'bd," *Theological Dictionary of the OT*, 383.

the exercise of dominion. The intimate relationship God had with the soil in the creation of *hā-ʾādām* suggests the intimate relationship he intended *hā-ʾādām* to have with the both the soil, its plants, and its inhabitants.

Adam's creation from the soil suggests a delicate handling of the natural resources of the earth to make something good, rather than those resources being there simply to meet human ambition. The creation of the woman particularly indicates the vital inter-connected relationship of God's creation. The woman, made from a rib, is intimately part of the man, and as such must not be merely used by him.

Humanity in the Edenic state must not selfishly use the resources of the created world, but rather lovingly serve and guard them. Genesis 2:15 indicates in shorthand form the core job description of human work: "Then the Lord took the man and put him in the garden of Eden to tend it and keep it." The plan for humanity to have dominion over the created world (Gen 1:26), specifically located in a garden, suggests this work, *ʾābad*, "tilling or serving," and *šāmar*, "caring or guarding," would be a pleasant activity. That maintenance-type work was given humans in the Edenic situation challenges both Volf's disparagement of "mere" maintenance[37] and the difficulty Goosen had in classifying the work of a repair mechanic from a co-creationist perspective.[38]

Naming indicates Relationship

The relational aspect of work is further emphasized by the first task given to *hā-ʾādām*: naming the animals and birds (Gen 2:19–20).[39] This indicates that *ʾābad* and *šāmar* was a shorthand description of the interactive aspect of human work. Naming clearly involves relationship. It also implies knowing and understanding the characteristics of the animals being named, and the role of human leadership over the animals.[40]

Cassuto suggested naming is a token of lordship.[41] Turner pointed out that God delegated naming the animals to *hā-ʾādām* (Gen 2:19), thus allowing him to demonstrate his authority in the world as God had showed his in naming the days of the week.[42] Sometimes in later Hebrew situations it was the mother who named a child, demonstrating her relationship with

37. Volf, *Work in the Spirit*, 101–2.
38. Goosen, *Theology of Work*, 69.
39. Stewart, "Redoing the First Work of Adam," 351–66.
40. Turner, *Genesis*, 29; Naidoff, "Man to Work the Soil," 5.
41. Cassuto, *Commentary on Genesis: Adam to Noah*, 130.
42. Turner, *Genesis*, 29.

the child, rather than her authority, which was being emphasized (see for example Gen 35:18; 1 Sam 4:21; 1 Chr 4:9, 7:16). However, Richard Davidson argues that naming is more indicative of discernment than of lordship, (for example when Hagar named God, Gen 16:13) which is significant when *hā-ʾādām* is asked to name the animals, see below.[43]

Thus it must be emphasized that the authority of *hā-ʾādām* over the animals was friendly, not dominating. It involved getting to know, that is, discerning, the creatures God had made, suggesting why God did not name the animals himself. It indicates God was giving *hā-ʾādām* opportunity to express his dominion and care for these creatures by having an intimate knowledge of and friendship with them.

Eugene Peterson noted an important aspect of naming: "What is unnamed is often unnoticed."[44] Peterson described his own experience with birds, and how until he became a birdwatcher and could name birds he never noticed them. As *hā-ʾādām* named the various kinds of animal, bird, and fish, and understood their special values, and needs, he could appreciate and empower them, or recognize their differing characteristics. This latter is implied in the text when *hā-ʾādām* discovers that none of the animals was an *ʿēzer*, "helper," fit for him, literally "one corresponding to him." By this negative evaluation, *hā-ʾādām* indicates he is learning what each animal is fit for and its intended place in God's scheme.

Naming Animals highlights Human Relationship in Work

The naming of the animals reinforces the fundamental relational nature of human work as God intended in an even more profound way. It shows that the secret of human identity does not lie in the power of naming, or even knowing about the animals.[45] The naming occurs after *hā-ʾādām* has been told about his work in the garden. The discovery that none of the animals was a *helper* fit for him suggests that *hā-ʾādām* may have been actively searching for someone to share the *ʿābad* and *šamar* of the garden, and especially to *enable* him be fruitful and multiply. The woman complements the man, without which he would be incomplete.[46]

---

43. Davidson, R., *Flame of Yahweh*, 31–33.

44. Peterson, *Working the Angles*, 155.

45. Kessler and Deurloo, *Commentary on Genesis*, 47.

46. Brown et al., *Jerome Biblical Commentary*, 12; McArdle, "Relational Person," 196.

The use of the word ʿēzer, "helper," to describe the woman's relationship with the man indicates God intended that purposeful activity should be a significant aspect of their oneness. However, the Hebrew ʿēzer is masculine, and is also used to denote *Elohim* and *YHWH* as helper (Gen 18:4; Deut 33:7). Therefore it implies no sense of inferiority.[47] They were one because they were fit for each other, and worked together. Westermann noted: "Human existence includes occupation, or work, v. 15b, and most important of all in community with other human beings, vv. 18–24."[48]

The Divine–Human Work Relationship

Immediately following the prologue, Gen 2:4–5 indicates God planned for humans to work in relationship with himself: "This is the history of the heavens and the earth when they were created, in the day the Lord God made the earth and the heavens, before [not yet] any plant of the field was in the earth and before [not yet] any herb of the field had grown. For the Lord God had not caused it to rain on the earth, and there was no man to till the ground." Twice the word *ṭerem* "not yet" is used, indicating a further development, a working relationship, a divine–human relationship that can only be recognized with awe. The productivity of the created earth would be the result of both God's activity (significantly described as sending rain) and human activity (working the garden).

Goldingay suggested that by giving humans work, God was sharing power in a manner that can only be described as love,[49] a concept emphasizing the relational quality of human work as God originally intended. The first work given humans was interactive (naming animals, Gen 2:19), indicating the broad sweep of human work involved more than "till the ground." "Sending rain" must be shorthand for the whole range of God's supernatural work in relationship with humanity. The pleasant aspect of the work God planned for humanity is captured by a pregnant observation made by Collins: "[O]ne purpose of redemption is to restore man to his proper working order."[50]

---

47. Davidson, R., *Flame of Yahweh*, 29–30.
48. Westermann, *Genesis 1–11*, 220.
49. Goldingay and Innes, *God at Work*, 8.
50. Collins, *Genesis 1–4*, 90.

The Dominion of Man and the Imperium of God

Naming the animals helped *hā- 'ādām* discover that animals had limitations. None of them was a suitable helper for him. This understanding aided his acceptance of the limits of his own function and authority, and by declaring one tree beyond his jurisdiction *hā- 'ādām* could recognize his accountability to God. The work of dominion given to *hā- 'ādām* was specifically over the sea creatures, birds, and the livestock (Gen 1:26), besides the care of the garden (Gen 2:15), and his work also included family relationships[51] resulting from the blessing of being fruitful and multiplying. God's instructions for work would provide the necessary boundaries (Gen 2:15–17), as the broad scope of the work required clearly defined limits.

Pope John Paul II noted that work given to humanity is summed up in the blessing: "fill the earth and subdue (*kābaš*) it; have dominion (*rādâ*) over the fish of the sea, over the birds of the air, and over every living thing that moves on the earth" (Gen 1:26).[52] Whether this blessing implies unlimited power over the created order, or whether there are limits to this power is now explored.

Rādâ, the Authority and Service of Kingly Dominion

Bruce Vawter observed that the term *rādâ* occurs relatively rarely in the Hebrew Bible, and usually in relation to kingship (1 Kgs 5:4; Ps 72:8, 110:2; Isa 14:6; Exod 43:4).[53] Some have regarded *rādâ* as mastery, not necessarily exploitation, but certainly involving compulsion and authority,[54] and that mastering the world is the implication of being made in God's image.[55]

However, the nature of *rādâ*, "have dominion," given in Gen 1:26–28 is explained and expanded in the work command of Gen 2:15–17 as *'ābad* "serve" and *šamar* "guard." Elsewhere this combination is used to refer to the work of the levitical priests in the tabernacle (Num 3:7–8, 18:7).[56] Therefore, although *'ābad* later meant "tilling the soil," possibly denoting manipulating it to extract the most from it, the word at this stage of the narrative means

---

51. Westermann, *Genesis 1–11*, 220.
52. John Paul II, *Laborem Exercens*, section 4.
53. Vawter, *On Genesis*, 57.
54. Goldingay, *OT Theology: Israel's Gospel*, 110.
55. Ibid., 109.
56. Mathews, *Genesis 1—11:26*, 209–10.

"serve," as in the sanctuary priesthood. Further, in Exodus 3:12, *'ābad* is used to denote Moses' worship at the burning bush,[57] suggesting the Genesis use also implies the human relationship with the Creator.

R. R. Reno suggested, "Dominion [*rādâ*] is not just the exercise of the social phenomenon of power," but rather it is "headship that guides and governs so that things can flourish according to their proper purposes."[58] *Rādâ* can also mean subdue in the sense of extracting something of value from the land, in the same way that honey is extracted from a comb, see Judges 14:9.[59] This implies that the land was not there just to meet human needs, but that humans should make the best use of the land for all its inhabitants, thereby empowering the entire creation. It implies a flow of blessing from God to his creation. This connected flow of blessing is implied in Gen 2:5, where it is stated God will send rain and humans will till the ground. Mathews said, "This appointment by God [to subjugate the world] gave the human family privilege but also responsibility as 'caretakers' . . . Human life then . . . is held accountable for the world God has created for humanity to govern."[60]

Rādâ in Concepts from Legal Practice

In ancient times, as in Victorian and Jacobean England (see below), ownership of land was intimately linked with the goodwill of the reigning authority, involving good relationship between the parties, and responsibility of the subordinate to the reigning authority. Linking *rādâ* with ancient concepts of kingly goodwill implies that land will be used in accordance with the policies of the reigning monarch.

In Victorian England the term dominion was used to denote various autonomous political entities that were under British sovereignty, that is, *imperium*,[61] such as those that became Canada and New Zealand.[62] Although these countries had self-government, they were expected to uphold British legal values and contribute positively to the British Commonwealth. A person renting a property is not responsible for its upkeep and

---

57. Ibid., 209.
58. Reno, *Genesis*, 54.
59. Entry "*rādâ*," def. 2, in Clines, *Concise Dictionary*, 414.
60. Mathews, *Genesis 1—11:26*, 164.
61. *Imperium* means "absolute power, supreme authority," *Pocket Oxford Dictionary*, 394.
62. Ibid., 241, entry "dominion."

maintenance, but a person who owns the property, who has *rādâ*, is responsible for its care and development, its *kābaš*. This concept of responsibility is reinforced in the Genesis text.

Dominion and Imperium

The excursion into historical legal concepts elucidates the meaning of dominion compared with the related concept *imperium*. Today dominion means ownership, but importantly it is ownership with limits.[63] Persons may own and have complete responsibility over their house and land, but it is still possible for the government of the day, with its overall *imperium*, to plan to put a road through the property, and despite their dominion, the owners must submit to the government authority.[64] Persons with dominion cannot use their property for illegal use, such as developing narcotic drugs or storing armaments.[65] Thus, someone with dominion does not also have *imperium*, the Latin word denoting the sovereignty and power of the state over the individual.

Genesis uses the ancient Hebrew term *rādâ*, denoting ownership related to kingship, to describe the gift God gave to humans after he created them. *Hā-'ādām* was given dominion, but under the sovereign power of God. The Genesis narrative later takes up the theme of land ownership, that is, dominion, at a very significant time. When God called Abram he promised to give Abram's descendants land which at the time was under the dominion of other peoples (Gen 12:7). This indicates that long after Eden, God still regarded it as his prerogative to give land to whomsoever he chose, that is, he retained the *imperium* to give dominion. But even Israel could not assume perpetual dominion. One of the major themes of the Old Testament is that any person's or group's right to the land, Israel included, is totally dependent on remaining within the will, or covenant, of God, (see, for example, 2 Chr 36:15–21; Dan 2:37, 5:18, 21, 26–28). The supreme monarch of the created order must therefore be God, and not *hā-'ādām*. This challenges the assumption that at creation humanity was given an unfettered perpetual dominion over the world.

---

63. Personal communications from Timothy John Matsis, Barrister and Solicitor, Invercargill, New Zealand, and Ronald Bower, Lawyer, Perth, Australia.

64. Personal communication Timothy Matsis.

65. Ibid.

Kābaš: Subduing to Make the Best Use

The Hebrew term *kābaš* indicates humans were to make the best use of the resources God was placing at their disposal. Although *kābaš* is usually understood to mean dominance and control, as expressed in modern concepts of the word subdue, it also includes the idea of service.[66] Robert Chisholm suggests that *kābaš* has the basic definition of "to bring under control for one's advantage," and he offers a paraphrase of Gen 1:28: "Have a lot of children and populate the earth! Harness its potential and use its resources for your benefit."[67] The term suggests humans will help the land produce what is needed for the diet of humans and other creatures God created.

Moltmann made the observation that the command to subdue the earth is connected with the provision of a plant-based diet for humanity and the animals (Gen 1:29–30). This makes humans stewards of the vegetation of the earth, and additionally, removes any suggestion that *hā-'ādām* had the right to lord it over animals by killing them.[68] Today it has been recognized that a plant-based diet is globally the most effective way of providing food for humans and caring for the earth.[69] Moltmann wished to separate the concept of subduing the earth from having dominion over the animals.[70]

The Eden Covenant

God's instructions to work (Gen 2:15–17) contain the basis for an interpersonal covenant between God himself and the human race,[71] "Then the Lord God took the man and put him in the garden of Eden to work it and keep it. And the Lord God commanded the man, saying, 'You may surely eat of every tree of the garden, but of the tree of knowledge of good and evil you shall not eat, for in the day that you eat of it you shall surely die.'"

These verses are recognized as the first covenant in the Bible.[72] It is beyond the scope of this thesis, but Collins described in detail why the passage should be regarded as a covenant. Referring to Hosea 6:7, he suggested the best translation of this somewhat difficult passage is "like Adam they

---

66. Clines, *Concise Dictionary*, 172.
67. Chisholm, *From Exegesis to Exposition*, 46.
68. Moltmann, *God in Creation*, 224.
69. Young, *Is God a Vegetarian?*, 41–51.
70. Moltmann, *God in Creation*.
71. Collins, *Genesis 1–4*, 138.
72. Dumbrell, *Covenant and Creation*; Collins, *Genesis 1–4*, 138.

transgressed the covenant," although *'ādām* could be a generic term for "men." Despite the lack of the word *bərît*, "covenant," in Gen 2:15–17, the verses have the characteristics of a covenant: they spell out the conditions for man, namely obedience to God's command; show what the punishment will be; and imply that continuing life is the reward for compliance.[73]

Goldingay also supported the idea of an Edenic covenant. "There are a number of covenants between God and humanity in Genesis-Exodus, of varying kinds. In the creation story, admittedly, there is no covenant. The implication may be that it is only when sin has entered into the equation that commitments need to be solemnly ratified and formalized. On the other hand, one of the covenants in Exodus is the 'permanent covenant' involved in keeping the Sabbath, which is a sign that looks back to creation (Exod 20:12–17). In this sense Genesis and Exodus do assume that creation involved a covenant."[74] Collins observed one of the key covenantal features of the whole passage (Genesis 1 and 2), taken up in other Scriptures, is the idea that God is the sovereign owner and ruler of his creation.[75] That is, he has *imperium*.

Brueggemann considered the tendency to focus on the prohibition in Gen 2:15–17 to the exclusion of vocation and permission unfortunate.[76] Instead of a negative prohibition the text is God's positive promise of life (eating freely), occupation (*'ābad* and *šamar*), and the on-going presence of God. Thus it can rightfully be considered the first covenant of grace between God and humanity.[77]

Co-creation and Human Work in the Eden Covenant

The Eden covenant offers two important clues regarding the human work status as intended by God in the perfection of the Eden garden. First, the work contract offered them is to serve, *'ābad*, and guard, *šamar*, the garden. Whilst to serve, that is to offer service, is noble, it implies that *hā-'ādām* has a status subordinate to the supreme sovereignty of God. This does not

---

73. Collins, *Genesis 1–4*, 112–14.

74. Goldingay, "Genesis and Exodus," in Rogerson et al., *Genesis and Exodus*, 18.

75. Collins, *Genesis 1–4*, 79.

76. Brueggemann, *Genesis: Biblical Commentary*, 46.

77. Ward and Venema suggest the "covenant of works" of Gen 2 was one of grace: God graciously offers life. Ward, R., *God and Adam*; Venema, Review of *God and Adam*, 242–48.

suggest that *hā-'ādām* can be regarded as a co-creator in the context of this serving role in the Garden of Eden.

Second, although the primary area in which *hā-'ādām* could be regarded as being a co-creator is in the area of reproduction, Gen 2:15–17 indicates a significant caveat. The gift of fertility bestowed on the human couple, and in fact on all creatures, is an astonishing one, and implies a level of comparability between God's creative ability and the reproductive ability of the creatures. But in the Eden covenant the origin of life is shown as the prerogative of God alone, and he bestows this privilege on those who choose to obey the covenant conditions. God did not warn that he would remove from the human couple the privilege of reproducing, but he did indicate they did not have the power to bestow unlimited life. Life remains firmly in the domain of God's *imperium*, and humans are subordinate.

Special Nature of the Covenant

The special nature of this covenant is highlighted by the Genesis text that follows it. The creation of a relationally fit *'ēzer* for *hā-'ādām* occurs after he discovers his lack of companion when naming the animals. Turner suggested this delay in the creation of woman helps emphasize her importance; she is vital in fulfilling both dominion and reproductive work.[78] The importance of relationship in achieving God's plans for human work is emphasized.

By making *hā-'ādām* aware of the importance and blessedness of human relationship, the importance and blessedness of relationship with God is emphasized. By giving the task of naming the animals, showing the subtle difference between men and women indicated by the different means God used to create them (God made man as a potter would, but he built the woman from a rib[79]), God shows that relationship does not mean sameness. By revealing differences between animals, between humans and animals, and between male and female humans, the naming process has emphasized that humanity is in the image of, but not the same as, or equal to, God.

The Tree of Knowledge of Good and Evil

The introduction of the tree of knowledge of good and evil indicates what God values in his relationship with humans: he wants them to live, but to

---

78. Turner, *Genesis*, 29.
79. Turner, *Back to the Present*, 39.

choose to live in relationship with himself.[80] John Scullion noted "'good and bad' is a mode of speech known as merism(-us), in which two extremes are mentioned to cover the whole, e.g., the heavens and the earth means the universe; God is he who 'forms light and creates darkness, who makes prosperity and creates adversity' (Is 47:7), i.e., God is creator of all and responsible for all."[81] Turner noted another expression that similarly uses two extremes to express merism, the idea of totality: from Dan to Beersheba means the whole country.[82] Therefore this tree represented knowing everything. By asking *hā-ʾādām* to name the animals God showed that he did want humans to know, but knowing involved appropriate relationship with God.

Division Between Good and Evil

Knowing good and evil hints at a tension that God did not intend humans should have to deal with. God repeatedly stated that his creation was good, indicating he intended humans to deal only with good. Eating from the forbidden tree would result in an on-going battle for humans to know what was good and what was evil. This is reflected in the curse pronounced on the serpent: "I will put enmity between you and the woman" (Gen 3:15). Eating from the forbidden tree would place the knowledge of good and evil into every person. Humans would not be good *or* evil, they would become good *and* evil.

This tension in understanding and intent is illustrated several times in the Genesis narrative. For example, the "good" Abram is "evil" when he lies about his wife's identity, and the "evil" Pharaoh understands "good" when he acknowledges that it is indeed not appropriate for him to have another man's wife (Gen 12:19–20). When Abraham perpetrates the same mistake with the Abimelech, it is to the "evil" Abimelech and not the "good" Abraham that God appears in a dream and reveals the severity of the situation (Gen 20:1–18). In this passage Abimelech claims that he is from a righteous nation (Gen 20:4) and God recognizes his "integrity of heart" (Gen 20:6). "Good" Isaac makes mistakes (Gen 20:6–11) and "evil" Esau shows a kind and generous spirit when he rejects Jacob's gift and offers to protect the brother who cheated him (Gen 33:9–15). Judah is an especially good example of good and evil playing out in the life of one person (Gen 37:26–27, 38:1–30, 44:18–34).

80. See Tonstad, "Message of the Trees," 82–97.
81. Scullion, *Genesis: A Commentary*, 39.
82. Turner, *Genesis*, 48.

But the Genesis narrative reveals the reason for this tension. Not only does God not abandon the disobedient human couple (see Gen 3:8-21) but he also continues to work on the behalf of humans. As conditions in the world prior to the Flood became increasingly evil, God revealed that his spirit had been striving with humans, but since they had been rejecting his overtures, he was about to remove his spirit and let evil take over (Gen 6:3).

This has important implications for understanding human work. It indicates that "good" people who profess to belong to God may not always produce good work. It also shows that people who may not obviously belong to God are capable of yielding to the striving of his spirit, and these may therefore produce "good" work. The critical issue is whether the performance of good work is due to the innate goodness of humans. As will be shown, the Genesis narrative indicates good work always comes as a result of God's work. It is also a warning against humans judging the long-term value of the work of other humans.

God's Imperium and Human Work Limits

Genesis 2:8-9 suggests humanity was given dominion over a very fruitful land with "every tree that is pleasant to the sight and good for food." This dominion included the presence of two special trees. Commenting on Gen 2:15, von Rad suggested: "That man was transferred to the garden to guard it indicates that he was called to a state of service and had to prove himself in a realm that was not his own possession."[83] Thus, von Rad recognized there were both responsibility and some kind of limit to the dominion offered humanity. Unfettered exploitation of the resources created by God was not the dominion given to humanity.

This "dominion but with limits," first implied with the mention of the two special trees in the garden (Gen 2: 9) becomes significant when the work of humanity is explained in Gen 2:15-17. "The Lord God took the man and put him in the garden of Eden to work it and keep it. And the Lord commanded the man, saying, 'You may surely eat of every tree of the garden, but of the tree of knowledge of good and evil you shall not eat, for in the day you eat of it you shall surely die.'" Many commentators[84] connect verse 15 (that announces the human responsibility to care for the created order) with the following two verses (which declare a prohibition), a limitation on

---

83. Rad, *Genesis: A Commentary*, 78.

84. See Collins, *Genesis 1-4*, 112; Westermann, *Genesis 1-11*, 220-22; Mathews, *Genesis 1—11:26*, 200; and Brueggemann, *Genesis: Biblical Commentary*, 46.

the activity and dominion of humanity is thus indicated. This limitation declares that God's *imperium* must be recognized. The prohibition is simple: *hā-'ādām* must not eat the fruit of one tree, but only one, in the garden (Gen 2:16–17). Although humans may eat, in fact are commanded to eat[85] from all of the abundant trees growing in the garden, there is one exception.

This single restriction is the sign of the *imperium* of God, and, if accepted, is a token of the presence and relationship of God in the lives of his created beings. Although Westermann suggested there is no rational basis for the prohibition to eat the fruit of the tree,[86] this must be refuted because the prohibition represents the supreme *imperium* of God. Calvin early recognized this and commenting on Gen 2:16 observed, "[I]n this way God designed that the whole human race should be accustomed from the beginning to reverence his deity."[87] Mathews suggested another aspect: "[T]he narrative sets the man in the midst of Eden to perform his managerial work, and God sets before him his first opportunity to express his obedient gratitude,"[88] that is, relationship. *Hā-'ādām* needed to recognize from whence all his blessings flowed. Waltke's suggestion is pertinent: "This unique prohibition confronts humans with the Creator's rule. The tree is good, but it belongs exclusively to God."[89] Although God did not give a reason for withholding permission to eat the fruit, he certainly made it very clear what the consequences of eating would be: You will *surely* die (Gen 2:17), or, "in the day you eat of the fruit of the tree, you will certainly become subject to death."[90] Although Westermann saw no rational base for the prohibition, he did recognize that it "opens up the possibility of a relationship to the one who commands."[91]

Arnold presents further evidence embedded in the creation account that suggests divine sovereignty, *imperium*, was the issue at stake for *hā-'ādām* with the prohibition placed on the tree. Drawing on biblical literary sources Arnold shows that the Sabbath institution at the end of creation was not simply a hymn of praise for the Creator similar to that for Marduk in the *Enuma Elish* and other ancient creation accounts, because it asserts that time is in God's domain.[92] "It summons the reader to *renounce dominion*

---

85. Naidoff, "Man to Work the Soil," 5.
86. Westermann, *Genesis 1–11*, 223.
87. Calvin, *Genesis*, 36.
88. Mathews, *Genesis 1—11:26*, 200.
89. Waltke, *Genesis: A Commentary*, 87.
90. Ben Zvi et al., *Readings in Biblical Hebrew*, 57.
91. Westermann, *Genesis 1–11*, 223.
92. Arnold quotes Brichto, *Names of God*, 69; Tsevat, "Meaning of the Biblical

over time and all the uses we humans have for time. The reader is invited to *acknowledge the lordship of the Creator* [emphases supplied] over time itself, and therefore renounce one's autonomy by embracing God's dominion over time and over oneself. Keeping the Sabbath is equated with acceptance of the sovereign lordship of God."[93] If Creator God, because of his sovereign lordship, retained dominion over time as Arnold suggested, he could also retain dominion over one of the trees he had created. Just as there appeared to be no obvious difference between the fruit trees in the garden, and no obvious difference between the days of the week, God's sovereignty declared there was a difference: one tree had its use withheld, and one day was set apart, sanctified and blessed.

Restriction means Freedom of Choice and Relationship

Martin Kessler and Karel Deurloo noted this restriction demonstrates two important principles. First, there is no freedom without limit. This is indicated in the preamble to the Ten Commandments where God begins the prohibitions by first pointing out "I am YHWH, your God, who led you out of Egypt, out of the house of slavery" (Exod 20:1). "That is to say, you are set free and you may live in freedom! . . . [prohibitions] only exist to protect humankind in the freedom granted."[94] Immediately following this announcement of freedom is the restriction to worship only one God. Whilst the truth of this principle may be difficult to accept, its importance cannot be over-emphasized.

The second related principle Kessler and Deurloo establish is that the prohibition indicates relationship with God. "Central in the commandment is the relationship with God. You are what you are in relationship to him who gives you breath. Breaking that relationship entails choosing death . . . Though he is dust, he lives by the breath that YHWH blows into his nostrils. He lives under the protection of the commandment not to eat of that one tree, for that would destroy this relationship."[95]

Cosden also recognized that broken relationship occurred when the fruit of the forbidden tree was eaten: "They chose to express their identities by doing their God-given work . . . autonomously and *apart from God*

Sabbath," 39–52.
93. Arnold, *Genesis*, 50.
94. Kessler and Deurloo, *Commentary on Genesis*, 45.
95. Ibid., 46.

[emphasis supplied]."[96] God did not intend that humans were to be left alone, without him, to manage the world as best they could. All the wisdom and knowledge of the Sovereign of the Universe was available to the human couple through their relationship to the divine (demonstrated later when God searched for them, Gen 3:8–9).

Choice means Life

Tonstad noted that Revelation, the book that describes the final return to Edenic conditions, presents no tree of knowledge of good and evil, but the tree of life is depicted as having two trunks, one on either side of the river of life (Rev 22:2).[97] The position of both the tree of life and the tree of knowledge of good and evil being in the middle of the garden (Gen 2:9, 3:1–3) raises the question: How can two things both be in "the middle"? Eve tells the serpent that it is the fruit of the tree (singular) in the middle of the garden that she has been told not to eat, or, she adds, touch (Gen 3:2–3; cf. Gen 2:9).

Tonstad suggested these trees, even in Eden, were one, as they are in Revelation. Westermann also suggested the possibility of just one tree.[98] "They" belong to God, who is the giver, the source, of everything, of both life and knowledge, so clearly demonstrated in the two creation pericopes. Mathews observed that the term "tree of life" occurs only in Genesis, Revelation, and Proverbs,[99] and Proverbs is concerned with the concept of wisdom: "wisdom is the tree of life" (Prov 3:13, 18). This supports the singleness of this tree, whose fruit, under God's dominion, was to be given to bring life to the humans.

The Challenge to the Good Quality of God's Work

The serpent's temptation in Genesis 3 focuses on God's prohibition regarding eating from the tree of knowledge of good and evil, but also questions the provision God has made for humans. The serpent distorts the perspective by misquoting both God's prohibition and provision. He said, "Did God

   96. Cosden, *Heavenly Good of Earthly Work*, 94.
   97. Tonstad, "Message of the Trees."
   98. Westermann, *Genesis 1–11*, 211–14.
   99. The references to Prov 3:18, 11:30, 13:12, 15:4; the LXX also uses the term in Isa 65:22, see Mathews, *Genesis 1—11:26*, 202.

actually say 'You shall not eat of *any* tree in the garden?'" [emphasis supplied] whereas God had in fact provided every tree, except one: "And out of the ground the Lord God made to spring up *every tree that is pleasant to the sight and good for food*. [Emphasis supplied] The tree of life was in the midst of the garden, and the tree of knowledge of good and evil" (Gen 2:9).[100]

The woman's response is reminiscent of the description of the trees provided: "the woman saw that the tree was good for food, and a delight to the eyes" (Gen 3:6). She recognized that God had created a beautiful world with abundant provision for her needs, but was asked to agree God had not provided all he should have to meet her desires, especially the desire to "make one wise" (Gen 3:6). The heart of the temptation is the offer to become "like God," knowing everything ("good and evil"). Thus the serpent questions both the quality of God's work and his relationship with humans by his failure to supply them with wisdom.

Serpent suggests God's Creation Work is Unfinished

Whereas the Genesis author has built up in chapter 2 a picture of abundant provision for the human couple: "Of every tree in the garden you may freely eat" (Gen 2:16),[101] and a finished work (Gen 2:1–3), the serpent's question and woman's reply infer otherwise. Eating the forbidden fruit will provide humans with knowledge to improve and perfect the created world so graciously given. Cassuto sums the response: *hā-'ādām* was "not content with what was given to him and desired to obtain more. He did not wish to remain in the position of a child who is under the supervision of his father and is constantly dependent on him; he wanted to learn by himself of the world around him; he aspired to knowledge, to become like God."[102]

The serpent's insinuation of imperfection is echoed in the doctrine of co-creation. The doctrine asserts that "*man*, created in the image of God, shares by his work in the activity of the Creator and that, within the limits of his own human capabilities, man in a sense continues to develop that activity, and *perfects it* [emphasis supplied]."[103] This endorses the serpent's assertion that God's work was not good, that it lacked something and was not finished.

---

100. Waltke, *Genesis: A Commentary*, 91.
101. See Collins, *Genesis 1–4*, 139.
102. Cassuto, *Commentary on Genesis: Adam to Noah*, 113.
103. John Paul II, *Laborem Exercens*, section 25.

Does God need Human help to finish the World?

The world humans now inhabit cannot be called very good, and neither is God's redemptive work finished, as the next pericope in Genesis portrays. But it seems unjustified, as co-creation suggests, that a now less-than-good humanity can assist God in perfecting his creation, even if those capabilities are recognized as limited.

To recognize the present imperfection of the world is self-evident, but the question becomes: How did it become imperfect and who is responsible for restoring it to the "very good" state that Genesis declares God originally pronounced it to be? When God gave hā-'ādām the work of caring for the garden (Gen 2:15) the world was in its original state of "very good." The serpent's suggestion that by improving human knowledge the incomplete (implied) created world could be righted is a serious aspersion against God's work and his assessment of it.

In contrast, the Genesis text asserts that humans, by accepting the serpent's insinuation and separating themselves from God, brought death into the world and made it imperfect and "not good." Since, despite all human effort, nothing has abolished death, it seems unlikely that humans are able to bring the world to perfection.

The Results of the Tragic Human Choice

Genesis states humanity accepted the serpent's offer to attempt to improve the provisions God had made for them, and rejected the beneficent sovereignty of God. They lost innocence, represented by their sudden awareness of total, exposed nakedness,[104] lost original relationship with God as shown by hiding themselves, and lost the right to eat of the tree of life (Gen 3:7–8, 22–23). This fatal choice suggests they may have lost some or all of their dominion, or some or all of their ability to care for the created world as God planned. As shown above, the supreme ruler is God, not hā-'ādām. The covenant with Abram, discussed later in this study, indicates that God continues to bestow dominion as he sees fit, and not as an inevitable continuation of the Edenic gift to all humans.

---

104. Davidson, R., *Flame of Yahweh*, 55–58. Davidson notes that the word for nakedness in Gen 2:25 is 'arom, meaning someone not clothed in the normal manner, whereas in 3:7 the word is 'erom, meaning total exposure, usually of a shameful nature.

Human Delusion of Autonomy

The Reformer Calvin taught that the first couple lost their dominion after their disobedience.[105] By accepting the serpent's proposition they accepted the serpent's offer to work entirely by themselves in their own wisdom, knowledge, and experience; they rejected God's *imperium*. Scullion suggested the woman's action implied: "[She] will experience, master, all; she will determine all, be autonomous. She will be independent of God; she, not God, will determine what is useful or harmful in life."[106] But the broken relationship with God spelt death, not a better life.

Emil Brunner observed, "The story of the Fall reveals the fundamental cause for the breach in communion: the desire to be 'as God.' *Man wants to be on a level with God*, and in so doing *to become independent of him*,"[107] and "[sin] is getting rid of the Lord God, and the *proclamation of self-sovereignty*" [emphases supplied].[108] Waltke suggested, "This unique prohibition confronts humans with the Creator's rule. The tree is good, but it belongs exclusively to God."[109]

Scullion said, "[T]he human person is confined within limits and, though intelligent and free to choose, *subject to God*. This is the meaning of the prohibition in 2:16–17, *a prohibition which imposes no hardship*, but is an expression of the limitations. The man and the woman *will not remain within their limitations*; they will *put themselves in the place of God*; they will be morally autonomous; they will be independent of God; *they will be God*; and when man and woman try to be God, they never do it very well"[110] [emphases supplied].

It is of interest that "In Islam the problem is self sufficiency, the hubris of acting as if you can get along without God, who alone is self-sufficient."[111] Or, as Sufi mystic Rumi wrote, "The idol of your self is the mother of all idols."[112] But tragically, as Turner pointed out, Eve actually now came under the dominion of the serpent.[113]

---

105. Discussed in Hart, "Teaching: John Calvin," 122–23.
106. Scullion, *Genesis: A Commentary*, 39.
107. Brunner, *Christian Doctrine of Creation*, 92.
108. Ibid., 93.
109. Waltke, *Genesis: A Commentary*, 87.
110. Scullion, "Genesis 1–11: An Interpretation," 13.
111. Prothero, *God is not One*, 32.
112. Chittick, *Sufi Doctrine of Rumi*, 82. Quoted in Prothero, *God is not One*, 32.
113. Turner, *Back to the Present*, 49.

Human Relationships Changed

The aspect of human existence highlighted in the first two chapters is relationship. Humans were made to relate to God (Gen 2:5, 3:8–9); to the ground and garden (Gen 1:29, 2:7, 15); to each other (Gen 1:26–28, 2:18, 21–24); and to the other creatures made by God (Gen 1:26–28, 2:19).

The Creator's intention that the couple work together "as helpers corresponding to each other" was eroded by the tree-side discussion with the serpent. By failing to support and help each other as the Creator designed, they became vulnerable to the destructive suggestions of the serpent. This indicates human relationship breakdown. Significantly, hā-ʾādām is silent although he was "with her" at the tree (Gen 3:6). Although the command not to eat of the tree of knowledge of good and evil was specifically given to hā-ʾādām (Gen 2:16) and the woman created after this (Gen 2:18–24), he is totally compliant when offered the fruit.

The equality between the couple has gone: the man will now rule over the woman, although she has the promise she will "yearn" for him (Gen 3:16).[114] But the curse God later pronounced simply recognized what had already happened: when the couple meet God in the garden, blame and reproach now characterized the relationship between them. The man retorted that it is both the woman and God who are responsible for the fruit-eating disaster (Gen 3:12).

Furthermore, the couple is now suddenly afraid of God and hide (Gen 3:8). The divine–human relationship has also been disrupted. In fact, the garden pericope ends with all human relationships seriously ruptured: between God and humanity (Gen 3:8, 22–24), between man and woman (Gen 3:12, 16), and between the man and the ground and its products (Gen 3:17–19).

Human Work Changed

Human work was introduced as a divine–human co-operative partnership (Gen 2:5) and a helpful companionship (Gen 2:18). Although the focus of the Genesis prologue was God's work, human work was an integral part of the Edenic covenant (Gen 2:15–17). The now-broken covenant implies there will be a change in the work situation of humans. After eating the forbidden fruit, the couple's first self-perceived problem is nakedness (Gen 3:10), but this is effectively remedied only by a work of God (Gen 3:21). The

---

114. Davidson, R., *Flame of Yahweh*, 73.

text of this passage thus clearly indicates human effectiveness has not been improved by eating the forbidden fruit.

Humans fail to Clothe Themselves

In their first recorded work after attaining their newfound knowledge, the couple chose fig leaves to provide coverings for themselves. However, this work using their own wisdom and knowledge gave at best temporary relief. The fig leaf garment, ḥăgōrâ, "a belt or loin cloth,"[115] did not cover them, because they needed to hide from God when he came searching for them (Gen 3:8). It would therefore be reasonable to assume that the declared result of eating the fruit, that is death (Gen 3:17), was already taking effect, and the leaves were withering and dying in the manner familiar to all humans ever since.

In highlighting the couple's choice of fig leaves, which have the appearance of being large and substantial, the Genesis author almost humorously presents the futility of unaided human wisdom and effort, and the on-going need for divine help. Lest this seem to be trivializing important salvific principles it is important to note, in the context of understanding human work, how transitory was the human solution to the problem of nakedness, compared with the durable clothing God provided.

Thus even before the curses are pronounced, the text shows that acceptance of the serpent's offer of increased knowledge has not been fulfilled. Contrary to the serpent's alluring promise, the couple actually know very little, not even the basics of how to clothe themselves effectively. Westermann observed this lack of success in human work after the serpent encounter and wrote, "Both God in 2:8f and the couple in 3:7f know that something is not good; both 'create' something to help the situation. [God creates a woman, the couple 'create' ḥăgōrâ from fig leaves.] But there is the widest gulf between what is actually done in each case . . . It is only the encounter with God that shows the couple's efforts to make something to counter their nakedness has not been successful, and that ultimately the serpent is not justified. The aprons that man and woman made do not hide them from God."[116]

---

115. Clines, *Concise Dictionary*, 108.
116. Westermann, *Genesis 1–11*, 252.

God's Work Clothes the Couple

What the human couple fails to achieve, God does for them. Genesis 3:21 records that God made for them, probably in a shocking first encounter with creature death, durable and substantial clothing from animal skins, the *kutōnet*, "a long shirt-like garment."[117] The verb used to describe God's action in making the garments has already occurred eleven times in the creation pericopes, *'āśâ*,[118] and thus links God's creative and redemptive power.[119]

God declares Human Work Changed

The work of humans is now portrayed as significantly changed from the divine–human co-operative of Gen 2:5 to the painful struggle intimated by God's response to *hā-'ādām* eating the forbidden fruit. Henceforth both female work (bearing children) and male work (tilling the soil) would be characterized by *'iṣābôn*, toil and pain. These opening chapters of Genesis thus challenge the basic assumptions of co-creationism: first, that God did not finish his original creative work, second, that work is the fundamental dimension of humanity, and third, that sin has not changed human work.

God's Rescue Work for Humans Continues

God's response to the emergency presented by the human choice to desire autonomous knowledge above relationship with their Creator is immediately one of intense activity. Although his creative work was declared finished (Gen 2:1), God must now continue to work to rescue the couple from their terrible predicament. There is a new cluster of verbs in the text applying to divine activity that occurs after the couple eat the fruit. Humans who are unable to clothe themselves now urgently need God's help, and there is no indication that their own work can rectify the situation.

Thompson noted (see Table 3) the text highlights this human need of divine work. In Genesis 3, many different verbs are used to indicate the

---

117. Clines, *Concise Dictionary*, 185.

118. Mathews, *Genesis 1—11:26*, 255; Thompson and Ostring, "God's Labor of Love."

119. It has been argued that in clothing the couple God is inaugurating them as priests, see Davidson, R., *Flame of Yahweh*, 58. But this is anticipating later scriptural developments.

intense activity of God in meeting the human predicament, but chapter 3 echoes the previous chapters by repeating key verbs already employed earlier to describe God's creation work.[120] Six verbs from the previous chapters are repeated, while eight additional ones describing God's ongoing, active, and progressive involvement with his creation are employed, giving a total of fifty-three verbs employed a total of 119 times in the first three chapters of Genesis to depict divine creative "work." God was very busy!

This description of God's continuing work for human need is noteworthy. While in Gen 2:15 *hā-ʾādām* was to guard/keep the garden, upon his expulsion, God himself took over the task, according to 3:24.[121] This is further confirmation that there is ineffectiveness in the human ability to perform. It indicates there has been a dramatic change, not only in the nature of human work, but also in the human ability to perform work. Although God's work of creation was finished (Gen 2:1–3), his work to rescue humanity from their difficulties clearly has not.

---

120. Thompson and Ostring, "God's Labor of Love."
121. Thompson, "Divine Work."

Table 3. Yahweh Elohim's Work According to Creation Pericope 3, Genesis 3:1–24

Verb	Gloss	Occurrences	Peric. 3 total	Peric. 1 & 2 total	Grand total
'āśâ * qal	"Y. El. made"	3:1, 21	2	11	13
hlk * hithp	"Y. El. walking about"	3:8	1	0	1
qārā' # qal	"Y. El. called out"	3:9	1	5	6
'āmar # qal	"Y. El. said" (finite vb.)	3:9, 11, 13, 14, 16, 17, 22	7	12	20
	"Y. El. said" (partic.)	3:17	1		
ṣwh # piel	"Y. El. commanded"	3:11, 17	2	1	3
nātan * qal	"Y. El. gave"	3:12	1	2	3
šît # qal	"I will set"	3:15	1	0	1
rbh # hiphil	"I will multiply"	3:16	1	1	2
'ārar # qal	"come under curse"	3:14, 17	2	0	2
lbš * hiphil	"Y. El. clothed"	3:21	1	0	1
šlḥ * piel	"Y. El. sent out"	3:23	1	0	1
grš * piel	"Y. El. drove out"	3:24	1	0	1
škn * hiphil	"Y. El. caused to dwell"	3:24	1	0	1
šāmar * qal	"to guard/keep"	3:24	1	0	1
14	TOTAL VERBS	TOTAL OCCURRENCES	24	32	56

Verbs of Yahweh Elohim's *actions* are marked with *
Verbs of Yahweh Elohim's *speech/speaking* are marked with #

But Human Work Continues

However, the final directive of God to the couple in chapter 3 is important. "Therefore, the Lord God *sent him out* from the garden of Eden, *to work* [emphases supplied] the ground from which he was taken. He drove out the man, and at the east of the garden of Eden he placed the cherubim and a flaming sword that turned every way to guard the way to the tree of life" (Gen 3:23–24). God thus retains the right to expel humans from at least part of their area of dominion. The couple no longer has any right to their dominion over the garden. God with his sovereign *imperium* can give or take away that dominion.[122]

But, somewhat surprisingly, despite his incompetence and reduced ability, despite relationship difficulties, hā-'ādām is sent out from the garden to work. God did not abandon humanity to their shameful nakedness. Furthermore, embedded in the curse pronounced on the serpent, is the suggestion that humanity still has a choice about whether to work with the serpent or with God. When there is "enmity" there are two opposing influences, implying an ongoing need for choice.

The Genesis narrative thus gives no warrant to assume that after eating the forbidden fruit either human dominion, or work in that dominion, would be the same as God had originally intended. And there is a large question over whether humans have sufficient knowledge to manage on their own.

Answering the urgent question, do humans *know* how to *work* on their own, seems vital for the remainder of the Genesis narrative. It is noted that God does not remove the gift of work, and the couple is specifically sent from the garden to work (Gen 3:23). Although human work was not the focus of the first three chapters, the narrative implies it now may be. The couple is not abandoned: the use of eight additional verbs in Genesis chapter 3 indicates the continuing personal work commitment God makes towards humanity.

Summary

Genesis begins with God's work, and a large number of verbs are utilized to portray this. The first creation pericope ends with the Sabbath, emphasizing God's sovereignty, and the second pericope ends in marriage, emphasizing the importance of relationship. Humans were originally made to relate to God (Gen 2:5, 3:8-9); to the ground and its vegetation (Gen 1:29, 2:15); to each other (Gen 1:26-28, 2:18, 21-24); and to the other creatures made by God (Gen 1:26-28, 2:19).

The gift of dominion, the term used to embrace the work lovingly given humanity, depended on, and was restrained by, the human choice for right relationship with their sovereign God. Significantly, it was through his instructions for work that God indicated both his sovereignty and his commitment to a relationship with humanity. These instructions (Gen 2:15-17) contain the basis for a covenant between God and the human race, and indicate dominion with limits.

122. Westermann, *Genesis 1-11*, 195, 257.

The knowledge dubiously promised them by the serpent did not prove sufficient to perform the basic task of clothing their own nakedness. God stepped in to make coverings for them (Gen 3:21). The work of humans has thus undergone significant change, from the initial co-operative partnership envisioned in Gen 2:5, to one of painful struggle.

6

Doing It Our Way: The Primordial Curses, Genesis 3:14—11:26

Human Work from God's Perspective

AFTER THE PROLOGUE THE primordial narrative establishes a picture of human work from God's perspective. The theme of work supports the assertion made in this chapter that the curses found in the primordial narrative all focus on problems with human work and elucidates that the wrong attitude to work is what God regards as the greatest of human sins.

Human Relationships and Work after Eden

The Genesis narrative shows the human choice to try to develop the world according to human knowledge resulted in a breakdown of all human relationships and a drastic change in the nature of human work. The primeval narrative elaborates these disastrous results. Examples of human relationship breakdown abound, such as Cain and Abel (Gen 4:8), Lamech and an unnamed man (Gen 4:23), the generalized antediluvian violence (Gen 6:11), and Noah and his son Ham (Gen 9:22). The behavior of the antediluvians resulted in a complete breakdown of human relationships: interpersonal relationships, relationship with the environment, and relationship between God and humans, causing God aching anguish (Gen 6:6). The activity of the antediluvians is described as "wicked" and "violent" (Gen 6:5, 11), and God condemns all their work to destruction. Details of human work activity involving the postdiluvians in the primordial narrative are limited to the

Tower narrative (Gen 11:1–9). Despite displaying ingenuity and energy in their work, God dooms the Tower builder's efforts. The primordial Genesis narrative is a recital of human failure. Human work after Eden is generally depicted as seriously displeasing to God

However, taking center stage of this bleak narrative is the work assignment of Noah. His skill, performed under directions from God, resulted in a project to save willing members of the human family. Thus, even in the grim primordial narrative there is hope. But, importantly, Noah's work did not perfect the world.

Putative Exposition of Primordial Narrative highlights Sin

Established exegesis of the primordial narrative sees it as an introductory exposition allowing elucidation of the remainder of Genesis.[1] Wenham suggested Genesis chapters 3–11 reveal "the hopeless plight of mankind without the gracious intervention of God . . . but the promises first made to Abraham in 12:1–3 begin to repair that hopeless situation."[2] Dumbrell stated, "Genesis 11:1–9 culminates the spread-of-sin narratives, which began in Genesis 3."[3] Surprisingly, considering the violence and corruption described in the antediluvian world, Dumbrell considered the Tower story shows "the spread of sin in Gen 3–11 is on an ascending scale."[4] Victor Hamilton regarded the patriarchal history as offering the solution to the sin problem outlined in the primeval history.[5] He neatly described his perspective of the Genesis narrative as moving "from generation (chs 1–2) to degeneration (chs 3–11) to regeneration (chs 12–50)."[6] Christian expositors have primarily focused on the nature of specific sins that lead to the resultant curses in the various primordial pericopes.[7]

---

1. Wenham, *Story as Torah*, 18–19.
2. Wenham, *Genesis 1–15*.
3. Dumbrell, *Search for Order*, 32.
4. Dumbrell, *Covenant and Creation*, 62.
5. Hamilton, *Book of Genesis Chapters 1–17*, 11.
6. Ibid.

7. Bergsma and Hahn, for example, argue that Ham's sin must have been maternal incest, not mere voyeurism, or the castration that has been postulated by some, for his grandson Canaan, and not Ham, to be the recipient of the curse. Bergsma and Hahn, "Noah's Nakedness," 25–40.

Robert Gonzalez recently challenged this division of Genesis on the basis of the sin problem, and others have recognized the challenge as valid.[8] Gonzalez asserted that the spread of sin in the patriarchal narratives has been largely unrecognized, although he concedes, "the main emphasis of the primeval history is on sin and the curse."[9]

However, the subject of the curses of the primordial narrative illuminates the fundamental nature of the sin involved. Gonzalez's suggestion that the patriarchs were not plaster saints[10] helpfully binds the primordial and patriarchal narratives in an intimate way, but whilst he saw the patriarchal narrative concluding with the sin problem unsolved,[11] it is asserted that the patriarchal narrative not only offers a valuable work perspective, but also offers a solution to the sin problem. Recognizing that all the curses are connected with human work identifies the aspect of human life where the wrong approach is most likely to be offensive to God.

Curse in the Primordial Narrative

The five blessings pronounced in the primordial story are matched in it by an equal number of curses. The five records of blessing are found in Gen 1:22, 28, 2:3, 9:1, 26.[12] God announces three of these at creation, and a fourth is made to Noah after the Flood catastrophe, and Noah pronounces one. This chapter proposes that "curse" in the Genesis narrative may be defined as a powerfully expressed negative pronouncement on human activity. Although Westermann suggests that the genealogies of chapters 5 and 10 indicate God's blessing of Gen 1:28 is being worked out in the primordial narrative,[13] and humans are being fruitful and multiplying, the drum beat rhythm of the record is "and he died" (Gen 5:5, 8, 11ff.), indicating curse is firmly in place. Curse, not blessing, dominates the primordial story.

All five of the curse narratives demonstrate a serious disruption of either human–human or divine–human relationship, or both. This underlines the importance of healthy relationship in the performance of human work, and stresses that good relationship and not merely productivity is a primary characteristic of healthy humans.

8. Tietz, Review of *Where Sin Abounds*, 830–32.
9. Gonzalez, *Where Sin Abounds*, 3.
10. Ibid., 4.
11. Ibid., 256.
12. Waltke, *Genesis: A Commentary*, 205.
13. Westermann, *Elements of OT Theology*, 88.

Meaning of Curse in Genesis

Use of the verb *'ārar*, "to curse," has several nuances, but of those recognized its meaning in Genesis seems to be "deprivation," which could be "a threat, but seems more likely to be stating a certainty if [someone] follows a certain course of action."[14] The verb can also mean to "inflict with a negative state as a consequence either of a physical condition or of divine choice."[15] Both these definitions imply that in the primordial curses, God is simply stating the new conditions of human work following the human choice to work according to their own knowledge.

As noted, God pronounces four of the primordial curses, and Noah utters the fifth. Although cursing may not be a dominant theme in the patriarchal narratives,[16] its portrayal in the primordial narrative makes it important background for the patriarchal stories. Efforts to determine the nature of particular sins that caused the curses are not always convincing,[17] but all the curses affect human work. It is therefore postulated that the five curses elucidate the manner of human working that meets with divine disapproval.

Blessing and Cursing from God indicates Covenant Relationship

The theme of blessing and cursing is prominent in Deuteronomy, and "scholars have long recognized that the structure of Deuteronomy appears to resemble that of an ancient Near East vassal treaty."[18] Thus, blessing and cursing are connected with the formalization of relationship between God and humans.

The First Primordial Curse, Genesis 3:14–19

The first curse is pronounced after the couple eat from the forbidden fruit. Significantly, this curse, pronounced by God, is not on the couple, although the serpent is cursed. The curses are directed towards their work. Man,

---

14. Aitken, *Semantics of Blessing and Cursing*, 81.
15. Ibid., 82.
16. Smith, G. V., "Structure and Purpose," 319.
17. See Davidsen, "Mythical Foundation of History"; Ross, "Curse of Canaan," 223–40; Bergsma and Hahn, "Noah's Nakedness"; Rice, "Curse that Never Was," 5–27.
18. Pate et al., *Story of Israel*, 43.

made from the ground, will now be dominated by it, and woman, made from the man, will be dominated by him in her childbearing role.[19]

The woman will experience 'iṣābôn, "pain," in childbearing, as well as 'ṣb, "sorrow" (Gen 3:16), and the man will experience 'iṣābôn, "pain," in tilling the ground (Gen 3:17–19). Both continue their co-operative areas of work, the woman's centering on family care and the man on economic pursuits.[20] The ground, originally under man's care and a "source of joy and life,"[21] becomes a source of pain in a wearisome existence. Children, part of the original blessing to multiply and fill the earth, will come only through pain. Although the pain the couple experience is "a perpetual reminder of sin's rewards,"[22] "the narrative conveys the pathos of a disappointed God rather than the rage of a divine judge."[23]

Curse Offers Hope

The divine curse, significantly first pronounced on the serpent, presents hope and the clear concept of opposing forces, of two significantly different approaches to life. "I will put enmity between you and the woman, and between your offspring and her offspring" (Gen 3:15) implies two hostile factions. This hints at a further chance for humans to choose their allegiance. Because of this enmity between humans and the serpent, humans are not forced to follow everything the serpent suggests.

The Curse is not Arbitrary: It Mirrors the Original Promises.

The first curses pronounced were not arbitrary. They were the natural outworking of the human choice of a god-devoid, or better, god-expelled, working environment. Reno observed that the punishments echo the promises of the garden.[24] Their dominion (the garden and its care) and their blessing (to multiply) would no longer be as effective or enjoyable. The curses thus reflect human ineffectiveness in performing the pleasant work humans were originally given to do (Gen 3:16–19). Patrick Miller's studies of the Hebrew

---

19. Turner, *Genesis*, 52.
20. Mathews, *Genesis 1—11:26*, 249.
21. Ibid., 252.
22. Ibid., 253.
23. Turner, *Genesis*, 45.
24. Reno, *Genesis*, 94.

prophets indicate that in God's later dealings with humanity the divine penalty inflicted for sin always mirrored the offence,[25] a principle applicable to the Edenic situation.

Levine's argument that there is a chiastic structure in the curses of Genesis 3 indicating the man is least guilty, the woman more guilty, and the serpent most guilty, is not convincing.[26] The punishments declare that the work of the man and woman will now be preformed with 'iṣābôn, pain and suffering. Roberto Ouro suggested a more convincing chiastic structure of Genesis 2–3 connecting the second creation pericope with the curses pronounced.[27] The center of this chiasm is the disobedience of the couple and the punishments are related to the work covenant.

Work has Undergone Significant Change

The Genesis narrative clearly indicates that the nature of human work has undergone significant change since the man and his wife chose to eat from the forbidden tree. God's original intention for humanity to have dominion remains, but the human ability to undertake the responsibility of dominion effectively can no longer be assumed. Not only has the couple demonstrated incompetence in coping with the basic task of covering their own nakedness,[28] but God's curse response to their act of taking the fruit recognizes they will now struggle to perform fundamental, life-sustaining work. Humanity does not have an unqualified ability to serve and to care for the created world, their dominion, and to assume so is not doing justice to the text.

Before any pronouncement of curse from God on human work, the Genesis author with gentle humor indicates that after eating the forbidden fruit, the effectiveness of unaided human work is questionable. Their nakedness was only successfully covered by an act of God (Gen 3:21). Thus the first curses pronounced are simply recognition of humanity's limited ability, the natural outcome of a working environment from which God has been expelled.

---

25. Miller, P., *Sin and Judgment*, 121–39.
26. Levine, "Curse and the Blessing," 193.
27. Ouro, "Garden of Eden Account," 219–43.
28. This recognizes their immediate work assignment to cover their physical nakedness, whilst not excluding the spiritual nakedness of guilt and shame.

The Second Primordial Curse, Genesis 4:1–24

The second curse is pronounced on Cain after he murders his brother, but this murder is closely connected with his attempt to worship by bringing products of his work as an offering.

Work Highlighted in Genesis 4

After the expulsion from the garden, Genesis chapter 4 highlights work. The work of family making, crop-growing, shepherding, cattle ranching, music-making, and metallurgy are all highlighted in this single chapter.

The first human work described is family making (Gen 4:1), a pre-eminence that continues the theme of working in relationship. In Eve's triumphant cry after the birth of her first child there is the hint of defiance. Cassuto considered her cry could mean, "I have created a man equally with the Lord,"[29] and that the text could be paraphrased, "The first woman in her joy at giving birth to her first son, boasts of her generative power, which approximates in her estimation the Divine creative power. The Lord formed the first man, and I have formed the second man . . . I stand together (i.e., equally) with Him in the rank of creators."[30] Turner agreed that Eve may have felt some defiance of God at this event.[31] The explanation of the boy's name indicates acquisition, as in purchase,[32] and by extension Doukhan suggested it means "to achieve."[33] But no word of condemnation from God is recorded at the birth, perhaps God even enjoying Eve's delight at what he had originally planned she should accomplish. Some consider Eve's cry suggests the couple thought she had produced the seed that was to destroy the serpent.[34] However, although Cain's name may intimate achievement, his brother is called Abel, *hebel*, meaning a breath, or worthlessness.[35]

The text notes the occupations of the brothers (Gen 4:2), which Westermann saw as "significant."[36] The importance of this focus on work becomes clearer as the pericope unfolds. The brothers' work could be seen as

---

29. Cassuto, *Commentary on Genesis: Adam to Noah*, 198.
30. Ibid., 201.
31. Turner, *Genesis*, 36.
32. Clines, *Concise Dictionary*, 397.
33. Doukhan, "Center of the Aqedah," 14.
34. Kaiser, W., *Toward and OT Theology*, 37.
35. Clines, *Concise Dictionary*, 85.
36. Westermann, *Genesis 1–11*, 293.

fulfilling God's command to till the ground and care for the creation (Gen 2:15). But in the pericope work is truncated. Cain is a "worker of the soil," ʿōbēd, but he does not šamar, "guard," it. Abel is a "shepherd of sheep," rōʿēh, which doubtless would have involved guarding them, but there is no mention of his working the soil. Already the idea of working with God to care for and preserve his creation has been supplanted by mere division of labor and job description. It is also noteworthy that the brothers' occupations are complementary, and there should be no reason to expect any conflict between them.[37]

Embedded in the Genesis 4 genealogical facts following the Cain and Abel narrative (Gen 4:17–22) is significant occupational information: "Jabal . . . father of those who dwell in tents and have livestock"; "Jubal . . . father of those who play the lyre and pipe; and Tubal-cain . . . the forger of all instruments of bronze and iron" (Gen 4:20–22). Cassuto recognized these names all come from the Hebrew verb root, *ybl*, meaning to yield, or produce,[38] suggesting Cain and his family believed they were able to circumvent the double curse God placed on the ground, and it was either yielding to their satisfaction, or by their inventions they hoped it would. Parallel with all this hard work, the Genesis author portrays a tragic moral decline and relationship breakdown. Lamech, the seventh generation from Adam in the Cainite line, has two wives, and boasts of murdering a young man for striking him (Gen 4:23–24).

Whereas Westermann saw the recital of the inventions and work achievements of the descendants of Cain as important evidence of human progress in skills,[39] Mathews, observing that this progress is recorded only in the Cainite line, suggested the arts and sciences are the invention and discovery of human knowledge, and do not indicate any divine origin.[40] For this line of humanity, which does not recognize the leadership of God, work has become a defining characteristic. "Cain's family is a microcosm; its pattern of technical prowess and moral failure is that of humanity."[41] This emphasis on human achievement and work in the Cainite line contrasts with the line of Seth, which is defined simply as those "calling upon the name of the Lord" (Gen 4:26). There is no mention of any technological achievement in this branch of humanity, although that they had skills is later clearly demonstrated by Noah's ability to build the ark.

---

37. Cassuto, *Commentary on Genesis: Adam to Noah*, 203.
38. Ibid., 234.
39. Westermann, *Genesis 1–11*, 343–44.
40. Mathews, *Genesis 1—11:26*, 54–63.
41. Kidner, *Genesis*, 78.

Work and Worship

In Genesis 4 work and worship are intimately related. When conflict erupts in this story, it is a good example of what Turner calls the unpredictable narratival sections of Genesis.[42] God's discrimination between the offerings brought by Cain and Abel is a surprise; both brothers came to worship.[43] When Cain brought his offering, notably from his work, the fruit of the ground, his offering was rejected. But his brother's offering, also from his work with the flock, is accepted.

Confining the study to the Genesis text, the rejection indicates something was wrong with either the offering, the motivations for bringing it, or perhaps God himself.[44] Since the pericope began with work, keeping this focus indicates the curse pronounced on Cain suggests either a work performance or an attitude to work that was unacceptable. The text offers clues for the discrimination between the two offerings, so God cannot be charged with unreasonable bias.

Cassuto noted the text uses two expressions to emphasize Abel's offering was the best kind because he brought the firstborn and the fat.[45] Cain however, brought only the "fruit of the ground," rather than the firstfruits that were later specified as acceptable offerings (Exod 23:16, 19). Cain's offense therefore seems to involve both an indifferent attitude, one he clearly displayed when God tried to talk with him, as well as a second-rate offering. The possibility that Abel was trying to outshine Cain is not supported by the text.

God was willing to discuss the issue with Cain. "So the Lord said to Cain, Why are you angry? And why has your countenance fallen? If you *do well*, will you not be accepted? And if you *do not do well*, sin lies at the door. And its desire is to rule over you, but you should rule over it" (Gen 4:6–7). The repetition of the phrase "do well" in God's speech to Cain not only suggests a reference to work, as the *hiphil* form of the verb *ṭwb* designates what one does, how one acts,[46] but the repetition designates emphasis. Cain,

---

42. Turner, *Genesis*, 27.

43. This apparent irrational favoritism has led to the inconsistent suggestion that God's blessings appear restricted, that there is enough for only one at a time, e.g., Abel vs. Cain, Jacob vs. Esau, and signifying a damning indictment against monotheism which inevitably leads to violence: see Schwartz, *Curse of Cain*. Brueggemann, Review of *Curse of Cain*, 534–37, with some reservations, endorsed the value of this perspective, but this evaluation shows no appreciation of the work aspect of the narrative.

44. Schwartz, *Curse of Cain*.

45. Cassuto, *Commentary on Genesis: Adam to Noah*, 205.

46. Clines, *Concise Dictionary*, 139.

however, does not respond to God; not even God could persuade him to change.[47] Cain considered his work offering adequate, and God should be satisfied with his effort. The small issue of being responsible for the care, the šamar, of an irritating younger brother who was receiving undeserved accolades (in Cain's opinion) was not part of his concern. Cain rejects God's sovereignty by refusing to accept God's assessment of his work and worship, and he irrevocably severs any relationship between himself and his brother.

Cain's god is His Work

The curse pronounced indicates Cain's primary sin was to think his own strength had brought forth the fruits of the ground. If murder were his primary crime, then a punishment corresponding to that would seem more appropriate. But punishment is directed towards his work activity (making the most of the fertility of the ground). It appears his sin (or rather sins, of arrogance, murder, and unrepentance) was regarded as more serious than his parents' sin, and as a result he becomes the first human to be cursed in the Genesis narrative.[48] The text says: "And the Lord said, 'What have *you* done? The voice of your brother's blood is crying to me from the ground. And now, *you* are cursed from the ground, which has opened its mouth to receive your brother's blood from your hand. When *you work* the ground it shall no longer yield to *you* its strength' [emphasis supplied]" (Gen 4:10–12).

The ground was the friendly recipient of Abel's tragically spilled blood, offering no warrant that it be cursed. However, Goldingay makes the important suggestion that there is an unrecognized link between humanity and nature, so if Cain will not be his brother's "watcher" then the ground will be.[49] The curse affects Cain's use of the ground ("when you work the ground it will no longer yield its strength") and his apparent assumption that its productivity resulted from his personal effort. This gives warrant to the suggestion that Cain's offering was unacceptable because he assumed the fruit he brought as a gift to God was the result of his own hard work and industry; work was his god. God, he thought, should be appreciative of his, Cain's, impressive endeavors. But God, in effect, said, "'The land is mine (Lev 25:23)' and it produces because I made it fruitful (Gen 1:11) to give its abundance to you for food (Gen 1:29). You think you can work without me, and so you shall. But you will now find that the ground is not fruitful because of your efforts. You will wander looking for fruitful land." Cain must

47. Turner, *Back to the Present*, 61.
48. Westermann, *Genesis 1–11*, 306.
49. Goldingay, *OT Theology: Israel's Gospel*, 153.

learn that the fertility of the ground he ascribed to his own personal effort was in fact due to God's blessing.

That this curse, or the removal of blessing on land fertility, was a general one seems to be implied by Cain's fear that people would blame him for their heavier workload, and desire to kill him for it. God mercifully marks him to spare him. But the land now is under a double curse, Adam's and Cain's, and humanity's unaided ability to care for their land is uncertain. Furthermore, when Cain allowed work to become his god, his relationships were seriously disrupted.

Relationship with Brother Broken

Cain's angry reaction to God's assessment of his offering (Gen 4:5), and worse, his murdering his brother, come as shocking intrusions into the serene pastoral family setting. In the Eden situation, disruption of good relationship was the first result of the human desire to be like God (hiding from God, Gen 3:8; and blame, Gen 3:12, 13). Now the break in human relationship is complete: murder offers no hope of restored relationship (Gen 4:8). However, Cain's contemptuous reply to God, "Am I my brother's keeper [šamar]?" (Gen 4:9), indicates that the knowledge of God's original plan to work in relationship was not unknown.

Relationship with God Broken

It is significant that after his encounter with God, Cain "went away from the presence of the Lord" (Gen 4:16). First his relationship with his brother, now his relationship with God is completely broken. Although he goes to the land of Nod, the land of wandering,[50] as God told him (Gen 4:12), he does not remain a wanderer. Cain's wandering was more spiritual than physical, demonstrated by the fact that after the birth of his first son, he settled and built a city, naming it Enoch after his son (Gen 4:17). He abandoned his agricultural work and settled into his own city, defying God's direction that he be a wanderer.[51]

Abraham was also called to a life of walking, *hālak*, from place to place, with the notable difference that he would walk where God told him: "Go . . . I will show you" (Gen 12:1). Cain is told to *nûʿ* and *nûd*, wander, indicating

50. Clines, *Concise Dictionary*, 260.
51. Turner, *Genesis*, 39.

aimlessness, whereas Abraham's *hālak* is directed. Cain however, begins his wandering by *going away* from the presence of the Lord.

Relationship with the Ground Broken

Finally, Cain's relationship with his environment is broken: the ground will no longer yield him its strength. Although Cain expresses no remorse at the loss of relationship with his brother, and chooses to go away from God, he is distressed about alienation from the ground, the focus of his labors. "My punishment is greater than I can bear," he moans, "Behold, *you have driven me today away from the ground* [emphasis added]," adding apparently as an afterthought, "from your face I shall be hidden" (Gen 4:13–14).

The Third Primordial Curse, Genesis 8:21

The third curse is the Deluge that destroyed almost all the inhabitants of the earth. After its occurrence, God claims the Flood was the result of his curse, *qll* (Gen 8:21).[52] He promises he will never again curse the ground because the intention of the thoughts of man's heart are only evil continually (Gen 8:21), the same assessment God made before the Flood (Gen 6:5), with the additional information that the earth was violent and corrupt (Gen 6:11–12). Goldingay asserted that nowhere else in the Hebrew Bible are humans described as being as bad as God's pre-flood assessment.[53] Violence, destructive activity, appears to be the deciding factor in God's determination to destroy his creation (Gen 6:13).

The work style of the antediluvians is implicit rather than explicit in the narrative of the Flood. Throughout Genesis, the *tôlēdôt*, "generations," sections that alternate with narratival sections contain vital information that unlocks the "unpredictable" narratival portions.[54] The *tôlēdôt* of chapter 5, preceding the Flood pericope, does not merely list the descendants of Adam; it has two significant asides that illuminate the background to Flood. The drumbeat-like, formulaic regularity of its boringly predictable, but true-to-life description of the lives of Adam's descendants: "So-and-so

---

52. The softer translation "dishonor" does not seem appropriate, but the related meaning to esteem lightly, indicating a lack of interest or concern, assures humanity of God's on-going care, see Clines, *Concise Dictionary*, 395–96.

53. Goldingay, *OT Theology: Israel's Gospel*, 164.

54. Turner, *Genesis*, 27.

lived *x* years, and fathered a son, So-and-so lived after he fathered the son *y* years and had other sons and daughters, so all the days of So-and-so were *z* and he died" is realistic. The sheer monotony of the recital makes any deviation noteworthy.

The first aside draws attention to the life of Enoch, seventh from Adam in Seth's line,[55] who is characterized by walking with God, a twice-stated fact: "When Enoch had lived 65 years, he fathered Methuselah. Enoch walked with God after he fathered Methuselah 300 years, and had other sons and daughters. Thus all the days of Enoch were 365 years. Enoch walked with God; and he was not, for God took him" (Gen 5:21-24). Walking with God was also a characteristic of Noah, a man who found favor in the eyes of the Lord: "Noah was a righteous man, blameless in his generation. Noah walked with God" (Gen 6:8-9). Westermann recognized that the phrase "walking with God" means a way of life morally pleasing to God, and results from an obedient attitude to God. The same phrase occurs in Gen 17:1, where Abram is admonished, "I am God Almighty; walk before me and be blameless."[56]

This *tôlēdôt* statement indicates walking with God was worthy of comment; subsequent events in the lives of both Enoch and Noah suggest it signifies something God desires in his relationship with humans. If the sin of Adam, and then of Cain, was to refuse to work in a relationship with God as sovereign, to consider work could be accomplished primarily by human effort, then walking with God suggests Enoch and Noah were notable for their acceptance of God's sovereignty and their willingness to work with him. But they were apparently exceptions to the general work approach of their contemporaries.

The second aside in the *tôlēdôt* of Adam offers an unambiguous clue regarding the work behavior of the antediluvians. Lamech (in Seth's line), the father of Noah, bemoans the painful toil that characterized his generation (Gen 5:29), and names his son *nōaḥ*, Noah, which sounds like the Hebrew for rest, in the hope that "this one will bring us relief from our work and the painful toil (*'iṣābôn*) of our hands, because of the ground the Lord has cursed."

While Lamech was feeling burdened with relentless work, from God's perspective every human intention was only evil continually (Gen 6:5), and the results of all their work was *ḥāmās*, "violence," that filled the earth (Gen 6:11). Things were so bad from God's perspective that he was grieved in his

---

55. Enoch, the seventh in Seth's line, contrasts dramatically with Lamech, the seventh from Adam in Cain's line.

56. Westermann, *Genesis 1-11*, 358.

heart (Gen 6:6), wished he had never made humans, and determined to wash it all away and start afresh (Gen 6:13). The apparent harshness of this decision clearly responds to the *ḥāmās*, the violence, of life on the earth at that time, and the lament of Lamech hints this was connected to relentless human working.

To work without recognizing the need for God was the significant issue in the Eden tragedy. Thus, the lament of Lamech (Gen 5:29) suggests that humanity, in continuing its attempt to work in its own knowledge, without guidance from God, was destroying the very physical structure of the earth. Several exegetes and commentators, for example Westermann,[57] Gary V. Smith,[58] Turner,[59] and Reno,[60] have noted that the Flood narrative reverses the creation narrative.

Therefore, it was not purely an "act of God" that returned the world to chaos, but chaos was already occurring from violent human work activity unguided by divine knowledge. Cassuto and Turner noted that the concepts corruption, violence, and destruction all come from the same Hebrew root.[61] Thus chaos and destruction began before the Flood actually occurred. A house "filled with violence" does not only have violent deeds done in it, but its very structure is damaged. It was towards this violence and chaos that God directed the most violent response meted out: destruction of the earth and its inhabitants. Genesis 6:1–4 implies that even in the area of reproduction humans were not performing to God's standards.

The work efforts of humans made such a violent mess of the world that the only merciful thing to do was start over again. This destruction included not only the work of God, the once "very good" creation that now "grieved, '*ṣb*, him to the heart" (cf. Gen 1:31, 6:6), but also all the works of violence that humanity had done in the earth. Lamech's words indicating the busy, exhausting life of the antediluvians are thus highly significant. Humans, ordained by God to serve and guard creation (Gen 2:15) are actually *destroying* it. "So the Lord said, "I will *destroy* man whom I have created from the face of the earth, both man and beast, creeping things and birds of the air, for I am sorry that I made them" (Gen 6:7). Turner pointed out that the tragic '*ṣb* (*hithpael*, "to be sorry") and '*iṣābôn* that were pronounced on the first couple now lodge with God himself.[62]

---

57. Westermann, *Creation*, 22.
58. Smith, G. V., "Structure and Purpose."
59. Turner, *Genesis*, 46.
60. Reno, *Genesis*, 128.
61. Cassuto, *Commentary on Genesis: Adam to Noah*, 51–53; Turner, *Genesis*, 46.
62. Turner, *Genesis*, 45.

This violence related to the way humans perceived their dominion. Thinking they "owned" the world and everything in it, and conceivably frustrated by the decreased productivity of the land, it appears they were violent in their attempts to achieve their goals. Lamech's lament identifies his belief (and anger?) that God caused the cursed ground and their increased workload: "This one will comfort us concerning *our work and the toil of our hands*, because of *the ground which the LORD has cursed* [emphases supplied]" (Gen 5:29). Inadequate food supply caused by poorly productive soil could lead to wars over fertile land, highlighting the issue of "dominion." Throughout human history war over land ownership has been one of humanity's most violent of works.

Violence may also have involved the way humans were working to obtain their food. Young proposed the violence of the antediluvians involved wholesale destruction of life forms.[63] He suggested humans may become so conditioned to violence against the animal world that it is no longer recognized, citing many examples in the contemporary meat industry. These examples include factory farming of veal, egg-producing hens in crowded cages with wholesale destruction of male chicks, pigs confined to tiny cages, and so on. Supporting this hypothesis, it can be noted that preservation of animal forms was an important part of Noah's God-given work (Gen 6:19–21). This included "clean" animals that could be eaten, as well as "unclean" animals that were apparently simply for human and divine enjoyment, as well as performing the important role of scavengers cleaning the environment (Gen 7:8). And as further evidence, Jesus singled out eating as a significant aspect of antediluvian behavior (Matt 24:37–39), giving warrant to the idea that food was involved in the perpetuation of antediluvian violence.

Noah's God-given Work

But Noah, the man who walked with God, was not idle: he was given specific work to do. Walking with God is thus not a state of mindless plodding, of maintaining the status quo, or even enraptured meditation. At the center of the pericopes highlighting the problems of human work, the Genesis narrative presents an example of human work performed in co-operation with the divine. Noah did not initiate the work he was given; the controlling factor at this stage of his life was God's initiative.[64] God gave Noah detailed instructions about the construction of the ark (Gen 6:14–16, 19–21), but Noah's technical skill was used to carry out the orders. The record is

---

63. Young, *Is God a Vegetarian?*, 43–50.
64. Reno, *Genesis*, 117.

repeated for emphasis: "Noah did all that the Lord had commanded him" (Gen 6:22, 7:5). Noah was both able and willing to work with God.

Noah's work made no sense to the people around him, or they would have entered the ark he made. "Noah is not pleasing to his generation, but he finds favor with God."[65] His work was not driven by his own or cultural foresight, wisdom, and initiative. Rather, he is willing to do exactly what God tells him to do, in ways God tells him, no matter the reaction of his contemporaries.[66]

Noah, interestingly, was not asked to transform the society of his time. This is significant given the severe problems that existed in the world (its ḥāmās and wickedness, Gen 6:5, 11, 12), as well as God's decreed destruction (Gen 6:7, 13). However, the ark of safety was not for Noah and his family alone, nor merely for the benefit of all humanity. The focus of relationship is wider. As in the Garden of Eden, Noah is invited to care for God's creation. This time care will take place in a time of terrible crisis, but it is care for God's total creation that is Noah's primary work. In caring for creation he will also save himself and his family. Interestingly, the record indicates that he saved a great many more animals than humans, as at least two "of everything" on the face of the earth went into the ark with him and his family (Gen 7:7, 9).

Noachian Covenant includes Animals and their Care

The work of caring for creation is emphasized by God's commands and covenant when Noah leaves the ark: "Then God said to Noah, 'Go out from the ark, you and your wife, and your sons and your sons' wives with you. Bring out with you every living thing that is with you of all flesh—birds and animals and every creeping thing that creeps on the earth—that they may swarm on the earth, and be fruitful and multiply on the earth'" (Gen 8:15–17). The equality given other creatures along with humans is startling.

This is further emphasized when God renewed the covenant: "And God blessed Noah and his sons and said to them 'Be fruitful and multiply and fill the earth . . . Behold, I *establish* my covenant with *you* and with *your offspring* after you, *and with every living creature that is with you, the birds, the livestock, and every beast of the earth with you, as many as came out of the ark; it is for every beast of the earth* [emphases supplied]'" (Gen 9:1, 9–10). The covenant clearly shows God's continuing commitment to his

---

65. Ibid., 116.
66. Ibid., 117.

total creation, and his willingness to work with humanity. It is remarkable for its inclusion of the "lower" creatures of the world and mirrors the original blessing on both the creatures and humanity (Gen 1:22, 28). Although not explicitly stated as "you look after them," it is implied, and certainly what Noah and his family had been doing for the year they were together in the ark (Gen 6:19–21, 7:6, 13). But although the human responsibility to care for all of creation is thus clearly emphasized, and a good foundation for a sound ecological approach to work is endorsed, the critical factor in the wellbeing of all creation is the blessing of God.

Changes in Dominion after the Flood

However, the new covenant made between God and humanity after the Flood indicates a significant change in the dominion of humanity over the animals.[67] God said, "The fear of you and the dread of you shall be upon every beast of the earth, and upon every bird of the heavens, upon everything that creeps on the ground, and on all the fish of the sea. Into your hand they are delivered" (Gen 9:2). The original dominion given Adam has *not* been restored to its previous state. Whereas naming the animals, suggesting friendly relationship, began the original dominion, now it is dread and fear that characterize this dominion. This fear of humans is protective for the animals, suggesting a lack of fear for humanity was a factor in allowing violence to be perpetrated on them in the antediluvian world.

In Eden vegetation provided food for all the created creatures (Gen 1:29–30, 3:18). Now, after the Flood, with the destruction of all life forms except those protected on board the ark, permission is given for animals to be killed to supply Noah and his family with essential food (Gen 9:3–5).[68] But notably, just as in Eden, there is a restriction in the dietary provision God makes, suggesting not only God's care and concern, but also his *imperium* (Gen 9:3–5; cf. Gen 2:16–17). This time eating blood is strictly prohibited. As in Eden, the penalty for failure to comply is death. This dietary restriction is one of many similarities between the Creation and Flood narratives. Whilst no reason was explicitly given for the withholding of the fruit of the tree of knowledge, this time the reason for the restriction is clearly given: blood is equivalent to life, and life comes from God, the Creator (Gen 9:5).

The Flood narrative began with the concept that hard, painful work became violent and destructive, the major factor in causing the deluge; it ends indicating the original dominion of humanity has changed. Turner

67. Ibid., 124.
68. Ibid.

noted that while the gift of reproduction remains unchanged, dominion over the animals has been significantly modified, and there is silence on the subject of subjugation.[69] This indicates the provisions of the blessing of (Gen 1:26–28) are not still in force.

The Fourth Primordial Curse, Genesis 9:25–27

Noah pronounces the most enigmatic curse of the primordial narrative on his son Ham. No pericope better demonstrates the "unpredictable narratival" sections of Genesis than does the final episode of Noah's story. This last pericope of the Noah narrative tragically shows that the Flood has changed nothing.[70]

Winemaker Pericope echoes Garden Narrative

Noah "began to be a man of the soil," developed a vineyard, and drank of the wine made from the grapes (Gen 9:20). Then Noah in his drunken stupor became uncovered in his tent (Gen 9:21).[71] The pericope's reference to Noah's concern about the soil rather than the creatures is reminiscent of Cain rather than Abel; his nakedness echoes the Eden tragedy.

There is little textual evidence to support the conclusion of Westermann and others that Noah's developing wine from his vineyard was a blessing, the fulfilment of his father's prayer for relief from hard work (Gen 5:29).[72] The pericope presents cursing as the primary result of Noah's work producing intoxicating wine. Turner[73] and Wenham[74] much more convincingly demonstrate that the story has eating fruit and nakedness as central motifs, as in Eden, suggesting a serious lapse in Noah's behavior.

---

69. Turner, *Genesis*, 52.

70. Ibid., 54.

71. The word *šakar*, "drunk," also occurs in Gen 43:34, where it refers to the brothers of Joseph being "merry" with him, see Goldingay, *OT Theology: Israel's Gospel*, 183. However, it should be noted that this was also a situation where the brothers were not in full control of themselves.

72. For example, Westermann, *Genesis 1–11*, 360; Waltke, *Genesis: A Commentary*, 159.

73. Turner, *Genesis*, 54.

74. Wenham, *Story as Torah*, 35.

Ross commented, "the . . . narratives represent various beginnings, none of which appear particularly virtuous," and that the verb used to describe Noah's "first" in growing grapes is also associated with the hunting activity of Nimrod, and the "beginning" of work on Babel.[75] Ross also pointed out that while wine may alleviate to some degree the painful toil of working the ground, the Old Testament is generally negative about drunkenness, and the story clearly shows the degrading effects of it.[76]

Ham's Disrespect

Noah's youngest son Ham "sees" his nakedness, whereas the other sons, Shem and Japheth cover it. The text twice emphasizes that these two sons blinded themselves to their father's plight: "Their faces were turned backward, and they did not see their father's nakedness" (Gen 9:23). Ross suggested that Ham's crime is an affront to his father's dignity, and thus merits an affront to his own family honor.[77] Despite study and speculation regarding the nature of the crime committed by Ham, there is no clear biblical picture of it beyond simple voyeurism.[78] Davidson argues persuasively from the Hebrew that there is no basis for making the fall of Noah a sexual fall.[79] Suppositions that it was a disfiguring or abusive sexual crime are not persuasive. Whilst maternal incest[80] might explain why the curse was pronounced on grandson Canaan and not on Ham, the Genesis author was generally not at all squeamish about clearly describing sexual sin, even in the patriarchal narratives, for example, the rape of Dinah (Gen 34:1–31), the incest of Reuben (Gen 35:22), and the prostitution and incest of Judah (Gen 38:15–30). There is no reason why he would refuse to be more explicit in the Noah pericope than elsewhere.

Noah's Curse on Canaan

When Noah woke from his wine (Gen 9:24), he made surprising pronouncements on Ham's family, committing them to lives of servitude. Noah's curse

75. Ross, "Curse of Canaan," 226.
76. Ibid., 227.
77. Ibid., 231.
78. For the arguments against castration, or that Ham had an incestuous relationship with his mother resulting in the birth of Canaan, see Yamauchi, "Curse of Ham," 46–47.
79. Davidson, R., *Flame of Yahweh*, 142–45.
80. Bergsma and Hahn, "Noah's Nakedness."

is enigmatic because the curse is not pronounced directly on his son Ham, who saw his nakedness, but on his apparently innocent grandson Canaan. Gene Rice enumerated a long list of scholars who tried to work out the difficulties of the curse of Noah being on Canaan and not Ham.[81] Rice's own resorting to Wellhausen's theory of the composite character of the Hexateuch[82] merely leaves us with poor redaction as an explanation. However, there is another approach.

Noah's Curse a Prophecy that highlights Work

However, since Noah was regarded as a man of God (see Gen 6:8, 9, 22, 9:1–17), the traditional concept that his was a prophetic utterance seems reasonable. A prophetic utterance regarding work was made at Noah's own birth (Gen 5:29), and he was named *nōaḥ* in the hope that he would bring rest to the overburdened workers of his father's society. Noah's own prophecy indicates that the family of Ham will not enjoy any rest, but will instead become servants. The type of servant indicated is *'ebed*, meaning a family servant, not a servant that has the current meaning of slave or serf.[83] Although this curse has too often been applied to legitimize the slavery of some races, there can be no textual evidence for this.[84] The three young men were brothers, with nothing to distinguish them on racial or ethnic lines. Canaan, shockingly, appears to have done nothing wrong. But the curse's focus illuminates the problem again developing in the human family: it highlights work. Work will consume their lives. The fact that the curse is presented as poetry emphasizes its significance. Three times Noah presents the curse as Canaan's servitude, thus strongly emphasizing work. The curse is servitude, not race.

> "Cursed be Canaan;
> a servant of servants shall he be to his brothers.
> "Blessed be the Lord, the God of Shem;
> and let Canaan be his servant.
> "May God enlarge Japheth,
> and let him dwell in the tents of Shem,
> and let Canaan be his servant." (Gen 9:25–27)

---

81. Rice, "Curse that Never Was."
82. Ibid., 18.
83. Goldingay, *OT Theology: Israel's Gospel*, 185.
84. Rice, "Curse that Never Was."

Work in the *tôlēdôt* of Noah verifies the Prophecy

This work-focused prophetic explanation gains weight when the focus on the work of Ham's sons is noted in the *tôlēdôt* section of the sons of Noah (Gen 10). As in the *tôlēdôt* of Adam, it is the small asides that are revealing.

The descendants of both Japheth and Shem are presented simply as individuals whose multiplying families inhabit various parts of the earth (Gen 10:2–5, 21–31), and thus show the blessing of God. But the sons of Ham do things, grand things. Notably Nimrod, grandson of Ham, is a mighty one in the earth, a mighty hunter (Gen 10:8–9). Significantly, it is this Nimrod who builds anti-God cities that later figure prominently in biblical narrative: Babel in the land of Shinar, Nineveh in Assyria (Gen 10:10–11). Work as achievement is the focus of this family.

In Genesis there is an implied disapproval of city builders: the cursed Cain is the first to build a city (Gen 4:17), and the descendants of the cursed Ham become noted for their city building.[85] This negative attitude becomes significant in the pericope of the Tower of Babel. Recognizing the work aspect of the curse, and reading the pericopes beyond Gen 9:24–27 to observe what occurs in them, clarifies the prophetic nature of Noah's curse. As noted, *'ārar*, a curse, might be a "threat, but seems more likely to be stating a certainty if [someone] follows a certain course of action."[86]

The Fifth Primordial Curse, Genesis 11:7–8

The fifth curse is not formally described as a curse in the text, but the negative assessment of God prevents the success of the Tower of Babel project, and is thus effectively a curse.

Meticulous Literary Structure of Tower Pericope

Many commentators have noted the care taken in writing the Tower of Babel narrative, recognizing it as a masterpiece of Hebrew story telling. Von Rad considered it the capstone of the primeval story, and of special

---

85. Goldingay however, does not consider that Genesis condemns the city as such, Goldingay, *OT Theology: Israel's Gospel*, 154.

86. Aitken, *Semantics of Blessing and Cursing*, 81.

significance in the Yahwist narrative.[87] Wenham noted many evidences that the Tower narrative had been carefully written: "The Tower of Babel is a short but brilliant example of Hebrew story telling... Word play, chiasmus, paronomasia, and alliteration are just some of the devices used to unify and accentuate the message of the tale."[88] He sums up saying he considers it a "finely crafted piece."[89] Cassuto called it a "fine example of biblical literary art," offering many reasons and detailed examples of different literary devices used to validate his assessment. These include the drumbeat alliteration of the Hebrew letters *bet*, *lammed*, and *nun*, and frequent use of certain words such as language (five times), or similar sounding words like *šem* "name" and *šam* "there." Cassuto observed that unlike the creation and flood stories, there is no parallel to this story in Mesopotamian writings.[90] Waltke recognized the pericope is in a chiastic form, beginning and ending with language, and pivoting on the phrase "and the Lord came down."[91] This widespread agreement about the careful construction of the pericope suggests the author took considerable technical trouble with it because he meant it to be both noteworthy and noted.

Tôlēdôt highlights the Achievements of Ham's Descendants

Literary features in the *tôlēdôt* of Noah's sons (Gen 10:1–32) provide clues that not only elucidate the puzzle of the pericope of Noah's cursing of Canaan, but also the Tower narrative. Again, the small excursions from the genealogic material in *tôlēdôt* alerts the reader to issues involved. As noted, it is Ham's sons, the active servants, who are building the Tower. The curse of Noah on Canaan therefore prepares the reader to discover it is Ham's descendants, the compulsive achievers, who build great cities and empires. The reader is thus forewarned that there could be something unacceptable about the Tower, and human-exalting hard work may be involved.

Nimrod, the "mighty hunter," does not fit the picture of abject servitude. Goldingay saw him as the first historical hero.[92] But the text's rapid-fire enumeration of his significant achievements demonstrates work is the center of his life (Gen 10:8–12). Turner recognized that Nimrod's name

87. Rad, *Genesis: A Commentary*, 143.
88. Wenham, *Genesis 1–15*, 234.
89. Ibid., 238.
90. Cassuto, *Commentary on Genesis: Noah to Abraham*, 226–34.
91. Waltke, *Genesis: A Commentary*, 176.
92. Goldingay, *OT Theology: Israel's Gospel*, 187.

could be translated "we shall rebel,"[93] interesting evidence when considered in conjunction with the judgment later pronounced on the city's Tower builders. Turner also noted Nimrod is a mighty warrior, a *gibbôr*, alluding to the *gibbôrîm* who were displeasing to God before the Flood[94] (Gen 6:4). As Enoch was twice described as walking with God (Gen 5:21–22), and Noah twice noted as doing what God commanded (Gen 6:22, 7:5), so the narrative emphasizes, not twice but thrice, that Nimrod is mighty, a mighty one, a mighty hunter (Gen 10:8–9). Nimrod, with all his mighty human accomplishments, is a *gibbôr*, a member of a group that in the Genesis narrative does not please God.

The Primary Sin of the Tower Builders

Dumbrell noted the Tower narrative (Gen 11:1–9), "present[s] the logical conclusion to a set of narratives whose purpose is to expose . . . human failures" and that, "the spread of sin in Gen 3–11 is on an ascending scale."[95] The Tower pericope utilizes the typical style of inscriptions of Neo-Babylonian colossal-building accounts intended to achieve a memorable name for the builders.[96] But Andrew Giogetti suggests because no divine permission was given for the building (the norm for a Mesopotamian project), the Genesis account sabotages the hubris of the Neo-Babylonian accounts and depicts curse instead of the expected blessing that should result from the builders' activity.[97] This highlights the builders' sin of hubris.

Turner and Harland, however, proposed the primary fault was failure to obey God's command to "be fruitful and multiply and fill the earth."[98] God's action in "dispers[ing] them from there over the face of all the earth, and [so] they left off building the city" (Gen 11:8), is reminiscent of the curse of wandering laid on Cain. Thus the primary sin was huddling together and failure to fulfill God's command to "fill the earth."[99]

For contemporary readers, the Tower narrative is surprising, even shocking, because the activity depicted seems innocent, even laudable. Some suggest the pericope has nothing to do with sin and punishment but

---

93. Turner, *Genesis*, 58.
94. Ibid.
95. Dumbrell, *Covenant and Creation*, 62.
96. Giogetti, "'Mock Building Account,'" 1–20.
97. Ibid.
98. Turner, *Genesis*, 30–33; Harland, "Vertical or Horizontal," 515–33.
99. Turner, *Genesis*, 30–33.

is simply an account of the origin of world culture.[100] Yet although the word curse does not appear in the narrative the efforts of the builders were condemned, and effectively cursed. It seems plausible that the desire to build and achieve a name, suggesting hubris from work achievement, was the primary sin of the Tower builders. But, both interpretations of the sin of the Tower builders indicate a refusal to accept the sovereignty of God.

Babel: No Apparent Moral Failure

There is no suggestion in the Tower narrative of sexual moral deterioration, no illegitimate efforts to usurp the land or goods of others, nothing, in fact, to indicate an ethical problem. It seems that if ever there was a group of people that could and should serve as role models for developing a theology of work, this is the group to study. Even God recognized their success.

There is one problem: they choose to work, to make a name for themselves, without any reference to God's plans. They act against the express will of God, to scatter and "fill the earth" (Gen 9:1), rather than to concentrate in a single area within a large central city. The key to the success of their project was corporate unanimity. The narrative suggests God himself declared this when he observed, "they are one people . . . nothing that they propose to do will now be impossible for them" (Gen 11:6). United they would stand, even, they thought, against God.

Babel: The Appeal of Human Achievement

Several authors agree[101] with Dumbrell's encapsulating comment: "Babel expressed a naïve and total confidence in what human achievement could effect,"[102] and that the aims of the Tower builders represent an arrogant usurpation of the rights and prerogatives of God. Turner and Mathews see in the "come let us" of Gen 11:4 echoes of God's activity in the creation of humanity,[103] which exhibits an assumption of divine prerogative. Any work approach that usurps the position or characteristics of God is idolatry.

Mathews compared the focus of this desire of humanity to achieve power independently from God with Eve's choice to eat the fruit to become

---

100. Hiebert, "Tower of Babel," 53.
101. See comments following in texts from Turner, Mathews, and Westermann.
102. Dumbrell, *Covenant and Creation*, 63.
103. See Turner, *Genesis*, 60; Mathews, *Genesis 1—11:26*, 466.

"like god."[104] Westermann suggested that the basic motif of the story is people wanting to demonstrate their greatness by a work of their own hands, and behind this is the attitude described by Isaiah: "You said in your heart, I will ascend to heaven; above the stars of God I will set my throne on high . . . I will ascend to the heights of the clouds, I will make myself like the most high" (Isa 14:13-14).[105] Dumbrell agreed with Westermann that what is presented in Genesis 11 is a search by society for a center to be realized within themselves.[106]

Thus Turner, Mathews, Westermann, and Dumbrell all suggested the motivation for the Tower's construction was the same fatal belief that motivated Eve to take the forbidden fruit. "To be like God" (Gen 3:5) through a work of their own hands fails to recognize God's sovereignty. The builders wanted to "reach heaven," and to resist being "scattered over the face of the earth" (Gen 11:4), a wish in direct opposition to the express will of God (Gen 9:1). W. Lee Humphreys suggested God's action in coming down to the Tower builders mirrors what must be inferred from the Eden situation, that God came down to talk with the human couple, suggesting he reasserts his sovereignty.[107]

Whose Own Might is Their God!

What the text most clearly describes is not the Tower builders' worship, or even their moral attitudes, but their work. They fit the description Habakkuk penned later: "guilty men, whose own might is their god!" (Hab 1:11b). Avivah Zornberg, using thoughts from Jewish midrash, suggested, "The post-Flood generation, the builders of the Tower of Babel, have as their motto, 'Me and not You.'"[108] The primordial narrative ends with a pericope demonstrating that one of the greatest of human sins is to work full of pride in one's own, or corporate, achievements. Kidner suggested the Tower story displays the pride of humans in their accomplishments in a manner similar to contemporary pride in space projects.[109]

Waltke noted the "postdiluvian tower builders are the spiritual heirs of the line of Cain, not of Seth, as these comparisons show: both migrate

---

104. Mathews, *Genesis 1—11:26*, 466.
105. Westermann, *Genesis 1-11*, 554.
106. Dumbrell, *Covenant and Creation*, 61.
107. Humphries, *Character of God*, 76.
108. Zornberg, *Beginning of Desire*, 55.
109. Kidner, *Genesis*, 109. Cassuto, *Commentary on Genesis: Noah to Abraham*, 225; Mathews, *Genesis 1—11:26*, 323; Reno, *Genesis*, 131, all make similar comments.

eastwards (4:16; 11:2); both build a city to establish a secure place and meaningful existence without God (4:17; 11:4); both are proud manufacturers (4:19–24; 11:3–4) and both are judged by being forced to migrate (4:12–13; 11:8)."[110] He suggested, "these city builders are futilely attempting to find significance and immortality in their own achievements,"[111] that is, through their work.

Language Essential for Community Co-operation

"Nothing that they propose to do will now be impossible for them," said God (Gen 11:6). Therefore, God declared, the Tower-builders' efforts would not achieve success. Whilst not precluding God's supernatural intervention in distorting language, Cassuto offered an interesting concept. He noted what is usually translated as "that they may not understand" literally means "that they may not hear."[112] Listening to parliamentary, board, or other group discussions readily demonstrates that a common language does not guarantee hearing or understanding between two parties! This suggests that as with the previous curses, the "curse" may simply be a statement of the situation. However, God's clearly stated intention and action was to confuse their language: "Come, let us go down and there confuse their language, so that they may not understand one another's speech" (Gen 11:7). Confusing language destroyed the chance for corporate harmony, and perhaps recognized that relationships were already severely strained during the Tower-building project.

The Hebrew verb translated šāmaʿ, "to hear," also means, by extension, "to obey, or give heed to, and respond to,"[113] and suggests the Tower-builders' failure to obey God's directives. By confusing language, God set in motion circumstances that forced their reluctant obedience to fill the earth. Cassuto's suggestion about hearing is consistent with the proposal that all the curses presented in the primordial Genesis narrative reflect humanity's defiance of God in their work (they did not hear, obey, šāmaʿ), rather than the condemning utterances of an autocratic being.

Cassuto's insight regarding the builders not hearing or understanding may also suggest a powerful struggle for personal supremacy occurring amongst the Tower-builders. Though the text indicates that the desire to

---

110. Waltke, *Genesis: A Commentary*, 177.
111. Ibid., 179.
112. Cassuto, *Commentary on Genesis: Noah to Abraham*, 247.
113. Entry "šāmaʿ," especially def. 2, in Clines, *Concise Dictionary*, 469.

make a name was a corporate one, this corporate culture would doubtless infect all the workers and their attitudes. With everyone dreaming of making a "name," it would be very disappointing for many to be hard at work merely pushing a barrow-load of bricks. It would be easy for tempers to flare, for words to be misunderstood and misconstrued.

Nehemiah's Project illustrates Good Human Work

However, the words "come let us" also occur in another biblical building project narrative. The major differences between the two narratives highlight the attitude problem at Babel, but also indicate that human achievement and human initiative *per se* were not the issues in the Tower pericope. In Genesis, for example Noah and Joseph, and in the Nehemiah pericope discussed below, God is presented as intending that humans will have the satisfaction of accomplishing significant goals and working for large projects.

When postexilic Nehemiah exhorts his fellow Jews to "Come, let us build the wall of Jerusalem," he is quick to point out that "the hand of my God had been upon me for good" (Neh 2:17-18). He meticulously records the names of all those involved in the project (see Neh chap 2), so that he takes for himself no honor and glory. When he meets opposition, he says, "Our God will fight for us" (Neh 4:20). He offers intimate personal details of the builders, showing a friendly relationship with them. He acknowledges that women as well as men were included in the project, for example: "Shallum the son of Hallohesh, ruler of half the district of Jerusalem repaired, he and his daughters" (Neh 3:12). And he records that all classes of society were involved in the project: priests, goldsmiths, perfumers, and merchants (Neh 3:1, 8, 32).

Nehemiah was interested in his people and their welfare, a fact particularly revealed in the pericope in chapter 5: Nehemiah fought a vigorous campaign against those charging usury from poor and needy Jews. Further, he did not exact any of the legitimate allowance due his position as governor for the twelve years he was in office (Neh 5:14, 18). Nehemiah's "come, let us" was a genuine cooperative based on concern for the needs of others, but above all a commitment to "my God." When the wall was finally finished, the surrounding nations "perceived that this work had been accomplished with the help of our God" (Neh 6:16). The motivation for Nehemiah's building project was obedience to God's commands to bring glory to God's name.

By contrast, the Tower-builders explicitly state that their motivation was to bring glory to themselves.

Danger of Idolatry of Community Projects

The Tower-builders were explicitly concerned to "make a name for ourselves." As Reno perceptively, yet frighteningly, observed: "Devotion to the collective projects [i.e., work] of society is very tempting, because it has the form of self-sacrifice that can seem similar to the life of devotion to God . . . The only alternative to the worship of a finite good made into an idol is the worship of the one true God, the lord and creator of all. Without a predominating love of God, love of neighbour will be come a limitless project, and the good things we seek for each other 'is only the beginning of what [we] will do' (Gen 11:6)."[114]

The Contemporary Appeal of a Babel Work Ethic

It is easy to question why this apparently laudable primordial civil engineering construction scheme should be doomed to failure by the express will of God. In contemporary "developed" societies, industry is a greatly admired, commendable feature of any nation or person. Contemporary readers may sympathize with the aims and objectives of the Tower-builders. The "project of Babel has been making a comeback. Ever since the beginning of the seventeenth century, when men like Bacon and Descartes called mankind to the conquest of nature for the relief of man's estate, the cosmopolitan cream of the city of man has guided many of the best minds and hearts throughout the world."[115]

Dumbrell observed that what Babel's inhabitants undertake at first sight appears to be a promising effort at social co-operation.[116] There is much about the Tower-builders and their intentions that seem laudable. They were co-operative, industrious, inventive, and ambitious, to name just a few of their apparently commendable characteristics. Their "Come let us" indicates a desirable willingness to cooperate with one another in achieving goals. They are willing to make brick for stone, a necessity in the area they

---

114. Reno, *Genesis*, 133.
115. Kass, "What's Wrong with Babel," 59.
116. Dumbrell, *Covenant and Creation*, 59.

were building due to a lack of masonry, but nevertheless indicating a high level of industriousness. Using bitumen for mortar was ingenious and made the most of their natural resources. Finally, their desire to "make a name" to achieve distinction for themselves, is a goal that resonates well with the pressures on, and aims of, both contemporary education and business.

However, as Turner pointed out, this desire to make a name for themselves was in striking contrast to all previous namings in the Genesis narrative, where the normal pattern is for a superior (or prior) to name an inferior (or successor).[117] Contemporary culture calls "making a name" being successful. It is both the warp and the woof of the fabric of culture. It is the dream as much in the hearts of those who do not achieve, as it is in those who do. "Reaching heaven" shows willingness to achieve the best a person can,[118] but it also suggests a desire to rival God.

Two Approaches to Work

The accumulating primordial pericopes show that although work itself is good and was given to *hā- ʾādām* in the garden, and Noah was asked to build the ark, there are two ways to work: a God-dependent, God-directed way, and a human-dependent, God-defying way. God's way is caring for, serving, the creatures of God's creation, human and otherwise, doing specific tasks God asks to be done, such as building the ark, and, most notably, "walking with God."

The pericopes of eating the forbidden fruit and Cain's rejected offering indicate that failure to recognize that success is due to the blessing of God is to effectively curse it. To thoughtlessly or wilfully destroy the natural world and its resources to achieve human aims dooms the world and all its inhabitants to ultimate destruction. Working towards any goal, no matter how worthy, without recognition of God is mere slavery and drudgery. To work for self-exaltation is presented as a very serious sin. The Tower narrative indicates that to work primarily to achieve personal distinction is most displeasing to God.

---

117. Turner, *Back to the Present*, 97.

118. The problem could have been a lack of trust in God's promise that he would not destroy the world by flood, see for example Turner, *Back to the Present*, 97. But it was more likely the long-held Jewish concept that they simply defied God's command to fill the earth. The point being made here is that for contemporary readers it is hard to recognize what was the sin of the Tower-builders.

The primordial narrative is therefore a dismal recital of human attempts to achieve without God, and the results unvaryingly declare this work is cursed, as shown schematically below.

Table 4: Schematic Presentation of All Primordial Curses, Genesis 3–11

Cause of Curse	Curse Pronounced by	The Curse	Effect on Work
Rejection of God's Sovereignty: Eating from the forbidden tree	God (Gen 3:16–19)	Woman: pain in child-bearing Man: work ground in sweat of brow	Increased hardship to perform basic functions
Rejection of God's Sovereignty: brought self-exalting offering	God (Gen 4:11–12)	Cain cursed (unspecified, and the ground will no longer yield its strength)	Further increased difficulty in producing food
Wickedness (rejection of God's sovereignty) and Violence (rejection of responsibility to care for created world)	God (Gen 8:21)	Almost everything destroyed	All human work destroyed except Noah's ark.
Rejection of father's authority	Noah (Gen 9:24–27)	Servitude on Ham and his descendants	Descendants of Ham recognized for their work focus and achievements (Gen 10:6–12)
Defiance of God / rejection of divine sovereignty	God (Gen 11:7–8)	Language Confused, workers scattered so building Tower abandoned	Tower building project abandoned

The Tower of Babel is Essential Backdrop to the Call of Abram

The Tower story, however, forms the essential backdrop to the call of Abram, because it was from the culture of the Tower-builders that Abram was called. Thus the work focus of Abram and his descendants deserves scrutiny. Westermann's suggestion that human achievement is a concern primarily of the primeval story but not of the patriarchal narratives[119] invites examination of human work in the patriarchal narratives.

The primordial narrative indicates that human work, corporate or otherwise, can become a dangerous threat to the human acceptance of the sovereignty of God. Therefore the assertion that all human work is an act of co-creation with God seems open to challenge, as is the assertion that: "Man is the image of God partly through the mandate received from his Creator to subdue, to dominate, the earth. In carrying out this mandate, man, every human being, reflects the very action of the Creator of the universe."[120] That "every human being" is carrying out the mandate of God through their work is not given warrant in the pericopes that follow the Creation narrative.

Recognition that an existence focused on the hubris of human achievement is not pleasing to God calls into question the assertions that "work is the means whereby man *achieves dominion*," and "through work man not only transforms nature, adapting it to his own needs, but he also *achieves fulfilment* as a human being and indeed, in a sense, becomes "more a human being.""[121] The primordial narrative indicates there must be careful thought about what human work is actually accomplishing.

The first man and his wife could not clothe themselves without the intervention of God. Cain, in both his work and worship, was not acceptable to God. The antediluvians were corrupt and violent in their activities; they and their work were both destroyed by God. The feverish work of Ham's descendants was not a blessing but a curse. And the Tower-builders are clearly portrayed as not carrying out work that fulfilled God's plans.

Laborens Exercens expresses a commendable desire to include all human work under the umbrella of co-creation,[122] but Hauerwas' suggestion that by attributing such a high status to human work we risk idolatry[123] is verified in the light of the work of the Tower builders. Hauerwas' concern

---

119. Westermann, *Genesis 1–11*, 18.
120. John Paul II, *Laborem Exercens*, section 4.
121. Ibid., section 9.
122. Ibid., section 4.
123. Hauerwas, "Work as Co-Creationism," 47–49.

regarding the suggestion that sin may have affected work but did not change its essential nature,[124] also seems more than justified by the picture portrayed in the primordial narratives, Genesis 3–11. This accords with Dumbrell's proposal that the Tower narrative "presents the logical conclusion to a set of narratives whose purpose is to expose . . . human failures" and that, "the spread of sin in Gen 3–11 is on an ascending scale."[125]

Whilst it is true that God has not removed the human ability to work, the unfolding Genesis narrative makes it increasingly difficult to consider all human work as carrying out a co-creation mandate of God. Genesis presents the human struggle to accept the sovereignty of God, and the natural human tendency to worship the work of human hands.

Summary

After the two creation pericopes, the primordial narrative of Genesis presents a series of five situations where human activity is cursed. Each of these "curses" impacts human work. It is shown that the curse is not an arbitrary pronouncement of divine wrath, but rather a declaration of the inevitable result of humans working outside relationship with God. This indicates there are two approaches to work: one depends on human wisdom and knowledge, and the other is working in co-operation with God. And, most sobering, the primoridal curse narratives suggest the greatest human sin is to reject the sovereignty of God and to work with hubris in one's own accomplishments.

---

124. Ibid.
125. Dumbrell, *Covenant and Creation*, 62.

7

Blessing: The Patriarchal Narrative Signature Tune

AFTER THE DISHEARTENING RECITAL of curse and wearisome work in the primordial narrative, it is encouraging to discover that blessing is the central concept in the whole Genesis narrative. "Blessing . . . is the over arching concept in the book of Genesis."[1] The centrality and importance of this concept cannot be overstated. Westermann "approached the study of Old Testament theology as an interchange between and integration of divine blessing and saving history."[2] He gave creation a place of theological importance, and considered blessing, a divine power that gives life and wellbeing to the human habitation and to humans themselves, is a major expression of creation.[3] This focus on creation blessing also brings in the concepts of eschatology, as the new heaven and earth corresponds to the creation at the beginning,[4] and as discussed, creation as presented in Genesis is solely the work of God.

Blessing as a Genesis theme has been noted by many.[5] Waltke noted that while "blessing" occurs only five times in the whole primordial narrative (Gen 1:22, 28, 2:3, 9:1, 26), suddenly blessing is concentrated five times in the call of Abram (Gen 12:1–3).[6] This balances the five curse situations found in the primeval narrative. John Sailhamer thought the multiple blessings in the call of Abram indicates a call to "return to God's original plan

1. Wenham, *Story as Torah*, 22.
2. Sommer, "OT Theology as the Dialectic," 103.
3. Ibid., 105.
4. Ibid.
5. Scullion, *Genesis: A Commentary*, 102; Smith, G. V., "Structure and Purpose," 311; Westermann, *Genesis 12–36*, 575; Wenham, *Story as Torah*, 22; Armstrong, *In the Beginning*, 51.
6. Waltke, *Genesis: A Commentary*, 205.

of blessing all peoples of the earth," the original creation blessing of Gen 1:28.[7] P. D. Miller stated, "The call of Abraham helps to make clear that the God of biblical faith . . . is clearly bent towards blessing and mercy towards the human creature . . . When Yahweh sent Abraham out, it was to bring about blessing, not curse."[8] Fretheim expressed his "career-long" concern to reinstate creation theology to its central place,[9] including its aspect of blessing, and he noted with approval the significant exposition of creation given in Goldingay's theology.[10] Fretheim suggested that blessing may have been the basic perception in Israel's understanding of God as creator.[11]

In this chapter the meaning of living and working in blessing is explored, and it is proposed that to live this way brings an encouraging perspective to the Edenic concepts of dominion and *imago Dei*.

Blessing: Signature Tune of the Patriarchal Narrative

The Hebrew *brk*, to bless, in the total of its verb and noun forms, appears in Genesis eighty-eight times, more than in any other book in the Old Testament.[12] This compares with 310 times in the rest of the entire Old Testament.[13] Blessing from God, as noted, is encountered in the very first chapter of the Genesis narrative, as God blesses the birds and fish (v. 22) and the humans (v. 28) that he has made. In these cases, blessing is specifically connected with "being fruitful and multiplying."

The theme of blessing occurs so frequently in the patriarchal narratives that Scullion poetically suggested blessing be called the "signature tune" of the patriarchal story.[14] Westermann considered, "The patriarchal community draws its life from blessing; it is due to God's blessing that children are born and grow up, that work is crowned with productive growth and expansion, that watering places are found and preserved, that the labour of the herdsman is fruitful."[15] Armstrong regarded the search for blessing

---

7. Sailhamer, *Genesis*, 21.
8. Miller, P., *Genesis 1–11: Studies*, 475.
9. Fretheim, *God and World in the OT*, xi.
10. Goldingay, *OT Theology: Israel's Gospel*, 42–130.
11. Fretheim, *God and World in the OT*, xv.
12. Mitchell, *Meaning of BRK*, 185; Wenham, *Genesis 1–15*, 275; Wenham, *Story as Torah*, 20, f.n.
13. Wenham, *Genesis 1–15*, 275.
14. Scullion, *Genesis: A Commentary*, 102.
15. Westermann, *Genesis 12–36*, 575.

as the major theme in the Genesis narrative, and the one around which the book is fashioned.[16]

David Clines defined the theme of the Pentateuch as, "the partial fulfilment—which implies the partial non fulfilment—of the promise to or blessing of the patriarchs. The promise of *blessing is both the divine initiative* in a world where *human initiatives always lead to disaster*, and a *reaffirmation* [emphases supplied] of the primal divine intentions for man."[17] This emphasis on blessing being associated with God's initiative, as opposed to the disastrous results of human initiative, is significant in the development of the theology of work from the Genesis narrative. The Genesis portrayal of blessing has the following characteristics:

Blessing is Connection with God

Alliteration links the Hebrew *brk*, "blessing," and the name of Abram,[18] an important linguistic link between the creation narrative and the renewal of God's benediction towards humanity in the patriarchal narratives. There is also word play between the Hebrew words *bārā'*, "to create (by God alone)," and *brk*, "blessing," intimating blessing is connected with the activity of God. Barth noted this connection: "Divine creation is divine benefit. What takes shape in it is the goodness of God. This is the character without which it would not be a work of God," and, "We cannot understand the divine creation otherwise than as benefit."[19] Barth considered that this benefit derived from "the covenant between God and man,"[20] or what he had earlier called "the supreme fellowship between God and [humanity]."[21]

Westermann regarded "The presence of God is an essential part of blessing . . . In the history of the patriarchs God's blessing (defined in part by God's presence) is one of the principle theological concepts . . . Here we can clearly observe how that which we today call success or happiness was at one time considered to be obviously anchored in acts of God, and to be the result of God's activity."[22]

Gary Smith suggested the Genesis author interprets the lives of the patriarchs from the theological viewpoint of blessing. God's presence means

---

16. Armstrong, *In the Beginning*, 16–17, 29–31, 51, 61–78, 84.
17. Clines, *Theme of the Pentateuch*, 29.
18. Wenham, *Genesis 1–15*, 276.
19. Barth, *Doctrine of Creation*, 330–31.
20. Ibid., 332.
21. Ibid., 260–61.
22. Westermann, *Joseph: Studies*, 22.

blessing, and conversely God's absence means curse. Smith declared, "Life or death depends on whether man receives from God a blessing or a curse. The blessing is the will of God stated in its most basic form. Its existence is of primary importance, for without God's blessing men and animals are not able to flourish. The blessing is related to the world of nature as well as the course of history. The world as a whole, and individuals as well, are dependent on God because of the blessing . . . The *blessing given to Adam and Noah is essentially the same as that given to Abram* [emphasis supplied]."[23]

Blessing is Fruitful Abundance

The first Genesis blessing is fruitfulness and multiplication (Gen 1:22). This blessing on birds and fish was repeated for humanity (and implied for the land animals) (Gen 1:28). Thus blessing, in its primary Genesis form, means abundance and reproduction. Blessing involves the maturation of life, multiplication, and the bearing of fruit.[24] Waltke noted, "Because of God's blessing, the natural world is teeming with life. Blessing is God's gift of potency and power,"[25] and Westermann also recognized the importance of this.[26] Blessing is repeated after the tragedy of the Flood (Gen 9:1), and bursts with stunning frequency throughout the patriarchal narratives. Blessing thus has the quality not only of quantity, but also of exuberance, of sufficiency, abundance, and the profusion of availability.

The blessing of fruitfulness, fertility, is Abraham's primary understanding of his blessing when he responds to God's promise of "exceeding great reward" (Gen 15:1) with, "Lord God, what will you give me, seeing I go childless?" (Gen 15:2). However, early in the patriarchal narrative the general fruitfulness God promised is demonstrated when Abram and Lot decide to separate because the land could not sustain their abundant flocks and herds (Gen 13:6).

Blessing is God's Power

As Waltke noted above, blessing is the bestowal of God's power that enables humans to achieve God's intentions. The curses of the primordial

---

23. Smith, G. V., "Structure and Purpose," 311.
24. Sommer, "OT Theology as the Dialectic," 106. In this passage Sommer is discussing the Genesis concepts of Claus Westermann.
25. Waltke, *Genesis: A Commentary*, 69.
26. Westermann, *Genesis 12–36*, 575.

narratives demonstrate what happens when humans are not working under the blessing of God. They do not achieve God's intentions, and neither do they achieve their own. The renewal of the blessing promises to Abram and his descendants is accompanied by striking achievements, such as Sarah's pregnancy in her old age (Gen 21:1–2), Isaac becoming *gādôl*, "great," in the eyes of his neighbors (Gen 26:12–13), and Joseph's remarkable career (Gen 39–41).

Blessing gives Hope for the Future

An important consequence of fruitful abundance is that it gives an assurance for the future. This assurance of a future through fruitfulness is notably supported in the pericope of Noah. Amidst a world frighteningly devastated by the flood waters, God promised Noah: "Be fruitful and multiply, and fill the earth . . . Behold I establish my covenant with you and with your offspring after you . . . And God said: This is the sign of the covenant which I make between me and you . . . I set my bow in the cloud, and it shall be for the sign of the covenant . . . the waters shall never again become a flood to destroy all flesh" (Gen 9:1, 8–9, 12, 15). Noah and his family could look forward to a future assured by God himself, and were regularly reminded of this by the beautiful rainbow.

The blessing of reproduction indicates that life is to be sustained into the future;[27] it is the assurance of hope for a future. This assurance of a future is repeated in all of the blessing promises given by God to Abram and his descendants: "Then the Lord appeared to Abram and said, 'To your offspring will I give this land'" (Gen 12:7).

Blessing is Goodness and Completeness

Blessing in the Genesis narrative is associated with goodness, completeness, and a well-finished product. Repeatedly in the first chapter of Genesis, God pronounced what he had made as good, and blessed it. The only condition God recognized as *lō tôb*, "not good," in the original perfection of the garden is being alone (Gen 2:18). Thus, humans were not good and blessed until they were complete, that is, male and female, and in relationship. This relationship is specifically one of helpfulness, implying occupation (Gen 2:18).

The blessing of chapter 1 is pronounced when both the male and the female have been created in the image of God, but it is subsequently shown

---

27. Sommer, "OT Theology as the Dialectic."

in chapter 2 that this blessing could only be bestowed on the completed couple. It is of note that the longest chapter in the Abraham narrative, Genesis 24, is the one describing the search for a wife for Isaac. The gift of Isaac the son was not complete until he had a wife.

At the end of Creation, when God pronounced that everything he had made was "very good" (Gen 1:31), he finished his work of creation by pronouncing a day of rest and blessing it (Gen 2:1–3). Thus the text emphasizes that completion, goodness, and blessing are inseparably linked. Moltmann stated, "[I]n the theological tradition of the Western churches creation is generally presented merely as the 'six day's work.' The seventh day, the Sabbath, was often overlooked . . . The resting God, the celebrating God, the God who rejoices in his creation, receded into the background. And yet it is only the Sabbath which *completes* [emphasis supplied] and crowns creation."[28] The connection between goodness, completion, rest, and blessing is profoundly brought together with the institution of the Sabbath.

Blessing: Covenantal Relationship with God

Mitchell, in his detailed study of the meaning of *brk* in the Hebrew Bible, came to the conclusion, "The factor that makes a blessing a blessing is the relationship between God and the person blessed . . . The type of benefit God actually bestows when he blesses is of secondary importance."[29] He observed, "God's blessing is a visible sign of his favor," and other people can say, "we have seen quite clearly that Yahweh is with you because God has blessed you (see Gen 26:28, 39:2–6)."[30] Westermann, as noted earlier, regarded "The presence of God is an essential part of blessing."[31]

The essential connection between relationship with God and blessing is emphasized in the negative primordial narrative. If it is God's presence that brings blessing, then his absence results in "curse"; thus God can be said to "cause" by either his presence or absence, both blessing and cursing. Broken God–human relationships, separation from God, result in cursing.

Relationship is highlighted in the call of Abram. Scullion noted the call shows "God's blessing proceeds from his will to form a relationship between himself and Abraham and through Abraham with his descendants and 'all the clans of the earth.'"[32] Although God repeatedly promises to bless Abram,

28. Moltmann, *God in Creation*, 6.
29. Mitchell, *Meaning of BRK*, 165.
30. Ibid., 166.
31. Westermann, *Joseph: Studies*, 22.
32. Scullion, *Genesis: A Commentary*, 107.

Abram is also called into relationship with God ("Go where I ask") and in relationship with others by being a blessing to them. The Hebrew of "you will be a blessing" is a command, not a promise,[33] emphasizing its importance.[34] It is Abram's relationship with God that brings the blessing, and it is the relationship between Abram and his descendants with the other families of earth that determines the latter's being blessed or otherwise. This is a striking concept. It suggests that to selfishly try to enjoy the benefits of relationship with God is not possible; that there is no blessing unless there is an extension of relationship beyond the self to God and other humans. The patriarchal narratives emphasize the blessing of relationship in a variety of ways.

The repetition of the word covenant (clearly denoting relationship) ten times in Gen 17:1–14, when God renames Abram as Abraham, is significant. It suggests that the great name Abraham was promised in Gen 12:1–3 was actually the covenant relationship between Almighty God and himself. Covenantal relationship with God is the greatest blessing. The covenantal presence of God is not passive, or accidental. It involves choice and deliberate action, symbolized by the rite of circumcision, given when God promised to "establish" his covenant with Abraham and his descendants (Gen 17:9–11).

That the absence of God brings the reverse of blessing, that is, a curse, is demonstrated in the Abraham narrative by the destruction of the cities of Sodom and Gomorrah. Before their destruction (their effective curse, although the word *'ārar* is not used), God presented Abraham with the opportunity to learn that the inhabitants of the cities had completely divorced themselves from him, and that there were not even ten god-connected righteous people in the cities (Gen 18:16–33).

The horrible results of this separation starkly contrasts with God's expressed desire to connect with Abram, to bless him (Gen 18:17–21), and inform him: "The Lord said, 'Shall I hide from Abraham what I am about to do, seeing that Abraham shall surely become a great and mighty nation, and all the nations of the earth shall be blessed in him? For I have chosen him, that he may command his children and his household after him to keep the way of the Lord by doing righteousness and justice, so that the Lord may bring to Abraham what he has promised him.' Then the Lord said, 'Because the outcry against Sodom and Gomorrah is great and their sin is very grave, I will go down to see whether they have done altogether according to the outcry that has come to me, and if not, I will know'" (Gen 18:17–20). It is

---

33. Turner, *Genesis*, 64.

34. See ibid. Although Dumbrell was uncertain of the importance of this command there can be only two possibilities: either Abram will bless God, or he will bless other people.

significant that even in this tragic situation God is still willing to "go down" (reminiscent of the Tower narrative, Gen 11:5) to see the situation for himself, and to attempt to connect with the cities of the plain.

Blessing is Completion that leads to Rest

The creation pericope clearly connects completion with rest (ceasing work) and blessing when God celebrates his completed creation work by instigating and blessing the Sabbath day. Thus the concept of blessing progresses from abundance and fertility into the dimension of time when God initiated this day for "ceasing." God pronounced that everything he had made was "very good" (Gen 1:31), but he finished creation by declaring a day for ceasing and blessing (Gen 2:1–3).

Moltmann observed that the aspect of celebration and rejoicing in the seventh day has often been overlooked.[35] The connection between goodness, completion, rest, and blessing is beautifully brought together with the institution of the Sabbath. Like God, humanity must take time to rejoice and celebrate; this cannot be done in relentless activity.[36]

Genesis seems generally silent on the valuable topic of rest after humanity's exit from the Garden of Eden, but Lamech's lament and Jacob's Jabbok experience highlight the special aspect of blessing that means ceasing from work. On the threshold of the overwhelming disaster of the Flood, Lamech, the father of Noah, indicates the very unrested, unblessed state of the arduous work culture in which he was living. From the depths of his exhaustion he cries out, "Out of the ground that the Lord has cursed this one shall bring us relief from our work and the painful toil of our hands" (Gen 5:29), and he names his first born son Noah, meaning rest. Whilst his culture may not have valued rest, Lamech through bitter experience had learned to appreciate it.

When Jacob at the Jabbok pled with his assailant to bless him, he was blessed with a name change and, surprisingly, a dislocated hip (Gen 32:24–31). Relentless work had dominated the life of Jacob, and the blessing for which he had yearned for at least twenty years came to him, at least partially, in the form of an injury that precluded the continuation of this relentless work.

---

35. Moltmann, *God in Creation*, 6.
36. Ibid.

Blessing is Joy

Blessing includes joy and happiness. When God visited Abraham and told him that his wife Sarah is blessed and will at last have a child he repeated the information twice, indicating certainty (Gen 17:16). Sarah would finally bear the long-awaited son. God then instructed the incredulous Abraham, who fell on his face laughing at the preposterous idea, to call this son Isaac, meaning laughter (Gen 17:15–19). Although the immediate context is that Abraham (and later Sarah herself, Gen 18:10–12) laughed at the notion that the aged Abraham and the aged and postmenapausal Sarah could conceive a son, this laughter need not be derisive. Their amazement was turned into true joy when Isaac was born (Gen 21:6).

The blessed joy of Isaac's existence is clearly shown when God tests Abraham most severely. Isaac is described as "the son whom you love," the blessing, the joy, the one who makes you laugh (Gen 22:1–2).

Blessing is a Circle returning Praise to God

Surprisingly, blessing is something humans can offer God. The use of the term blessing in this situation is perhaps better rendered as thanks, but Hebrew does not use the word "thanks" in this situation.[37] However, the benedictory aspect of thanks which are "returned" to God makes the use of the term "blessing" perhaps more accurate than merely thanks, which simply recognizes benefit. Melchizedek, the priest-king of Salem, recognizing the source of the stupendous victory Abram and his helpers achieved over Chedorlaomer and the three confederate Mesopotamian kings, cries triumphantly, "Blessed be God Most High who has delivered your enemies into your hand!" (Gen 14:20). Abraham's faithful servant, successful in finding a wife for Isaac, bows his head and prays, "Blessed be the Lord God of my master Abraham . . . the Lord led me to the house of my master's brethren" (Gen 24:26–27).

For Westermann, praise, prayer, and offering were the appropriate humans responses to God. Meditation on divine acts of blessing was also an important part of this response, leading to the recognition of the goodness of God. Importantly, recognizing the blessing and goodness of God enables humans to understand that they cannot live fulfilling lives apart from God.[38]

---

37. Scharbert, J., "brk," in *Theological Dictionary of the OT*, vol. 2, 305. "Therefore the verb [brk] with God as object was used only when one wanted to give thanks for a saving, helping deed."

38. Westermann, *Elements of OT Theology*, 153–216.

Humans can Bless Each Other

Humans blessing each other is first recorded in the immediate postdiluvian world. In the first few chapters of Genesis blessing remains in the realm and privilege of God. But in the pericope of Noah's response to the behavior of his sons, blessing (and cursing) recognizes something humans can offer other humans. This becomes more frequent in the patriarchal narratives: Melchizedek blesses Abram (Gen 14:19–20); Jacob craves blessing so much that he even attempts to steal a blessing from his father Isaac and brother Esau (Gen 27:11–30); Jacob blesses his sons (Gen 49:1–27) and grandsons (Gen 48:6–20), and even the Pharaoh of Egypt (Gen 47:7).

In the Genesis narrative, the human ability to bless others being contingent on prior blessing from God is implicit rather than explicit. However, the only people who bless others are those who have received God's blessing, people like Isaac (Gen 25:11), Jacob (Gen 32:28–29), and Joseph (Gen 39:3, 23). Importantly, in the later pericopes of the Moabite King Balak's attempts to get Balaam to curse Israel, it is revealed that a person can bless or curse others only with God's permission (Num 22:35, 23:11–12, 25–26, 24:10–13).

God's Blessing Contingent on Obedience

The importance of obedience in obtaining God's blessing is shown by the implied loss of blessing when the man and woman disobey the command not to eat from the tree of knowledge of good and evil. Their original blessings (fertile ground and children) are now presented as the subjects of painful curses (Gen 3:14–19).

The blessings pronounced on Abram are clearly dependent on his willingness to obey the command "Go!" (Gen 12:1). It is only because "Abram departed as the Lord had spoken to him" (Gen 12:4) that there was any certainty that the blessings would flow. This demonstrates that acceptance of the sovereignty of God remains a vital aspect of the God–human relationship.

However, not until the terrible testing of Abraham in chapter 22 is there confirmation that obedience and total commitment are the critical factors that make blessing possible. Although obedience was clearly a part of the original call of Abraham: "Go!" so Abram went (Gen 12:1, 4), the blessing pronounced upon Abraham after his ordeal with Isaac is voiced immediately. The original blessings are repeated, and emphasized by expansion: "I will *surely* bless you, and I will *surely* multiply your offspring *as the stars of heaven and as the sand that is on the seashore.* And your offspring shall posses the gate of his enemies, and in your offspring shall all the nations of earth be blessed, *because you have obeyed* my voice [emphases supplied]" (Gen 22:17–18). Abraham's willing obedience to the command to offer Isaac appeared to be the death knell of all the promises given to him, and his life's work, but the text reveals the opposite. Through his obedience the blessing became certain.

The Cycle of Blessing

The scope of blessing is thus wide, but importantly, blessing in the Genesis narrative is always connected with God. Thus it can be said that blessing is portrayed in the Genesis narrative as a circular flow pattern, a beneficial cycle that includes at least the following:

Table 5: Blessing

Blessing is a major theme of the Genesis narrative.
Blessing always originates as a gift from God to his creation.
Blessing involves multiplication of both humans and the creatures of nature.
Blessing implies an abundant provision of life-sustaining supplies.
Blessing is power.
Blessing offers an assurance of a meaningful future.
Blessing implies intimate relationship with God.
Humans who are blest by God will have a positive, beneficial relationship between other humans. God's blessing can be shared between humans.
Blessing means goodness and completion, implying rest, peace, joy, and contentment.
Blessing means happiness.
Blessing is the reward for obedient commitment and sacrifice.
Blessed humans return blessing, as thankful praise, to God.

Adam's Blessing of Dominion: The Original Human Work

The call and promises of Abram that initiate the "signature tune of blessing" which dominates the patriarchal narrative have been recognized as a renewal of the original blessings bestowed at creation.[39] It would therefore be useful to re-examine those creation blessings.

The Creation blessings were reproductive fertility and dominion.[40] Collins asserted that although the Fall of humanity impacted the created world, it was humanity that "fell from the task" and not the dominion that was lost.[41] However, Calvin held that humanity lost their dominion over this world because of the Fall, but their dominion was restored by Christ's sacrificial death.[42] Issues and ideas surrounding the concept of dominion and the related one of *imago Dei* will now be re-examined.

Land Ownership absent from Blessing Promised Abram

It is conspicuous that of all the blessings offered to Abram, dominion as land ownership was notably only a promise. After Abram had obeyed the call and was physically present in the land, God appeared to him, saying, "To your offspring will I give this land" (Gen 12:6–7), but the land was still not given to him.

Even later, when Abram voiced serious concern about his continued childlessness (Gen 15:2–3), God covenanted that there would be both offspring and land, but warned there would be a long time of sojourning in a strange land, no less than four hundred years (Gen 15:13–21, 17:8), before the land would be given to Abram's descendants. It seems the ownership aspect of human dominion was not a crucial factor in God's blessing. In fact, Abram's call stressed utter dependence on God more than power, authority, or ownership.

---

39. Smith, G. V., "Structure and Purpose," 311.
40. Arnold, *Genesis*, 126; Fishbane, *Biblical Interpretation*, 372–73.
41. Collins, *Genesis 1–4*, 183.
42. Hart, "Teaching: John Calvin," 123.

Eden Dominion is over Creatures, not Resources

The original Eden dominion focused on the other creatures God created, rather than on the land: "And God said, 'Let us make man in our image, after our likeness. And let them have dominion *over the fish* of the sea and *over the birds* of the heavens and over *the livestock* and over all the earth and *over every creeping thing* [emphases supplied] that creeps on the earth.' . . . And God blessed them. And God said to them, 'Be fruitful and multiply and fill the earth and subdue it and have dominion *over the fish of the sea* and *over the birds* of the heavens and *over every thing that moves* [emphases supplied] on the earth'" (Gen 1:26, 28). Repeated twice, a typical Hebrew literary emphasis technique, dominion is identified as being over the other creatures. Whilst subduing the earth is noted as under the umbrella of dominion (Gen 1:26), when God blesses the couple they subdue the earth (to multiply and fill it) but have dominion over the animals (Gen 1:28). Moltmann noted this important distinction: that dominion was over the animals, and subjection of the earth was for the purposes of food.[43]

That the creatures were to be objects of care rather than for human use is demonstrated in the next two verses (Gen 1:29–30). God gave humanity fruit and seed-bearing plants for food, and to every beast of the earth, every bird of the heavens, and everything that crept on the earth he gave green plants for food. Thus in the context of the creation pericope dominion is the care of creation, and not the use of creation.

This focus on other creatures emphasizes the caring and relational aspect of the original human dominion, and perhaps explains why Abram was not given any land. That he had animals is revealed early in the narrative. In fact Abram had so many animals that "the land could not support" both his flocks and those of his nephew, Lot (Gen 13:5–6). The focus here is on the animals and their needs, and not on land that Abram does not own.

This delay in achieving land ownership is noteworthy. If dominion in the Edenic situation meant the care and leadership of the animal kingdom, it is conceivable that the call of Abram could emphasize something not previously appreciated by Adam and his descendants. The original dominion was to care, not to have. The call of Abram therefore emphasizes by repetition

---

43. Moltmann, *God in Creation*, 224. Moltmann wrote: "[T]he beginning teaches that human lordship over the animals has to be distinguished from human subjugation of the earth for the purposes of nourishment, and distinguished more clearly than is the case in the traditional theological doctrine of the *dominium terrae*, for this doctrine throws the two together and intermixes them, with disastrous consequences for the world."

that firstly, all blessing comes from God, and secondly, that Abram himself is to respond to others in blessing. Having kingly dominion was not the essence of the Edenic blessing, and therefore was not part of the Abramic blessing.

It is noteworthy that dominion over land had not yet occurred when the Genesis narrative ends (Gen 50:25). In fact, dominion over land had not occurred when the Torah's account ends on the borders of Canaan (Deut 3:23–27, 34:1–5). Furthermore, the tribe of Levi, who served in the tabernacle, conspicuously had no land inheritance, only villages scattered throughout the land owned by their brethren: "You shall have no inheritance in their land, neither shall you have any portion among them. *I am your portion and inheritance among the people of Israel* [emphasis supplied]" (Num 18:20). Tragically, when the descendants of Abraham eventually obtained dominion over the land they did not put their ownership to good use, and after much prophetic warning they once again lost dominion over the land (2 Chr 36:14–21). This implies there is a question about the outright dominion of humanity over the land. God retains the right to bestow dominion of land ownership on whomsoever he chooses. However, the dominion of care is given to all who accept God's sovereignty in their lives.

The political and religious leaders of first-century CE Palestine were intensely focused on regaining their lost dominion over land, but by this focus they lost sight of the blessing (the incarnate God) in their midst.[44] This was exemplified by the Zealots, who "uncompromisingly faithful to their God, Torah and land, fought valiantly for the holy city and temple against the conquering Roman armies, and then held out for another three years atop the fortress of Masada."[45] It is therefore asserted that to make dominion over the land the key concept in a theology of human work is a misleading focus.

Imago Dei: Working to Bless or to Dominate?

Closely connected with the concept of human dominion has been that of *imago Dei*. There has been considerable discussion throughout Christian history, continuing to the present, on the meaning of this phase, and Goldingay said, "Interpretation of the image of God is the history of western understanding

---

44. For a detailed description of Jewish attempts to wrest their land from the Romans, see Josephus, *Wars of the Jews*. For an archeological perspective of Jewish nationalistic activity see Davies, "Under Seige," 65–83.

45. Horsley, "Zealots: Their Origin," 159.

of humanity."[46] Nathan Macdonald suggested that the "relationship between *imago* and dominion finds its background in those Near Eastern texts that speak of the human king as the divine image, a representative of the deity who acts as his vice-regent on earth," and he noted James Barr regarded this "functional" opinion as the most influential today.[47] Another view of *imago Dei* is Barth's "relational" interpretation, which focuses on the male-female nature of humanity and the Trinitarian nature of God.[48] Both of these views seem applicable in the Edenic context. Goldingay's suggestion that in order to understand the concept of *imago Dei* we must understand both what it means to be God and what it means to be human seems most reasonable,[49] but it leaves us with the realization that we cannot fully know God, and we are far from knowing what being human is all about.

Cotter suggested "[t]o be in God's image means to be blessed with the responsibility of ruling the world in such a way that it is the ordered, good, life-giving place that God intends it to be."[50] Hollenbach considered dominion involved continuing the creative activity of God and that this creative activity is part of the *imago Dei*.[51] Pope John Paul II stated, "Man is the image of God partly through the mandate received from his Creator to subdue, to dominate the earth."[52] He emphasized that work is important because man is important. These ideas see humans as the primary beneficiaries of the dominion given them, without appreciating that humanity was given dominion to care for the animals. Richardson opposed the idea that *imago Dei* might mean sharing the creative activity of God, declaring humans are vice-regents on earth to do God's will.[53]

It seems reasonable to conclude that the call of Abram indicates what is the true way of imitating "the character and ways of God,"[54] that is, to be in verity the *imago Dei*. It is to respond to the command "be a blessing." The call emphasizes submissive obedience, upon which the blessing depends.

---

46. Goldingay, *OT Theology: Israel's Gospel*, 102.
47. Macdonald, "Imago Dei and Election," 304.
48. Ibid., see for full discussion.
49. Goldingay, *OT Theology: Israel's Gospel*, 102.
50. Cotter, *Genesis*, 18.
51. Hollenbach, "Human Work," 63.
52. John Paul II, *Laborem Exercens*, section 4.
53. Richardson, *Genesis 1–11*, 55.
54. Wright, *Walking in the Ways*, 13–45, quoted in Collins, *Genesis 1–4*, 131.

Work: Imago Dei or Self-Actualization?

The idea that the goal of human work is to be a blessing contrasts with current idea that work is a source of self-actualization.[55] Volf and Ben Witherington have noted the Western postmodern obsession with work is connected with ideas of self-actualization and authentication. Volf said: "The contemporary religion of work has little to do either with worship of God or with God's demands on human life; it has to do with 'worship' of self and human demands on self."[56] Witherington asked, "Is my sense of identity so bound up in what I do that I have become a compulsive workaholic just to validate my existence and give myself a sense of importance, worth and value?"[57] Thus, responding to God's call to go from the culture of "Babel" will cause approaches to work to be diametrically opposed to current ideas on work in Western culture.

Abram is not called to make a great name for himself. A name is part of the packaged gift resulting from obedience to the call. His obligation was to be a blessing, not to transform the world. Abram is not presented as someone achieving self-actualization and authentication, but somewhat disgracefully as someone unable to create what he most desires, a legitimate son. He has no prospects of ever having a legitimate child because his wife, twice stated for emphasis, is barren (Gen 11:30). It is only through the blessing of God's power that he can achieve this goal.

Abram is thus utterly dependent on God for the fulfilment of the promised blessings. In this total reliance on God, the promised blessings most truly point back to the promises of God to *hā-ʾādām* and the conditions God had envisioned in the beginning. Abram was not asked to resolve the imperfections of his family, neighbors, and community, nor was he given any instructions about how to possess the promised land. Rather, as Waltke pointed out, Abram's call expands his perspective on blessing from himself to the whole world,[58] a clearly different perspective from the "ourselves" of the Tower-builders' viewpoint.

---

55. Blustein, *Psychology of Working*, 115ff.
56. Volf, *Work in the Spirit*, 129.
57. Witherington, *Work: Kingdom Perspective*, 155.
58. Waltke, *Genesis: A Commentary*, 203.

8

The Literary Structure of Genesis

THE TRADITIONALLY CONCEIVED GENESIS structure, consisting of two parts, primordial and patriarchal, has been useful. As noted, Hamilton considered the patriarchal history offered the solution to the curse/sin problem outlined in the primordial history, and the Genesis narrative moved "from generation (chs 1–2) to degeneration (chs 3–11) to regeneration (chs 12–50)."[1] However, the fundamental idea in this structure is sin, regarded as concentrated in the primordial story.

But Gonzalez challenged this concept, contending that the spread of sin continues into the patriarchal stories with no significant change. He did not see the call of Abram and the patriarchal narratives as the solution to the problems of the primordial story, noting the many sins perpetrated by the patriarchs and their families, and that "Joseph, ['Yahweh's agent for blessing and the savior of the promise'] ends up dead in a coffin and the sons of Israel stranded in Egypt, far from the Land of Promise. So the patriarchal narrative, like the primeval narrative, leaves the problem of sin and the curse ultimately unsolved."[2] However, I argue the Genesis narrative does offer a solution to the sin and curse problem, and an analysis of its structure offers the key.

This study is not a literary analysis of Genesis per se, but by utilizing the theme of work it is asserted the Genesis narrative emerges as having the classic form of a chiasm. This elucidates the problem of "unfinished business" encountered at the end of Genesis, and has important implications for developing a theology of work from the Genesis narrative.

---

1. Hamilton, *Book of Genesis Chapters 1–17*, 11.

2. Gonzalez, *Where Sin Abounds*, 264–65. Gonzalez considers instead that the realistic and truthful presentation of the patriarchal characters endorses the doctrines of divine inspiration and sanctification.

Evidence of Intentional Authorship

To describe the book of Genesis as having structure presupposes that there is something intentional about its composition. Use of the term "author" rather than "redactor" seems reasonable if evidence of an intentional arrangement of the material can be demonstrated. The term "redactor" suggests an editing of material, particularly for legal purposes,[3] whereas the Genesis narrative shows a careful overall literary plan. The traditional structure of primordial and patriarchal parts gives evidence of editing, but the proposed structure denotes significant intention. That pre-existing material is utilized is recognized, but the arrangement of that material appears deliberate.

Smith observed the important relationship between structure and meaning, recognized in the syntactical study of language, and also in the conscious and unconscious development of longer forms of oral and written communication.[4] He noted that unfortunately the source criticism of Genesis offers little to those interested in the structure of the book, because of its assertion that the book was composed by different authors over a long period of time, and cobbled together by a redactor late in Jewish history.[5] Turner noted that partly as a reaction to the fragmentation of the text in the traditional historical-critical methodologies there have been several recent attempts to demonstrate structural coherence of large sections of the narrative, but he suggested there has been more success with the structure of individual passages than with over-all structure (discussed further below).[6] The following are evidence suggesting the text was arranged with a definite plan in mind.

The tôlēdôt Framework

Several recent exegetes observed the *tôlēdôt* forms a significant structural device of Genesis.[7] Although Westermann supported the documentary approach to Genesis, he recognized the importance of this genealogical information, suggesting it be given "proper significance"; that the whole of Genesis has two types of writing, the narrative and the enumerative.[8] Turner

---

3. See entry "Redact": "to censor or obscure a part of a text for legal or security purposes," *New Oxford American Dictionary*.
4. Smith, G. V., "Structure and Purpose," 307.
5. Ibid.
6. Turner, "Genesis," 351.
7. For example, Turner, *Genesis*; Mathews, *Genesis 1—11:26*; Cotter, *Genesis*.
8. Westermann, *Genesis 1–11*, 3.

noted the regular pattern of generations (the *tôlēdôt*) alternating with what he called "unpredictable" narratival material.[9] This *tôlēdôt* framework supports all of Genesis, and suggests a unified plan, so that the early chapters should not be divorced from the later.[10] Theological concepts conveyed in the primordial parts of Genesis would thus be followed through in the patriarchal.

Mathews noted the "prominent literary device" of the *tôlēdôt*; that the usual word for "generation," *dôr*, is not used, and that *tôlēdôt* usually means simply "begettings."[11] He recognized the word is used in Ruth 4:18, where it acts as a hinge device, pointing to elements in the previous section, yet focusing attention on the subsequent material. He suggested that the word functions similarly in Genesis.[12] This "looking forward while looking back" concept is significant in the overall Genesis structure. Mathews divided the book into twelve sections thus:

> The Creation of heaven and earth (1:1—2:3) (but note, no *tôlēdôt*)
>
> The *tôlēdôt* of earth's family (2:4—4:26)
>
> The *tôlēdôt* of Adam's line (5:1—6: 8)
>
> The *tôlēdôt* of Noah (6:9—9:29)
>
> The *tôlēdôt* of Noah's sons (10:1—11: 9)
>
> The *tôlēdôt* of Shem (11:10-26)
>
> The *tôlēdôt* of Terah (Abraham) (11:27—25:11)
>
> The *tôlēdôt* of Ishmael (25:12-18)
>
> The *tôlēdôt* of Isaac (25:19—35:29)
>
> The *tôlēdôt* of Esau and family (36:1-8)
>
> The *tôlēdôt* of Esau (36:9—37:1)
>
> The *tôlēdôt* of Jacob (Joseph) (37:2—50:26)[13]

The *tôlēdôt* framework thus links all parts of the Genesis material and is valuable evidence that it is a unified whole. The theme it most obviously supports is the creation blessing, that humanity was proliferating as God intended.

---

9. Turner, *Genesis*, 27.

10. Arnold, *Genesis*, 126.

11. Mathews, *Genesis 1—11:26*, 27.

12. Ibid., 33.

13. Ibid., 27-28. While some scholars either do not recognize the creation story as a *tôlēdôt* section or combine the two Esau *tôlēdôt* sections, there is agreement on the importance of this structural device for the book.

Gary V. Smith's Analysis of the Primordial Narrative

In his analysis of the structure of the primordial narrative (Gen 1–11), Smith suggested it consists of two parallel parts, each with the following pattern: first a blessing (Gen 1:28, and 9:1, 7) with its promise to multiply and fill the earth, followed by a sin (Adam, Noah) that led to a curse on the relationship between brothers (Gen 4, and 9:20–27), then after the curse comes expansion and genealogies (Gen 4:16–26, 5, and Gen 10, 11:10–32), and finally there is a curse on wider society (Gen 6, and 11:1–9) with the election of one man (Noah, Abram) to bring about God's plans.[14] From this assessment Smith argued that the rest of the Pentateuch is developed from the theological perspective of whether a man receives from God a blessing or a curse, that God's dealing with humans is consistent with his action in Genesis 1–11.[15]

Smith's analysis therefore suggests there is a repetitive pattern in the Genesis stories. However, a corollary of his structure is to ask: Why does someone receive blessing or cursing from God? The text suggests an important aspect of the answer to this question is whether or not the elected individual cooperates and works with God. This idea of working with God therefore provides a cohesive and useful approach to understand the meaning and purpose of Genesis as a whole.

The Theme of Blessing

As noted in the previous chapter, many have recognized blessing as a theme in Genesis. Waltke's observation that "blessing" occurs only five times in the primordial narrative (Gen 1:22, 28, 2:3, 9:1, 26), and then is concentrated five times in the call of Abram (Gen 12:1–3),[16] balances the five curse situations found in the primeval narrative, endorsing the suggestion that Abram's call is a bidding to return to the original divine plan of blessing.

But a call to return to the divine plan is not the same as saying "With Abram . . . begins the decisive implementation of the plan of God."[17] Some even suggest God did not set the gospel story in motion until the call of Abram.[18]

14. Smith, G. V., "Structure and Purpose," 317.
15. Ibid., 318.
16. Waltke, *Genesis: A Commentary*, 205.
17. Blocher, *In the Beginning*, 211.
18. Gibson, *Genesis*, 213.

The *tôlēdôt* framework supports blessing (being fruitful and multiplying) as a core Genesis narrative concept. Yet blessing was also notably a characteristic of the Sabbath day that concluded God's creation activity. As discussed in the previous chapter, the critical concept implicated in blessing is relationship with God.

Utilization of Classic Narrative Technique

Alter argued that literary art is crucial in biblical narrative: "What role does literary art play in the shaping of biblical narrative? A crucial one, I shall argue, finely modulated from moment to moment, determining in most cases the minute choice of words and reported details, the pace of narration, the small movements of dialogue, and *a whole network of ramified interconnections* [emphasis supplied] in the text."[19] In narrative, "there is story—events narrated—and discourse—the form given the narrative by the narrator."[20]

Narrative consists of five parts: First, there is a beginning and an ending; Second there is a catastrophe; Third a plan for rescue is plotted; Fourth characters develop; and finally, all parts have significance.[21] Alter offered a good Genesis example of the final point, when he demonstrated that the "supposedly interpolated story" of Tamar and Judah (Gen 38) is actually an essential part of the Joseph narrative (Gen 37–50).[22]

The curse pericopes are the intensification of the "catastrophe" of the Genesis narrative. The original catastrophe was when *hā- 'ādām* disregarded the prohibition to eat from the tree of knowledge. The primordial narrative fleshes out the results of that apparently simple act of defiance. The calls of both Noah and Abram begin the rescue plan and the character development aspects of the narrative. However, Gonzalez's emphasis on the Genesis narrative ending with Joseph being in a coffin far from the Promised Land poses the question: Is this a suitable resolution of the narrative tension?

---

19. Alter, *Art of Biblical Narrative*, 3.
20. Marguerat and Bourquin, *How to Read Bible Stories*, 18.
21. Peterson, *Working the Angles*, 120–21.
22. Alter, *Art of Biblical Narrative*, 3–12.

Cassuto's Assertion

Cassuto stated that it is a Golden Rule of Torah that the conclusion of a narrative should reflect the opening.[23] This suggests that the patriarchal stories are moving towards a significant conclusion (not a mummy in a coffin) that will bear some relationship with the beginning. Wenham noted: "we need to see individual stories within the context of complete books,"[24] which emphasizes the unity of the Genesis narrative message.

Chiastic Structure in the Book of Genesis

The concept of inclusion, that is, the ending of a narrative recalling its beginning, is implied in Cassuto's remarks. The story, the idea, folds back on itself, so that the parts the author wishes to emphasize may be at the beginning, the ending or, for a classic chiasm, also at the center. By "repeating" the concepts along the two arms of the chiasm the author reinforces the ideas presented. However, it must be noted that the "message" of a chiasm is not restricted to its central portion.

Examples of Chiasm in Genesis

The use of chiasm occurs early in the Genesis narrative literary structure, and there are many examples of it throughout the text. The first, and most simple, Gen 2:4, illustrates the principle. This chiasm emphasizes that God made everything, the heavens and the earth.

> A heavens
> > B earth
> > > C created
> > > C' made
> > B' earth
> A' heavens[25]

---

23. Cassuto, *Commentary on Genesis: Noah to Abraham*, 190.
24. Wenham, *Story as Torah*, 17.
25. Wenham, *Genesis 1–15*, 46.

Genesis Chapters 2–3

Ouro demonstrated a chiastic structure for Genesis 2–3, which shows overall intent and unity of thought between the chapters describing human placement in the Garden of Eden, and their expulsion from it. This chiasm emphasizes the original plan of God, God's crucial sovereign activity in formulating law and its enforcement, and the tragically decisive role of the disobedience of humans.

> A The placement of Man in the Garden of Eden (Gen 2:5–15)
>> B Divine Commandment and Organization of Human life (Gen 2:16–25)
>>> C Disobedience of Human Beings (Gen 3:1–7)
>> B' Divine Judgment and Reorganization of Human life (Gen 3:8–21)
> A' Expulsion of Man from the Garden of Eden (Gen 3:22–24)[26]

The Tower of Babel

Another example of a chiastic structure is found in the Tower of Babel pericope, which is, as already noted, very carefully crafted. Cassuto called it a "fine example of biblical literary art."[27] Wenham recognized the structure of the Tower narrative was chiastic,[28] calling it a "finely crafted piece."[29] Waltke delineated the pericope's chiastic form and demonstrated that it pivots on the phrase "and the Lord came down." The focus is thus actually on the activity of God, whereas on first reading human unity (as expressed in language) and work appears to be the center of attention.

> A All the earth one language
>> B People settled together there
>>> C said to each other
>>>> D Come now let us make bricks
>>>>> E A city and a tower
>>>>>> X And the Lord came down

---

26. Ouro, "Garden of Eden Account," 224.
27. Cassuto, *Commentary on Genesis: Noah to Abraham*, 226–34.
28. Wenham, *Genesis 1–15*, 234.
29. Ibid., 238.

  E' The city and the tower

  D' Come now, let us confuse

  C' [not understand] each other

  B' people disperse from there

  A' Language of the whole earth[30]

The Aqedah

Doukhan demonstrated that the pivotal story of the *Aqedah* has a classic chiastic structure. Doukhan suggests the central idea of the story is the tragic dialogue between Abraham and his son Isaac, but it is important to note that this is framed by Abraham's conversations with God. This pericope demonstrates that the message of a chiasm is not only at the center.

 A Dialogue between God and Abraham.

  B Abraham's walk

   C Dialogue between Abraham and Isaac

  B' Abraham's walk

 A' Dialogue Between Angel of God and Abraham[31]

The Last Words of Jacob and Joseph

Nicholas Lunn demonstrated another example of chiastic structure in Genesis. He showed that the last words of Joseph and Jacob has the following pattern:

 A Last words and death of Jacob (49:29—50:3)

  B Joseph's appeal to Pharaoh (50:4-6)

   C Funeral of Jacob (50:7-14)

  B' The brothers' appeal to Joseph (50:15-21)

 A' Last words and death of Joseph (50:22-26)[32]

This chiasm suggests the significant funeral at the end of Genesis might be that of Jacob rather than Joseph. Jacob's body is returned to Canaan, but

---

30. Waltke, *Genesis: A Commentary*, 176.

31. Doukhan, "Center of the Aqedah," 17-28.

32. Lunn, "Last Words of Jacob and Joseph," 164.

Joseph's awaits return to Canaan until, as he says, "God visits." Importantly, this chiasm also indicates that the last words of Joseph have significance similar to the last words of Jacob, and this will be explored later.

The Jacob Story

The largest block of chiasm that Turner recognized as having been generally accepted to show a chiastic structure is Fishbane's[33] landmark study of the Jacob story.[34] This structure is somewhat complex, but can be simplified thus:

A Oracle sought, Rebekah struggles in childbirth (Gen 25:19-34)

  B Interlude: strife, deception, blessing, and covenant with foreigner (Gen 26)

    C Deception, blessing stolen, flight from land (Gen 27:1—28:9)

      D Evening encounter with divine being (Gen 28:10-22)

        E Internal cycle opens: arrival, kisses, Laban at border, wages, deception (Gen 29)

          F Rachel barren, Leah fertile, Rachel fertile, Jacobs breeds (Gen 30)

        E' Internal cycle closes: depart, kiss Laban at border, wages, deception (Gen 31)

      D' Evening encounter with divine being (Gen 32)

    C' Deception planned, Blessing/gift returned (Gen 33)

  B' Interlude, strife, covenant with foreigner (Gen 34)

A' Oracle filled, Rachel struggles in childbirth[35]

Although Turner described this structure as "compelling" it is noteworthy that a significant part of the story (that includes the death of Rachel) must be regarded as a postlude standing outside the main composition. This suggests either that the Genesis compiler utilized chiastic structure but did not feel bound by it, or simply that the Jacob narrative does not have a regular chiastic structure.

---

33. Fishbane, "Composition and Structure," 15-38.
34. Turner, "Genesis," 351.
35. Ibid., modified Fishbane's structure.

A Favored Device

This recurrent use of micro chiastic structure in the Genesis narrative, and recognition that it has been used in at least one major block of the book, suggests it was a favored device of the author, and could therefore be found in the overall Genesis narrative. Turner suggested there has been more success in demonstrating structure in individual narrative blocks than for overall structure, and refers to suggested, but not universally accepted, plans from A. Quinn, T. E. Fretheim, G. A. Rendsburg, J. Blenkisopp, and D. A. Garrett.[36] Turner stated there have been few attempts to postulate a formal design for the whole book,[37] but he considers exceptions being the works of D. A. Garrett[38] and T. J. Prewitt.[39]

Theme of Work has a Chiastic Form in Genesis

But despite apparent lack of previous success to demonstrate an overall structure for Genesis, there is warrant to postulate a chiastic form for the narrative. Further, when the theme of work (a major theme[40]) is examined in the entire Genesis narrative, it can be presented as inclusion, and this expanded to an overall chiastic form. Whereas the themes of sin and even blessing have a somewhat homocentric focus, the theme of work in Genesis is primarily theocentric and only secondarily homocentric. Thus the dominating theme of successful work in Genesis is the work of God, which is contrasted with the ineffective work of humanity without God. The analysis of the first three chapters of Genesis indicates the work of God and the relationship of humans with each other and God are the focus of those early chapters. Therefore it is no surprise when the themes of work and relationship re-emerge at the end of Genesis.

---

36. Ibid., 351.
37. Ibid.
38. Garrett, *Rethinking Genesis*.
39. Prewitt, *Elusive Covenant*.
40. Hart, "Genesis 1:1—2:3 as a Prologue," 315, 336.

Table 6: Genesis Begins and Ends with a Work of God

God separated light from darkness (Gen 1:3–5)	God separated waters above from below (Gen 1:6–8)	God gathered waters, let dry land appear, and made vegetation (Gen 1:9–13)	God filled heavens with lights to rule day and night (Gen 1:14–19)	God filled waters with living things and heavens with flying things (Gen 1:20–22)	God made living things and humans (Gen 1:24–31)	God blessed the seventh day (Gen 2:1–3)
God sent Joseph before family to preserve life (Gen 45:5)	God sent Joseph before to preserve a remnant (Gen 45:7)	God made Joseph a father to Pharaoh (Gen 45:8)	God made Joseph lord of all Egypt (Gen 45:9)	God planned it (the brother's evil behavior) for good (Gen 50:20)	God will surely take care of you (Gen 50:24)	God will bring you up from this land (Gen 50:25)

Genesis begins with a seven-part declared work of God, the Creation (Gen 1:1—2:3), and ends with the final of Joseph's seven declarations of the work of God, involving the salvation of the patriarchal family from starvation and hope for their future (Gen 45:5, 7–9, 50:20, 24–25). There may be an allegation of contrivance to link the four declarations of Joseph when he discloses his identity to his brothers, with his three declarations after his father's death and when he is facing his own death. But the delay in the final utterances demonstrates the consistency of Joseph's position that God is the one who makes good, blessed things happen.

Joseph is clearly the main candidate in the Genesis narrative for someone who makes a name for himself in the manner of the Tower-style work culture, and he could be expected to demand recognition of this from others. His four declarations to his brothers ascribing honor and action to God alone could be seen as an emotional outpouring in a highly charged situation. But the final three declarations show that it is his consistent, established understanding that God is the one who overrules in the affairs of humans. Although he had admirable suggestions to make to Pharaoh about how to cope with the famine emergency in Egypt, he has nothing to offer the family about how to get back to Canaan, except to point them in confident assurance to the on-going activity of God. It is also significant that between the set of four and the set of three declarations of Joseph are incidents of blessing: the blessing of Joseph reuniting with his father (Gen

46:29–30), Jacob's blessing Pharaoh (Gen 47:7), Jacob blessing his grandsons (Gen 48:3–16), Jacob blessing all his sons (Gen 49:1–27).

The intervening Genesis narrative appears to offer a bewildering array of pericopes. The primordial narrative offers pictures of disastrous human activity when God is excluded, culminating in the Tower narrative. But the primordial narrative of Noah demonstrates the value of humans working with God. The patriarchal narratives begin with Abram's call to leave the Tower culture, and demonstrate the on-going struggle even "good" people have to allow God to work in their lives. Yet the patriarchal narrative offers several examples of people who successfully worked with God: Abram, Isaac, and the remarkable life of Joseph. Jacob's life begins in an atmosphere of blessing, but he is distracted by the Babel-equivalent of the Laban work culture. Only by leaving this culture can Jacob finally achieve blessing. Both the Abraham cycle of pericopes and the Jacob family cycle have seemed to defy symmetrical structuring,[41] but it is suggested that the theme of work binds these texts together in a meaningful way.

Genesis Narrative moves towards an Objective

Thomas Brodie argued for receiving the text of Genesis as a unity.[42] Then he noted: "At first sight the pattern of the stories in Genesis may seem erratic, disunified," but "[t]he whole book of Genesis moves systematically from episodes to continuous narrative."[43] He argues that in Genesis 1–11 there are primarily episodes, but the Abraham account, although episodic, is held together by a single figure.[44] In the account of Jacob there is almost continuous story, and notably this is the narrative to which the Genesis author has devoted most space. Jacob is introduced at the center of the book (Gen 25:21–26), and continues as a central or significant background figure until the last chapter, which refers to his funeral (Gen 50:4–14).[45] Brodie asserted by the time the reader arrives at the Joseph narrative, continuity is almost pervasive and episodes are an exception.[46] This development of narrative also applies to characterization, so that the most fully developed

---

41. Turner, "Genesis," 351–52.
42. Brodie, *Genesis as Dialogue*, 5–11.
43. Ibid., 12.
44. Ibid., 13.
45. Waltke, *Genesis: A Commentary*, 617.
46. Brodie, *Genesis as Dialogue*, 12–13.

characters of Genesis are in the Joseph narrative.[47] Further, the Genesis author devotes thirteen of fifty chapters to the Joseph narrative, indicating its significant interest.

The theme of work binds the primordial story together in a significant way, and this theme is also significant in the Jacob pericopes. Further, the dominance of the narrative and character of Jacob in the second part of Genesis raises the idea that the issues identified in the first part of Genesis may be highlighted in his life. It is therefore noteworthy that Jacob's life was dominated by work and blessing, and the issues relating to it: he worked to obtain a blessing from his father, he worked for his wives, he worked for his livestock, lastly he worked to provide for his children, his story records many commercial transactions, and, as recognized, he only begins to gain blessing when he leaves the Babel culture of his uncle.

These important observations imply that the Genesis author intentionally develops the text towards an objective. Brodie made the pregnant suggestion that the Joseph story "picks up the elements of the first story (Gen 2–4) and uses them in a radically new way."[48] This suggests insights into human work may be "episodic" in some of the earlier patriarchal narratives, but become more clearly developed in the Joseph narrative. It also gives warrant to the proposal that the entire Genesis narrative has a chiastic-like structure.

Suggested Chiastic-like Structure of Genesis

The Genesis narrative is immensely rich, with several themes and motifs embellishing it throughout. To specify the particularized Genesis pericopes in detail becomes rather complex and conceals the basic chiastic-like pattern, so for the purposes of this discussion a simplified general outline is presented thus:

---

47. Ibid.
48. Ibid.

A God's creation work described in seven parts (Gen 1–2)
  B Distrusting God leads to loss of position and expulsion—Adam (Gen 3)
    C Work, Fratricide, and sex (Gen 4)
      D Death on all (Gen 5)
        E Violence / one man called to work with God (Gen 6–9)
          F Table of Nations (Gen 10)
            G Pride in human work (Babel) leads to separation (Gen 11:1–9)
              H God calls a human to work with him—Abram (Gen 11:10—12:3)
                I Humans try to work for blessing in their own way (Gen 12–20)
                  J God performs a miraculous work to fulfill his promise of son (Gen 21)
                    X Abraham renounces lifework, trusts God, values wife (Gen 22–23)
                  J' God performs a miraculous work to provide a wife for Isaac (Gen 24)
                I' Humans try to work for blessing in their own way (Gen 25:1—28:9)
              H' God calls a human to work with him—Jacob (Gen 28:10–22)
            G' Pride in human work (Laban/Jacob/Esau) leads to separation (Gen 29–33)
          F' Esau's genealogies (Gen 36)
        E' Violence (rape and massacre) / one man called (Gen 32, 34—35:15)
      D' Death of Rebekah, Rachel (prematurely), and Isaac (Gen 35:8, 16–19, 29)
    C' Work, attempted fratricide, and sex (brothers and Joseph) (Gen 37–38)
  B' Trusting God leads to position and acceptance—Joseph (Gen 39–47)
A' God's saving work acknowledged by Joseph seven times (Gen 45:5, 7–9, 50:20, 24–25)

Chiastic Form highlights God and Relationship in Work

The end points of this chiastic structure focus on characteristic works of God (creation and salvation), and emphasize the extreme importance of these two concepts. The center of the chiasm focuses on the need for humans to acknowledge God as the primary source of their work success. Humans must give up their own claims to achievement and success and rely totally on the provisions of relationship with God (Gen 22:8), leading to blessings being assured (Gen 22:15–18). The center of the suggested chiastic pattern also, somewhat unexpectedly, highlights God's plan that human work should be performed in relationship (see further below). The self-made person is not a biblical concept. This focus on human relationship connects the beginning of the Genesis narrative and the institution of the marriage relationship with the conclusion of Genesis that focuses on the restored relationships within Jacob's family.

Defense of Suggested Chiastic-like Structure

Apparent in this chiastic structure is the disparity between the lengths of the corresponding parts. In the cited straightforward micro chiasms that occur throughout the book there is a clear correspondence in the "arms" of the chiasm, but this is not always the case with the suggested chiastic structure.

However, reference to the recognized *tôlēdôt* structure will demonstrate that whilst the *tôlēdôt* structure supports the narrative, it does not dictate the length of the narratival sections associated with it. Further, the *tôlēdôt* sections, presented as an unusual number of eleven, offer some endorsement for the proposed chiastic structure. Mathews considered that the creation of heaven and earth acts as a *tôlēdôt*, which would thus bring the number to a satisfying twelve sections, see above, but not all scholars accept this. There further seems to be some redundancy in the two *tôlēdôt* sections provided for Esau (Gen 36:1–8 and 36:9—37:1) and some would like to combine these as one. But, with the eleven *tôlēdôt* sections indisputably present in the book, the central one, that is, the sixth, deals with the *tôlēdôt* of Terah and the life of Abraham (Gen 11:27—25:11). This suggests that the narrative of the life of Abraham offers crucial material for understanding the whole text, as suggested in the proposed chiastic structure.

    A *tôlēdôt* of earth's family (2:4—4:26)
      B *tôlēdôt* of Adam's line (5:1—6:8)
        C *tôlēdôt* of Noah (6:9—9:29)
          D *tôlēdôt* of Noah's Sons (10:1—11:9)
            E *tôlēdôt* of Shem (11:10–26)
              X *tôlēdôt* of Terah (Abraham) (11:27—25:11)
            E' *tôlēdôt* of Ishmael (25:12–18)
          D' *tôlēdôt* of Isaac (25:19—35:29)
        C' *tôlēdôt* of Esau's family (36:1–8)
      B' *tôlēdôt* of Esau (36:9—37:1)
    A' *tôlēdôt* of Jacob (Joseph) (37:2—50:26)

A striking aspect of the *tôlēdôt* structure is the significant variability of the different *tôlēdôt* sections and the associated narrative portions, from a mere seven verses (the *tôlēdôt* of Ishmael) to 14 chapters (the *tôlēdôt* narratives of both Abraham and Jacob). Further, this *tôlēdôt* pattern demonstrates no special theme, except, as already noted, the blessing of proliferation.

There may seem to be some contrivance, or perhaps poor redaction, in the textual double *tôlēdôt* given for Esau. But, as has been noted, repetition in the Genesis narrative denotes emphasis. Pairing the two *tôlēdôt* of Esau with the single *tôlēdôt* of Noah's sons, the Table of Nations, as suggested in the proposed structure, offers an important concept. The apparently rejected family of Esau has the significance of the whole worldwide Table of Nations. They were part of the Abrahamic concept of "all the families of earth" that Abraham and his descendants were commanded to bless (Gen 12:1–3).

It is also acknowledged that there is slight displacement in these "F" portions of the chiasm, so that the genealogies of Esau that correspond to the Table of Nations in the primordial narratives actually occur after the violence in the household of Jacob, rather than prior as would match the primordial narrative and a simple chiastic structure. But the technique of displacing material to generate emphasis has been encountered previously in the Genesis narrative. The creation of Eve was delayed (displaced) to emphasize her value, and the pericope of the Tower of Babel was displaced from the Table of Nations to form the distinct background to the call of Abram. In terms of logical narrative flow of the book, this displacement of Esau's *tôlēdôt* can be justified thus: Not only does the narration of Jacob's family violence followed by peaceful Esau *tôlēdôt* proliferation contrast the two families is an arresting manner, but the emphasized double Esau *tôlēdôt* are more notable when described after the poignant reconciliation between Esau and Jacob (Gen 33) and the violent behavior of Jacob's family (Gen 34), which indicates they have no moral superiority over the Edomites.

The rich detail of the Genesis narrative is demonstrated in selected examples of how individual pericopes fit into the suggested chiastic structure. Under the general title of "humans try to work for blessing in their own way" are the compelling Abram-Lot-Hagar pericopes of I and the birthright struggles in I'. Under the umbrella of "work, fratricide, and sex" (the fratricide of Abel and the attempt on Josephs' life are clear) are the pericopes of the Judah-Tamar story in C' compared with the polygamy story of Lamech in C; furthermore, both these stories involve a significant portrayal of human work activity, as well as sexual aberration (Gen 38:12–26, 4:19–24).

Criticism of the D portions of the proposed structure as comparing two different genres, namely *tôlēdôt* material with narratival material, is possible. But as already observed, *tôlēdôt* material is vital for illuminating narratival material, and the two genres in the Genesis narrative work together to illuminate the concepts presented. Thus in the D portions of the chiastic structure, narratival material illuminates *tôlēdôt* material. The drumbeat dirge of the Genesis 5 *tôlēdôt* of Adam dulls the impact of the recurrent theme of death, and is balanced nicely in the *tôlēdôt* with the recurring theme of birth. But the recurring deaths in Genesis 35 are presented, for the first time in Genesis, with a pathos that underscores the pain of death. The reader is reminded that the muted presentation of chapter 5 is only possible because distant genealogical data is recounted. Genesis 35 is the powerful emotional foil of the muted march of death in Genesis 5. A simple place name "oak (or terebinth) of weeping" captures the family anguish at the loss of Deborah, Rebekah's nurse, and there is no birth to soften this pain (Gen 35:8). Jacob's anguish at the untimely loss of Rachel during childbirth is captured by his setting a memorial pillar, and his later remembrance of the event (Gen 35:18–20, 48:7). Finally, the death of Isaac demonstrates both pain and healing as his two sons come together peaceably for the burial (Gen 35:29). The death of Abraham also demonstrated this, but the estrangement between Isaac and Ishmael was not as stark and potentially lethal as that between Jacob and Esau.

Danger of Sinners-versus-Saved Mentality

The separation of the Genesis narrative into primordial and patriarchal parts can lead to a sinners-versus-saved, them-versus-us mentality, one that was tragically apparent in much of Jewish history (as illustrated in the

Jewish attitude to the Romans in the first century CE), and which has been all too commonly seen in Christian history (for examples, the Crusades, or as Donald Heiges observed, that a person's status as elect and part of God's own people in the Calvinistic tradition seemed to be confirmed by their being blessed and prospering in their work[49]). This problem seems also to be a concern of Gonzalez, who asserted the patriarchal stories do not solve the sin problem.[50]

All Humans Infected with Work Hubris

The suggested chiastic-like structure not only highlights the theme of God's work, but reveals no human is immune to sin and the appeal of attributing to his or her own unaided effort success in life. Tawney noted the "trick of the unsophisticated intellect and naïve psychology of the businessman who ascribes his achievements to his own unaided efforts," which Tawney attributed to the suggestion of Puritan moralists that "practical success is at once the sign and the reward of ethical superiority."[51]

The reward, the blessing, becomes the goal, illustrated in the Jacob narratives. Unfortunately the quip, "He is a self-made man and he worships his creator," becomes all too true. In the Genesis narrative this attitude is most clearly expressed by the Tower of Babel builders in the primordial narrative, and by both Laban and the Yahweh-worshipping Jacob in the patriarchal. Jacob's relentless pursuit of blessing for its own sake led him to cheat his brother and his father, brought him into bitterly competitive contact with his double-dealing father-in-law, and eventually even to the point of fighting God.

Themes of Sin and Blessing not Denied

This chiastic structure of Genesis utilizing the theme of work does not deny the importance of the theme of sin, or that both the primordial and patriarchal narratives give a clear picture of the curse consequences of sinful action. The theme of blessing clearly portrayed in the patriarchal narratives

---

49. Heiges, *Christian's Calling*, 58.

50. Gonzalez, *Where Sin Abounds*, 264–65. Gonzalez discusses in great detail the ethical failures of the patriarchs, although he conspicuously omits a study of Joseph.

51. Tawney, *Religion and the Rise*, 221.

is not rejected, but it is tied to the on-going activity of God rather than any human endeavor. God does not set blessing in motion and then let humans continue in their own "blessed" way. The message of Genesis is that blessing is a working relationship with God. The recurring issue throughout the book is the human tendency to mistakenly think it possible to achieve blessing through personal activity without God. This is compellingly demonstrated in the pericopes of Jacob that dominate the second part of the book.

The Importance of Relationship: Both Divine and Human

The chiasm highlights an important aspect of human ontology, and one closely tied to God's plan for work in the original creation pericope. At the center of Genesis is an emotionally fraught passage, Abraham's sacrifice of Isaac. Integral to Abram's call from God was the assignment to produce an heir. Abraham was successful in producing an heir through human methods, but this heir was rejected. To carry the blessing Abraham must work in God's chosen way, the apparently impossible way of producing a son by his infertile wife.

After a quarter of a century Abraham finally succeeded in siring the acceptable promised heir. God's later demand that he sacrifice this son Isaac must have seemed incomprehensible; perhaps Abraham's unquestioning acquiescence to the request is just as incomprehensible. The pericope highlights Abraham's need to acknowledge that Isaac was not his own achievement. Following Abraham's recognition that Isaac is the work of God and he, Abraham, must give him back to God, he not only receives a renewal of the promises, but God swears the blessing will surely occur (Gen 22:16–18).

But Isaac was the result of God working in the lives of two people, Abraham and, primarily, his infertile wife Sarah. So Abraham must not only recognize God's right to do as he chooses with his own achievement, just as Adam was intended to recognize God's right to make one tiny restriction in the garden, but Sarah's role must also be recognized.

The proposed structure highlights Sarah's role in the birth of Isaac. Although there are many deaths in Genesis, the burial of Sarah is unique and described in great detail in chapter 23, the twin heart of the proposed Genesis structure. The burial of Jacob is described lavishly, but is significantly shorter, fourteen verses as against twenty for Sarah. Moreover a telling sentence describing Jacob's funeral does not occur in the preparations for Sarah's: "Thus his sons did for him as he commanded them" (Gen 50:12). Sarah left no instructions for her own burial.

The text indicates Sarah became recognized and appreciated as the "helper fit for" Abraham (Gen 2:18), liberated from her previous position as the embarrassingly, shamefully barren woman twice used as a foil to protect her nervous husband (Gen 12:10–20, 20:1–18). She was the desperate instigator of an extramarital affair as the means to achieve a son (Gen 16:2), and was despised by her haughty and fertile Egyptian servant girl (Gen 16:4–6). But in her now-valued role, nothing would be spared for her funeral. Not even the apparently high price asked for the burial site caused Abraham to waver (Gen 23:14, cf. 1 Kgs 16:24 and Jer 32:9). Her beloved position is recognized in a simple sentence regarding her son Isaac: "So Isaac was comforted after his mother's death" (Gen 24:67b).

Thus, not only does this chiastic structure reveal God's intention that humans acknowledge that they can achieve success, that is, blessing, only through him, but it also shows the importance of God's original plan that humans work in cooperation with one another, especially in the marriage relationship. No one is a self-made man—or woman.

The Message of Genesis: Recognizing What God can Do

To recognize a chiastic structure for the entire book of Genesis is an effective tool in unpacking the text's emphasis. Whilst Gonzalez's concerns about a portrayal of "plaster goodness" in the patriarchal narratives is valid, his suggestion that the focus of Genesis is limited to the doctrines of divine inspiration and sanctification[52] dilutes the book of its power.

That power is a portrayal of what God can do: simply, anything. The book is packed with examples of how powerfully God works. Genesis begins and ends with powerful portrayals of what God can do. He can make a world. He can make a slave into a chief minister. He can destroy a world. He can make childless women mothers. He can rescue people from starvation. He can make a nation from brothers destroying themselves with their enmity. He can heal broken relationships. He can save a family or a nation. And notably he can make "bad" people good, conspicuously in the portrayal of Judah. The presence of God and what he does is called blessing, despite the human tendency to focus on the result rather than the cause when they think of blessing. The blessing of his presence is the benevolent intent of God for his creation, if only people would let him.

So the patriarchal narrative does not leave the problem of sin and the curse unsolved. The structure of Genesis offers an answer to the human

52. Gonzalez, *Where Sin Abounds*, 264–65.

predicament, which is the on-going need for the work of God. "God will surely visit you" (Gen 50:25).

But to recognize the full extent of what God can do requires humans to relinquish claims to their own, individual achievements. First, humans must recognize their dependence on him for all their significant achievements, and secondly, they must be willing to appreciate the contribution of others. Abraham's apparently horrendous call to sacrifice his son Isaac becomes the test representative of the universal human struggle to relinquish claims to personal achievement. And the beautiful but quietly understated pathos of the funeral arrangements for Sarah demonstrate how important, how God-designed, it is to honor those who have contributed to any personal success.

9

The Call and Life of Abraham, Genesis 12:1—25:10

THE CALL OF ABRAM (Gen 12:1–3) marks a significant change in the Genesis narrative, from the grim primordial curses to the optimism of patriarchal blessings. It is asserted that the narrative moves from the dismal recital of failed do-it-yourself human attempts to succeed in work, to the surprisingly contemporary-style struggles of the patriarchs to comprehend that work could be successful in partnership with God. Abram achieved no Nimrod-style architectural or civic engineering feats, but he did, finally, learn to work with God. Abraham's call has long been recognized not only as a model of the call of God to all Christians, but also their response to it.

The major part of the story of Abraham forms, together with the primeval story, one arm of the proposed chiastic structure of Genesis. His story begins with humans attempting to achieve great things themselves, and reaches its pinnacle with his willingness to respond positively to God's call to sacrifice his most cherished achievement. Yet this willingness to sacrifice brings unquestionable assurance that with God he will ultimately triumph. The story of Abraham does not present humans as merely helpless pawns of God, but does indicate that without God they are powerless to accomplish anything of true and lasting value.

Recognition of the Limited Focus

Recognizing the chiastic structure allows elucidation of the intent of the Genesis author, but due recognition of the patriarchal narratives' development of rich theological, character, and relationship themes is here noted. Focusing on the seemingly mundane topic of work and limiting attention to these other themes has at times been difficult. Yet this focus allows appreciation of the surprisingly contemporary and relevant work issues that engaged patriarchal concern. It is noteworthy that quality of relationship dominates the Genesis author's focus in the patriarchal narrative. Significantly, it is not patriarchal achievement that is highlighted, not even in the notable success of Joseph.

Criteria for "Work" in Patriarchal Narratives

Criteria were established for defining patriarchal work in order to provide a base for selection of narratival material examined. First, given the original Edenic promises, and promises of the Abrahamic call, producing progeny was a core patriarchal function. Concern for this dominates the narrative, and this was also an essential part of the original work given humanity (Gen 1:26-28). Second, sheer survival was essential work for the patriarchs, an issue God highlighted to Adam after he had eaten fruit from the tree of knowledge of good and evil, as discussed. Finally, incidents involving commercial transactions are regarded as work. Whilst there is no Edenic connection with this criterion, it resonates with contemporary conditions and occurs many times in the patriarchal narratives.

Political philosopher Hannah Arendt distinguished between labor—the expenditure of human effort—and work—the accomplishment of socially recognized, tangible achievements.[1] Acceptance of this dichotomy (which could be challenged) may appear to deprive the patriarchs of a great deal of "work," but the narrative includes several situations where the neighbors and associates of the nomadic patriarchs expressed appreciation for their relationship, and stated connection with them brought benefit to those concerned. This suggests the activities of the patriarchs do fulfill criteria for what can be regarded as work. However, Westermann's suggestion that the concept of achievement does not carry over from the primeval narrative to the patriarchal[2] is significant, as, with one exception, the patriarchs did not "achieve" things generally regarded as great (see as examples of primordial achievement, Gen 4:20-22, 10:8-12). The patriarchs made no inventions that are recorded, built no cities or towers, and developed no great laws.

---

1. See the arguments of Arendt, *Human Condition*.
2. Westermann, *Genesis 1-11*, 343-44.

Tower Work Hubris background to Call of Abram

The Tower story is out of chronological sequence,[3] but for a purpose. Its delayed position highlights the actions of the builders, and "lead[s] the reader forward in expectation to a better way."[4] The Tower narrative is thus carefully positioned to give it maximum impact as background material for the call of Abram. Separated from the Table of Nations, in which chronologically it fits, the author connects it to the genealogies of Shem and Terah that lead to the pivotal call of Abram. Five times in the Genesis 10 Table of Nations, tangential reference is made to events in the Tower story, but the narrative is not fleshed out.[5] Its delayed literary position connects it to the *tôlēdôt* sections of Shem and Terah (Gen 11:10–32), and the call of Abram.

The Tower pericope is thus essential background to understand all the implications of the call of Abram. Mathews stated, "[T]he tower event must be viewed against the backdrop of the primeval events collectively. For the thematic purposes of the author we have reached a pivotal passage on the development of his thesis for understanding the antecedent events of Abraham's call . . ."[6] The Tower narrative restricts the general primordial narrative focus on sin to issues in work. A later Jewish endorsement of a work connection between the Tower narrative and the call of Abraham is found in Hebrews 11:10, which states Abraham was looking for a city with foundations, whose designer and builder was God. This comment has relevance only if there was another city whose founder and builder was *not* God, yet was a serious contender for Abraham's loyalty. Dumbrell remarked that "the fame of the great centers of commerce in the Mesopotamian world can hardly have been far from the author's mind as God's promise of Gen 12:2 is recorded,"[7] and these centers included not only Abraham's birthplace Ur, but Babel and Nineveh, specifically mentioned in the narrative (Gen 10:10–11).

---

3. Dumbrell, *Covenant and Creation*, 59; Arnold, *Genesis*, 119.

4. Arnold, *Genesis*, 119–20.

5. Genesis 10:5 states, "peoples spread in their lands, each with his own language"; verses 9–11 state Nimrod began his kingdom with Babel, Erech, Accad, and Calneh before going to Assyria and building cities there; verse 25 states that in the days of Peleg (meaning division) the earth was divided; verse 31, "these are the sons of Shem . . . by their languages"; and verse 32, "These are the clans of the sons of Noah, according to their genealogies, in their nations, and from these the nations spread abroad on the earth after the flood."

6. Mathews, *Genesis 1—11:26*, 456.

7. Dumbrell, *Covenant and Creation*, 61.

Call to leave Babel Work

Work was clearly an issue at Babel, suggesting work was an important aspect of the call of Abram. The Tower-builders' desire to "make a name for ourselves" (Gen 11:4) forms a marked contrast with Abram's call and God's promise that he, God, will make Abram's name great (Gen 12:1–3). Reinforcing the daily work connection is Mathews' suggestion that the Tower story mirrors the attempt of humanity in the garden to achieve power independently of God.[8] This focus on human work and its motivation suggests the call of Abram involves the practicalities of daily living and working more than is generally recognized. The command to leave his culture and follow God reveals the author's deliberate invitation to compare the two pericopes. The call of Abram bursts with a cascade of blessing reminiscent of creation, and assures of God's continuing desire to relate to humanity.

Abram's call is described as the thematic center of the Pentateuch.[9] Luther thought it "one of the most important in all Holy Scripture,"[10] while Reno claims it is not possible to overemphasize the importance of this call.[11] The call, and Abram's responses to it, have implications that illuminate ordinary human work. Abraham's personal struggles to understand the full meaning of the call prove instructive, and his final acceptance of the call's implications (a working partnership with God to bless others) forms the center of the Genesis structural chiasm on the theme of work, and the foundation of God's plan for his people.

The Call of Abram

"Now the Lord said to Abram, 'Go from your country and your kindred and your father's house to the land that I will show you. And I will make you a great nation, and I will bless you and make your name great, so that you will be a blessing. I will bless those who bless you, and him who dishonors you I will curse, and in you all the families of the earth shall be blessed'" (Gen 12:1–3). Five times the word "bless" (or its derivatives) is pronounced in the call, counterbalancing the five curses of the primeval narrative.

---

8. Mathews, *Genesis 1—11:26*, 467. The divine plural appears in both accounts, Gen 3:22, 11:6, and both indicate divine distress over events that are occurring.

9. Waltke, *Genesis: A Commentary*, 208. Waltke earlier asserts that the call of Abraham is the key to "Primary History," and "Primary History, which traces Israel's history from the creation of the world (Gen 1) to the fall of Israel (2 Kgs 25), is all about what the New Testament calls 'The Kingdom of God,'" (44–45).

10. Luther, *Lectures on Genesis*, 253.

11. Reno, *Genesis*, 139.

After the quintet of tragic curse situations of the primordial narrative, this quintet of repeated blessing bursts with dazzling splendor into the Genesis story. This repetition cannot but arrest the reader's attention. Even at the time of creation, when things were pronounced "very good" (Gen 1:31), there were only three blessings (Gen 1:22, 28, 2:3), and only five blessings in the entire primordial narrative (Gen 1:22, 28, 2:3, 9:1, 26).[12]

Abram's Call repeats Creation and Noachian Blessings

Significantly, "the blessing given to Adam and Noah is essentially the same as that given to Abram."[13] Abram's call expands his perspective from himself to all peoples,[14] a clearly different outlook from the "ourselves" of the Tower-builders' viewpoint.

The call echoes the beginning of God's story with humanity in the garden and the repeated blessings bestowed at that time (Gen 1:22, 28, 2:1–3). Scullion observed, "God's blessing proceeds from his will to form a relationship between himself and Abraham and through Abraham with his descendants and 'all the clans of the earth.'"[15] Brodie declared there is a sense of complete accord with God's spoken word, and thus beneficent relationship, in three pivotal Genesis situations: the creation narrative (Gen 1:1—2:3), Noah's obedience (Gen 6:2, 7:5, 9:16), and now with Abram of whom it is recorded, "The Lord said to Abram . . . and Abram went as the Lord had told him."[16]

The Blessings of the Call

Cassuto considered the call of Abram consisted of seven blessings: 1) I will make of you a great nation; 2) I will bless you; 3) I will make your name great; 4) you will be a blessing; 5) I will bless those who bless you; 6) I will curse him who dishonors you, and 7) in you will all the families of the earth be blessed.[17]

---

12. Waltke, *Genesis: A Commentary*, 205.
13. Smith, G. V., "Structure and Purpose," 311.
14. Waltke, *Genesis: A Commentary*, 203.
15. Scullion, *Genesis: A Commentary*, 107.
16. Brodie, *Genesis as Dialogue*, 210.
17. Cassuto, *Commentary on Genesis: Noah to Abraham*, 312.

Remarkably, God's promise to bless is repeated to Abram seven times, a biblically significant number (Gen 12:1-3, 12:7, 13:14-17, 15:1-17, 17:1-21, 18:18-19, 22:15-18). These seven different occasions of blessing are all associated with difficult and challenging working situations that Abraham encountered. The difficulties are examples of the "obstacle theory" of narrative,[18] but the blessings are unforeseen. These obstacles are: leaving family of origin; finding the promised land occupied by Canaanites; the separtion of Lot from Abram; the threat of military reprisal for the rescue of Lot; the Hagar and Ishmael debacle; feeding unexpected strangers; and most notably, passing the ultimate test to offer Isaac as an offering.

A Great Nation

Being fruitful and multiplying was part of the Edenic blessing, so becoming a great nation is no surprise (Gen 1:26-28). What does surprise is that Abram personally would make a great nation. Twice the reader is informed that Abram's wife, Sarai, has no child and is barren, suggesting both the present fact of no child, and that she is incapable of having one (Gen 11:30). Thus Abram cannot carry out the most basic Edenic "work" given humans, to "be fruitful and multiply" (Gen 1:28). The text thus highlights the utter powerlessness of Abram to achieve by his own effort the first thing promised, and his total dependence on God to supply a solution to his predicament.

Yet in his utter dependence on God, Abram is clearly being asked to return to the original creation state. The fatal choice of *hā- 'ādām* and his wife to eat of the forbidden tree in an attempt to achieve power and independence from God is contrasted by this man's painful experience. This tragically powerless man is promised great things on the condition he trusts God and allows himself to be utterly dependent on God. As the narrative unfolds, delay in the fulfilment of the promise of nationhood serves to emphasize this dependence on God.

I will Bless

This apparently redundant clause emphasizes that it is God alone who will be the source of all blessing. The cause of blessing is "I," Yahweh, the one who is directly and personally addressing Abram, and who will personally guarantee and provide the promised blessing. It echoes the opening Genesis

---

18. Ellis, *Yahwist: Bible's First Theologian*, quoted in Helyer, "Separation of Abram and Lot," 81.

statement: "In the beginning, God." It reminds that God alone is the one who blesses.

A Name

The theme of "name" forms a vital connection between the Tower narrative and the call of Abram. Although von Rad saw the mention of a "great name" in the call of Abram as a "hidden allusion" to the Tower narrative, and that God will now give what "men attempted to secure arbitrarily,"[19] the allusion is not hidden. It is an overt reference by the Genesis author that connects the two pericopes in a critical way. The work motivation of the Tower-builders was self-exultation and an attitude that usurped the powers of God. Abram is called to something quite different. Unlike the Tower-builders, Abram will not strive to make a name for himself, but God will generously *give* him a "great" name.

Instead of self-centeredly slaving to burn bricks and build towers to make a name, God promises blessing if Abram will obey the command to go where God asks him to go and "be a blessing" to others. This is an incredible offer. Not only does it overflow with all the richness of grace for which the Abramic call is so splendidly famous, but it also echoes the life of two unique primordial characters, Enoch (Gen 5:22) and Noah (Gen 6:9), noted for their walk with God. Abram too is being asked to walk with God. Where he goes will be where God asks him to go, to wherever God commands him. Abram demonstrated his faith and obedience and the text states, "so Abram departed as the Lord had spoken to him" (Gen 12:4). God later makes this more explicit when he tells Abram "walk before me" (Gen 17:1).

Twenty-four years later, when he was ninety-nine years old, with only one "illegitimate" son whom God refused to recognize as the fulfilment of the promise, Abram was given a new name by God: Abraham, meaning father of a multitude of nations (Gen 17:5). When God gave this name, the setting was the formal renewal of the covenant, and institution of the rite of circumcision. Ten times in the passage (Gen 17:1–14), covenant is mentioned. This suggests the "great name" Abraham was promised was actually the covenant relationship between Almighty God, *'El Shaddai*, and himself.

The promise of name was socially linked, negatively, with the childless state of Abram's wife, Sarai. Wenham pointed out that it was through his children that a man perpetuated his name,[20] and without children Abram's

---

19. Rad, *Genesis: A Commentary*, 155.
20. Wenham, *Genesis 1–15*, 273.

name would die with him. Thus this promised blessing is again a surprise given Abram's circumstances.

Wenham observed, "every mention of the root 'to bless'... is a paronomastic allusion to Abram's name,"[21] as seen with the construct "I will bless," 'ăbārekəkā and 'abrām. Thus, the greatness of Abram's name is intimately connected with the promise of blessing both to Abram himself and those with whom he shared the blessing.

You will be a Blessing!

Turner pointed out that the Hebrew of this "blessing" is an imperative. It is not a promise, but a command: "Be a blessing!"[22] The promises God offers are thus at least partially dependent on Abram's willingness to obey this command.[23] Humphries suggested God is offering to become Abram's patron, proffering him security and a future, but also setting up expectations for his behavior, which include responding to this command to be a blessing to others.[24]

The command to be a blessing is at the center of the seven statements in the call.[25] Abraham must be "both a receptacle and a transmitter of the blessings of Yahweh."[26] This connects with the second clause in the call, and suggests Abram is being asked to work as God envisaged in the beginning, to bring blessing to all (Gen 2:5, 15). As noted, recognizing Abram's persistent childlessness, the command "be a blessing" is surprising. By the Table of Nations (Gen 10), the text emphasizes the importance of progeny and how unlikely it would be that a man who cannot have children could be a blessing.

Blessing the Blessers, Cursing the Curser

God promises to "bless those who bless you and dishonor the one who dishonors you." Interestingly, the text designates blessers as plural, but "he

---

21. Ibid., 276.

22. Turner, *Genesis*, 64. Humphries also recognizes the important command aspect of this phrase, Humphries, *Character of God*, 83.

23. Turner, *Genesis*, 64.

24. Humphries, *Character of God*, 83.

25. Pate et al., *Story of Israel*, 37.

26. Ibid.

who curses you" is singular (Gen 12:3), suggesting that if Abram obeys he is more likely to encounter blessing in others than cursing. These reciprocal clauses in the call also indicate God will relate to other people in response to the way they relate to Abram. Recognizing that Abram was asked to go into unknown territory among potentially hostile peoples, this is a comforting and reassuring promise of God's continuing presence and protection. By suggesting that others will generally respond in a positive way, the call emphasizes Abram's directive to be a blessing.

In You All the Families of Earth will be Blessed

This concluding blessing clearly connects with the central thought of the call, "Be a blessing!" It suggests that the hope for this world and all humanity rests with the obedience of this one man,[27] and this must be how Abram himself understood it. The promises are given to him personally, indicating they would be set in motion during his lifetime. The call is personal to Abram, and the promises are personal, but they would have relevance for his descendants and all the families of the earth.

A contemporary Jewish perspective considers the final portion of the call of Abram as both promise and command, recognizing that Abraham's descendants have brought blessing to the world through their contributions in medicine, science, literature, and culture, that is, their work.[28] This perspective suggests that for both ancient and contemporary Hebrew readers of the Genesis text, the immediate, practical, working aspect of the call of Abram in his daily life was recognized.

Land

The call of Abram does not offer land; it only hints at it: "Go . . . to a land I will show you." When Abram has obeyed the command to go and passed through the territory to Shechem, noting, perhaps with concern, that Canaanites were in the land, God appears to him and says, "To your offspring will I give this land" (Gen 12:6–7). Later, when Abram voiced concern about his continuing childlessness (Gen 15:2–3), God covenants that there will be both offspring and land, but before the execution of the land agreement there will be a very long time of sojourning in a strange land, no less than

---

27. Ibid., 38.
28. Bernis, *Rabbi Looks at Jesus*, 72.

four hundred years (Gen 15:13-21, 17:8). The call of Abram therefore focuses on the immediate blessing of God, and Abram's willingness to share that blessing with others, and not on land ownership.

Blessing Contingent on Walking with God

God's prerequisite command was simple but drastic: "Go!" It is significant that the Hebrew of the command is literally "Walk!" Although this walk was not specified as being with God, verse 7 suggests that Abram perceived God's presence was with him, and that is why he built altars. It suggests a friendly, intimate relationship between Abram and God, as a person walks with a friend, not with a crowd. As noted earlier, walking with God signifies God's preferred relationship with his people (Gen 5:22, 6:9).

Separate

God said: Go from your country. Go from your kindred. Go from your father's house: an increasingly narrowing focus of imperative matched only by a widening focus of promise.[29] Abram is asked to do something that requires remarkable courage and obedience.[30] The phrase "lek ləkā" (start walking, or go) occurs in the Bible only here and in the command for Abraham to take his son, his only son, his beloved son, to Moriah,[31] also a narrowing focus of emphasis, and another incredibly demanding directive from God to Abraham. These calls demand an all-or-nothing response. Kidner observed that the nearest biblical parallel to this all-encompassing imperative to renounce everything is not found in the Bible again until the Gospels.[32] There is no mention that Abram had significant possessions until after the Egyptian sojourn (Gen 12:16, 20).

Miller noted: "The call of Abraham helps to make clear that . . . God . . . is clearly bent towards blessing and mercy towards the human creature . . . When Yahweh sent Abraham out, it was to bring about blessing, not curse."[33] Thus, although Abram must make this all-or-nothing response,

---

29. Turner, *Genesis*, 64.
30. Humphries, *Character of God*, 82.
31. Waltke, *Genesis: A Commentary*, 301.
32. Kidner, *Genesis*, 113.
33. Miller, P., *Genesis 1-11: Studies*, 475.

in the covenants that God ultimately makes with him there are actually no conditions.[34] Abram must give up everything but is given everything.

That Abram himself recognized that his culture of origin was seriously antagonistic to his call is later implied by his refusal to allow his son to return to the family of origin, not even for the vital function of finding a wife (Gen 24:6). Abraham's grandson Jacob did return to the ancient home, and found, in the person of his uncle Laban, a self-centered and grasping work ethic (Gen 29–31), reminiscent of the Tower-builders' culture.

Significantly, Abram did not completely separate from all his family, but took his nephew Lot with him (Gen 12:4).[35] The reasons are not enunciated. Perhaps Lot was taken because Abram mistakenly believed that through this young man God would be able to achieve the promised blessings, recognizing the twice-mentioned fact of Sarai's childlessness. Perhaps Lot simply wished to join the expedition. But Lot was a source of anxious care for Abram, and his story serves as a significant foil to the Abram story.

Seven Blessings but only One Command

The inescapable prerequisite of the call is obedient separation, separation from everything except God. Abram is asked to separate from his family, country, culture, and its norms: "Get out of your country, from your family and from your father's house" (Gen 12:1). This command of God seems cruel. However, Kidner observed that Abram's part is simply to respond to the single command, *lek ləkā*, while the seven blessings, the "heaped up *I will's* reveal how much greater is the Lord's part."[36]

The call suggests the need for a new and radically different approach to living, worshipping and working. To be a blessing suggests that God plans to continue, as in the beginning, to involve humans in the work of caring, sharing power in a manner that can only be described as love.[37]

Abraham's Struggle

Abraham obeyed, but the unfolding text reveals he struggled with the tendency to revert to culturally conditioned behavior. Examples are his lying

---

34. Plaut, *Torah: Modern Commentary; Genesis*, 152.
35. Humphries, *Character of God*, 84.
36. Kidner, *Genesis*, 114.
37. Goldingay and Innes, *God at Work*, 8.

about Sarai in Egypt (Gen 12:13), his acceptance of Sarai's surrogate pregnancy suggestion (Gen 16:2), and his repeating the lie about his wife (Gen 20:2). Numerous times his story reveals the power of his previous do-it-yourself culture over his working life. The strength of his story is that he eventually triumphed in his walk with God.

Variety of Abraham's Work

On a daily basis, Abram's work was the routine associated with a nomadic cattle-breeder, and in this he was highly successful and generous.[38] The emphasis on his being a keeper of animals echoes the work of Abel (Gen 4:2). But his work was not limited to this, and it included several other impressive activities. He did build, but it was altars to God, not a city nor a tower.[39] When he moved on, these altars were left behind as permanent reminders of his priorities. He also proved to be both a capable army commander and an astute negotiator. But a dominant theme in the Abraham narratives is delay,[40] frustrating, aching, painful delay, because he could not accomplish his perceived core work achievement and produce an heir. After a ten-year wait, Abram's response to this delay was to utilize some self-help strategy, which brought no blessing, and possibly delayed the event by another 14 years.[41] In the end, he had to give up all personal claims regarding his heir before he could be absolutely assured of the blessing (Gen 22:16–17).

Abraham was recognized by others as materially successful. He achieved his dream of producing an heir from his long-term barren wife, and therefore was blessed. But all this success was attributed entirely to God (Gen 21:22, 24:1, 35). He appears disinterested in his material success, and it is others who note it (Gen 13:5, 21:22, 24:1).

Abram the Warrior

Abram's broad capability is shown when he rescues Lot from the marauding kings (Gen 14:1–17). Significantly, he was so trusted by his Canaanite neighbors that they were willing to risk their lives under his leadership in a very daring military campaign (Gen 14:13–14, 24).[42] Turner considered

---

38. Westermann, *Genesis 12–36*, 75.
39. Hamilton, *Book of Genesis Chapters 1–17*, 377–78.
40. Reno, *Genesis*, 163.
41. Wenham, *Genesis 16–50*, 13.
42. Turner, *Genesis*, 70.

that Abram was motivated in this daring escapade by his belief that Lot was his apparent heir, the perpetuator of the promised blessings,[43] but the text is implicit not explicit on this point. But clearly, he travelled long distances, risked his life, and God blessed his efforts. This suggests human work at times must be active, not merely a passive appropriation of divine blessing. Melchizedek blessed Abram for his decisive action in rescuing Lot.

Table 7: Abraham's Work

Work Activity	Suggested Modern Equivalent	His Strategy	Outcome	Reference
Building altars, offering sacrifice	Build church	Response (to God's Reiterating the Promise)	Long term witness to worship of God	Gen 12:7–8, 13:4, 22:1–19
Coping with Famine	Unemployment	Relocate to Egypt (own initiative); Hide identity, compromise wife to save himself	Materially improved, Pharaoh angry, expelled from country, disrupted relationship	Gen 12:10–18[35]
Mediating strife between herdsmen	Labor dispute / Commercial competition	Divide assets / Separate from Lot	God reiterated promises of blessing, but relationship with Lot in jeopardy	Gen 13:1–18
Rescuing Lot: Army general	Fighting exploitation, defending family	Gather allies. Reject opportunity for personal benefit	Lot rescued; Abram blessed by Melchizedek	Gen 14:1–24
Producing Child (core activity)	Self-actualization, Achieving the dream	Cohabit with Hagar	Strife, broken relationships	Gen 16:1–15
Training his household	Educator, leading his family	Unknown/ example	Oldest servant / Isaac notably continue the blessing	Gen 18:19

43. Ibid.
44. Kidner, *Genesis*, 116.

Work Activity	Suggested Modern Equivalent	His Strategy	Outcome	Reference
Offering hospitality to strangers	Enthusiastic approach to extras in job description[36]	Accept opportunity, enlist Sarah's help	Divine revelations (re Isaac and Sodom)	Gen 18:1–33
Digging wells	Routine trade work, irrigation	Persistence	Hostile neighbors note presence of God in his life and ask for treaty	Gen 21:22–34
Relinquishing ownership of life work		Total trust in God	Blessing assured	Gen 22:1–19
Buying burial site for wife	Commercial negotiation to provide for burial	Open honesty, no sharp dealing, "fair" price	All parties satisfied, Sarah honored	Gen 23:1–20
Finding wife for Son	Achieve dream and carry out patriarchal duty	Delegate responsibility	Goal achieved	Gen 24:1–67

Selfless Commercial Dealer

The commercial aspect and possibilities of this episode are implied in the Hebrew. Turner noted in Genesis chapters 14 and 15, the Hebrew verbs for giving, *ntn*, and taking, *lqḥ*, each occur seven times.[46] Significantly, the "reward" offered by God after this military expedition, *sākā* (Gen 15:1), denotes a laborer's wages.[47] The first word of the King of Sodom to Abram is "give me" but the first word of Melchizedek the King of Salem is "Blessing."[48] These words encapsulate the diametrically different approaches to life of the two men, and Abram is clearly aligned with Melchizedek. Significantly, the issue that started

---

45. Although hospitality to total strangers was a normal expectation in patriarchal times, Abraham's busy activity seems to have gone beyond the basic requirements, see Thompson, "Boundaries of Christian Hospitality," 327–32.

46. Ibid., 72.

47. Mathews, *Genesis 11:27—50:26*, 163.

48. Ibid., 146.

the war is rebellion against servitude (Gen 14:4).[49] But the pericope ends with Abram refusing any material advantage for himself, "lest the king of Sodom claim he made Abram rich" (Gen 14:22–23). Abram had already indicated he regarded God as his sole benefactor, and he thus also demonstrated his motives for this war were to benefit others, not personal gain.

Abraham the Negotiator

Abraham was a skillful negotiator. He defused the potentially serious disagreement between his herdsmen and Lot's by generously offering his young nephew choice of good land (Gen 13:8–9). He negotiated, albeit awkwardly, the minefield of difficulties between his embittered, childless wife and her conceited and haughty pregnant slave girl (Gen 16). He maintained interest and concern for his self-seeking nephew (Gen 18:16–33) and twice intervened on his behalf.[50]

He used the desire of Abimelech to make a covenant with him to draw attention to the unhelpful behavior of Abimelech's servants filling in the wells that Abraham's servants had dug (Gen 21:22–34). The timing of this complaint is impeccable, and not surprisingly the problem was quickly solved to the satisfaction of all parties.

Yet when he buys land to bury his wife, Abraham does not cavil over the price, but achieves his goal with "impeccable legality and a certain elegance."[51] The contract between him and Ephron follows the known legal patterns of the Ancient Near East,[52] but he did not strike a bargain.[53] He probably paid more than he needed to but did not desecrate the memory of his wife by caviling over prices.[54]

Abraham's Failures

Abraham failed in three situations that offer important insights. Each of these times, Abraham relied on his own knowledge and understanding and did not consult God for direction.

---

49. Scullion, *Genesis: A Commentary*, 225.
50. Kidner, *Genesis*, 133.
51. Scullion, *Genesis: A Commentary*, 275.
52. Plaut, *Torah: Modern Commentary; Genesis*, 221.
53. Ibid. His purchase price of 400 shekels can be compared with the 17 shekels Jeremiah paid for land (Jer 32:7), and the 6,000 shekels Omri paid for all of Samaria (1 Kgs 16:24).
54. Scullion, *Genesis: A Commentary*, 182.

Failure of Personal Initiative to Survive and Fear for Personal Safety

Abram's first failure involved his personal initiative and fear for his personal safety. Famine threatened all his family, but going to Egypt was Abram's own initiative; there is no indication God was consulted.[55] In Egypt, fear for his own personal safety (again without consultation with God) led to dishonesty regarding the identity of his wife and resulted in embarrassment and banishment (Gen 12:10-20). Although he materially benefitted by the sojourn in Egypt (Gen 12:16), his behavior caused plagues on the Egyptians (Gen 12:17) and he was ignominiously expelled. In this situation, and the one discussed below (Gen 20:1-18), Abraham's lack of trust in God seriously endangered Sarah's health and life.

Failure of Fear for Personal Safety

In the superficially similar situation with Abimelech, it was not starvation from famine that threatened, but Abraham's nervous perception that "There is no fear of God at all in this place, and they will kill me because of my wife" (Gen 20:11), which led to another deception about Sarah. Yet this Abimelech, the Philistine, is the first person recorded in Genesis to receive a dream from God (Gen 20:3).[56] Thus, the narrative portrays Abimelech as both receiving and responding to God's message (Gen 20:3-8), demonstrating that Abraham's perception and understanding of the "no fear of God in this place" was completely wrong, and his reliance on his own knowledge caused faulty behavior. Through God's intervention, Sarah was restored to Abraham, and the one thousand shekels Abraham was offered (Gen 20:16), a fabulously large sum,[57] suggests Abimelech was serious about making amends.

Despite these failures, God overruled events, both in Egypt and Gerar, to ensure neither Abraham nor Sarah was harmed or materially disadvantaged. In fact, in Gerar, the end result was positive good and a peace treaty signed between the parties, Abraham and Abimelech the King of Gerar (Gen 21:22-32).

---

55. Kidner, *Genesis*, 116.

56. Brodie, *Genesis as Dialogue*, 258.

57. A Babylonian laborer, normally paid half a shekel a month, would have to work for 167 years to earn such a sum, Waltke, *Genesis: A Commentary*, 287.

Failure by Accepting Sarah's Pragmatic Initiative

Abraham's major failure involved achieving his life dream: a son to carry on the name and the blessing. Sarah's reasonable human initiative to circumvent her childlessness with a socially acceptable surrogate wife[58] was shown to be unacceptable to God: "God said, 'No, but Sarah your wife shall bear you a son, and you shall call his name Isaac. I will establish my covenant with him . . . As for Ishmael, I have heard you . . . I have blessed him and will make him fruitful . . . into a great nation. But I will establish my covenant with Isaac" (Gen 17:19–21). The immediate result was relational failure, with strife between all concerned: Abram, Sarai, and Hagar (Gen 16:3–6). Although a son was born, he was not recognized as part of God's plan. This core "work" of producing a son to carry on the promises could be done only by relying on God's way.

This is a challenge to the co-creationist idea that all human work is furthering God's plan for this world. Although the goal to produce a son was God's plan,[59] it could be done only in God's way. However, Abram struggled with the situation, and the text clearly shows he loved the son of Hagar. He is the one who names Ishmael (Gen 16:15),[60] indicating he recognized their relationship, although doubtless Hagar had told him of her experience and what the angel told her the boy should be named, and that Ishmael too would have a multitude of offspring (Gen 16:10–11). Further, Abram pled with God to recognize Ishmael (Gen 17:18), indicating that Abraham had to surrender both his sons.[61] He could not boast either in his own achievement (Ishmael) or in what God achieved through him (Isaac).

These failures all demonstrate that the patriarchs and matriarchs were most likely to fail when they perceived themselves inadequate for the situation, yet acted in their own strength and wisdom. This is also conspicuous in the lives of Sarah, Isaac, and Jacob.

A Failure unless Utterly Dependent on God

The call of Abraham bursts with splendor into the dreary primordial narrative, but this did not result in an immediate understanding of God's ways. The promise of blessing was repeated to Abraham no less than seven times, emphasizing its importance and certainty, but he struggled to understand.

---

58. Hamilton, *Book of Genesis Chapters 1–17*, 444.
59. See for example Gen 12:7.
60. Hamilton, *Book of Genesis Chapters 1–17*, 458.
61. Waltke, *Genesis: A Commentary*, 303.

By utilizing their own knowledge and culturally acceptable work solutions, Abraham and Sarah probably delayed the promised son by at least 14 years.[62]

Abraham was a blessing to his unappreciative nephew, his neighbors, and within his family circle. But he took many years to understand the importance of the Edenic principle that he must work with God and that Sarah was his "helper fit for him": twice he endangered her wellbeing to secure his own safety. Yet at the center of the Genesis chiasm is found Abraham's total submission and trust in God (Gen 22:1–19), and his eventual appreciation of his struggling wife (Gen 23).

Abraham was not called to make a great name for himself. A name was part of the packaged gift that would result from obedience to the call. His obligation was to be a blessing, not to transform the world. He is not presented as someone achieving self-actualization and authentication, but as someone unable to achieve what he most desired without God's help. Abraham is introduced as having no legitimate children, and no prospects of ever having a legitimate child because his wife, twice stated for emphasis, is barren (Gen 11:30). Abraham is thus portrayed as utterly dependent on God for the fulfilment of the promised blessing. Perhaps in this total reliance on God the promised blessings most truly point back to the promises and the conditions God had envisioned in the beginning. Abram was not asked to resolve the imperfections of his family, neighbors, and community, nor was he given any instructions about how to possess the promised land. But, as Waltke pointed out, Abram's call expands his perspective on blessing from himself to the whole world,[63] a clearly different outlook from the "ourselves" of the Tower-builders' viewpoint.

Blessing in Abraham's Work Life

Four times, suggesting a global aspect, people pronounced Abraham a blessed person. Each of these times is associated with his work activity, and each time God is specifically identified as the source of blessing. First, Melchizedek notes Abram's blessed state after Lot is rescued (Gen 14:19). By giving Melchizedek the first-fruits of the plunder (Abram pays tithe) he signals that the Lord is victor.[64] Second, Abimelech king of Gerar, despite Abraham's failure to identify Sarah as his wife and the resulting curses pronounced on the king, recognized that Abraham had been a positive influence

---

62. Wenham, *Genesis 16–50*, 13.
63. Waltke, *Genesis: A Commentary*, 203.
64. Ibid., 227.

in the country (Gen 21:22). This positive influence is specifically associated with the activity of well-digging (see Gen 21:25). Third, the narrator, when Abraham is "old, well advanced in age," summarized his life and declared God had blessed Abraham in "all things," no doubt including his work as a herdsman (Gen 24:1). Fourth, Abraham's trusted servant, when delegated for the task of finding a wife for Isaac, enumerated Abraham's undeniably materially affluent status and ascribed it to God's blessing (Gen 24:35).

Abraham's Special Achievements

Most importantly, Abraham finally achieved unquestioning trust in God. Emphasizing that Isaac was solely the result of God's blessing and initiative, and not from Abraham's own hard-working achievement, Abraham is asked to sacrifice this son (Gen 22:1–2). The self-sacrifice involved in obeying this command was enormous, but gives clear indication that Abraham finally learned to trust God completely. Paul Borgman suggests that Genesis 22 indicates a work partnership: "Divine effort meeting full human response: this is the language of partnership perfected."[65] But although Abraham certainly had to respond to God's command, the critical issue seems rather that he was willing to renounce his "claim to fame" and accept God's sovereignty. Doukhan's study on the chiastic structure of Genesis 22 centers the pericope on the dialogue between Abraham and Isaac. This center contains significant passages of "silence," suggesting an emptying of all human hubris and a total acceptance of God's plan.[66]

As noted earlier, restricting attention to the mundane topic of work in the face of the rich theological material in the patriarchal narratives is difficult, and nowhere more so than in chapter 22, which is packed with theological meaning. However, there is one general theological concept in this kaleidoscopic chapter that is noteworthy in the context of work. JoAnn Davidson pointed out the many literary devices that indicate the emotional tension of the "test" Abraham is given (by none other than God), especially noting the significance of the fact that the word "love" is used for the first time in Genesis: "Take now your son, your unique/only son, whom you love" (Gen 22:2).[67] The immensity of Abraham's struggle to give up his most cherished achievement signals both the difficulty all humans have to surrender their cherished accomplishments, and the significance of actually doing this.

---

65. Borgman, *Genesis: Story We haven't Heard*, 93.
66. Doukhan, "Center of the Aqedah," 17–28.
67. Davidson, J., "Eschatology and Genesis 22," 243.

This sacrifice was not passive, either on God's part or Abraham's. Abraham's renunciation involved hard work, which noting the verbs describing his response demonstrates: he rose, saddled, took, cut wood, went, lifted his eyes, saw, said, took fire and knife, trusted ("God will provide"), built altar, laid wood, bound his son, reached out with the knife, took ram, offered ram, returned (Gen 22:3–10, 19). God also was active. He tested, called, said, provided, called, said, swore (Gen 22:1–2, 11–18). Working with God in the Edenic state required service, but in post-edenic fallen conditions it requires great human effort and courage. Central to the activity of God is "providing."

Sacrifice of Isaac

This self-sacrifice also involved Isaac, for without his co-operation the potential sacrifice would not have been possible. As mentioned above, Doukhan's study stresses the importance of the dialogue between Abraham and Isaac.[68] This suggests that it was not only Abraham who relinquished his plans and ambitions, but also Isaac. Abraham refers to his son as a young man, *na'ar* (Gen 22:5). Abraham was already an old man from whom Isaac could easily have broken free if there had been any struggle. The spiritual lessons from this pericope are well known, but the implications for ordinary work should not be overlooked. All human achievement must be submitted to God. Further, the pericope indicates the importance of truth that can be demonstrated, not just asserted.[69] This is one of the most important considerations in human work.

Obtaining a Suitable Burial for Sarah

When he obtains a burial ground for Sarah, Abraham is the model of courtesy and honest dealing. He is called a "mighty prince," or "great leader"[70] by his neighbors at this time, and they seem genuinely willing to give the requested burial ground free of charge, indicating their esteem (Gen 23:6). But Abraham's gallantry regarding Sarah's funeral highlights Sarah's role in the birth of Isaac. There are many deaths in Genesis, but the burial of Sarah is described in great detail, more than any other funeral (Gen 23). Unlike Jacob (Gen 50:12), Sarah made no requests for her burial.

68. Doukhan, "Center of the Aqedah," 17–28.
69. Arnold, *Genesis*, 202.
70. Scullion, *Genesis: A Commentary*, 181.

Abraham demonstrates in his arrangements for Sarah's funeral that she has become appreciated as the "helper fit for" him (Gen 2:18). Nothing would be spared, not even the apparently high price asked for the burial site (Gen 23:14; cf. 1 Kgs 16:24 and Jer 32:9). He recognizes that she is no longer the shamefully barren woman that he twice used as a foil to protect himself (Gen 12:10–20, 20:1–18), and even, perhaps, that he appreciated her desperation in instigating an extramarital affair to attempt to obtain a child.

Good Relationships with Family and Servants

Abraham's relationship with his oldest servant of many years shows both appreciation and a relaxed relationship. When the servant is asked to find a wife for Isaac (Gen 24:1–9, 12), he prays, not for his difficult job to be easier, but that kindness be shown his master, indicating an esteemed, even beloved relationship (Gen 24:12). Abraham's deathbed, notably, was the occasion for his rival sons to meet in reconciliation (Gen 25:9).

Abraham's Co-workers

In the Abraham pericopes there are several people who worked closely with him. The primary co-workers are two women, Sarah and Hagar, and two men, his nephew Lot and his trusted servant. It is useful to explore how the attitudes and contributions of these people impacted Abraham's effectiveness in his work.

The Contribution of Women

In the primordial narrative women are shadowy figures. Only four are named.[71] Naming in the creation pericope indicated authority and power,[72] so singling these women out by name suggests they wielded power and authority.

However, in the patriarchal narrative, women are much more prominent. Many are named and influence the course not only of their own lives,

---

71. The named women are: Eve, the mother of all living, and a cluster of three in the line of Cain. Adah and Zillah are the wives and apparently passive audience of the boasting murderer Lamech, seventh from Adam through Cain (Gen 3:20, 4:19), and contemporaries of the virtuous Enoch, seventh from Adam in the line of Seth (Gen 5:1–18). These women are the mothers of the inventive Jabal, Jubal, and Tubal-cain, and Naamah is their sister.

72. Turner, *Genesis*, 29.

but those of their families and posterity, indicating their increased power and authority. Sometimes the woman begins nameless in the narrative, but is later given a name, suggesting an increase in value has occurred over the years. For example, the young woman given to Rebekah by her family when she leaves to marry Isaac is known solely by her work, "her nurse" (Gen 24:59), but at the end of her life she is called "Deborah," and buried under a tree called Terebinth of Weeping (Gen 35:8). Not only is she now named, but the family response to her loss gives rise to a locality name that clearly indicates her value to them.

Like the servant woman who became Deborah, it seems women at this time were primarily valued for the service they provided to their community, a surprisingly modern situation.[73] Although, like Sarah and Rebekah, they could be noted for their good looks (Gen 12:11, 24:16), or like Sarah and Rachel, they could be desired for their good looks, they were valued for their ability to work hard.[74] The text records that Abraham, Isaac, and Jacob were very wealthy and had servants (Gen 24:35, 26:12–13, 31:1), but the wives of these men were willing to work hard. Their essential function was to bear children, and if they were unable to do so they could be despised (Gen 16:4). Although they had handmaidens, the responsibility of child rearing was primarily theirs. They were the cooks in the family, expected to drop everything to provide for visitors as needed (Gen 18:6). When Abraham invites three strangers to dine with him, he runs to Sarah, not the servants, saying, "Quickly, make ready three measures of fine meal; knead it and make cakes" (Gen 18:6). Women carried water from wells for the family, a significant burden in a hot climate (Gen 24:15). They cared for the flocks and herds (Gen 29:6).

The Work of Disabled Sarai

Sarai enters the patriarchal narrative seriously disabled. Later the text informs the reader she was very beautiful (Gen 12:11) and resourceful (for example, Gen 16:1–2), but the first information given is the double indictment that "Sarai was barren; she had no child" (Gen 11:30). "In stark contrast to all the fruitful progeny [of the *tôlēdôt* of Shem] there is barrenness."[75] A childless woman was an ignominious failure.[76] The double reinforcement of Sarai's childlessness sets the plot for much of the Abram-Sarai narrative.

73. See Bachmann, *Women at Work*.
74. Ibid.
75. Arnold, *Genesis*, 128.
76. Wenham, *Genesis 16–50*, 7.

Sarai was unable to perform the most important of womanly work, bearing children.

Table 8: Sarah's Work (with Hagar)

Work Activity	Suggested Modern Equivalent	Strategy	Outcome	Reference
Produce heir despite infertility	Lack of ability or experience	1. Pass job to someone else / exploit ability of others 2. Wait for God	Relationship stress, eventual success due to God's blessing	Gen 11:30 Gen 16:1–6 Gen 21:1–3
Expel Hagar and her son	Remove any opposition	Complain to superior	Hagar removed, but problem not solved; God intervenes to help the exploited	Gen 16:4–15, 21:8–19
Feed Strangers	Acceptance of routine work assignment	Accept opportunity	Personal Benefit	Gen 18:6–15

Sarai's Pragmatic Solution

God's rejection of Sarai's practical solution to her predicament, a child from her servant girl Hagar, adds to the tension. Although it is easy to sympathize with this attractive woman's attempts to pragmatically carry out the revealed will of God, she must have known that God had rejected Abram's equally practical solution to the problem, that of recognizing Eliezer of Damascus as his heir (Gen 15:2–4). Her first words in the Genesis text attribute her childless predicament to God (Gen 16:2), and her next words indicate she is determined to remedy God's mistake.[77] Her words, translated as "that I may be built up" by her maid's bearing children, echoes the attitude of the Tower of Babel workers.[78]

Wenham suggested that although she waited ten years for God to fulfill his promises (Gen 16:3), "Sarai's anxiety to have a child seems to have

---

77. Ibid., 12.
78. Brodie, *Genesis as Dialogue*, 237.

delayed the promise's fulfillment some fourteen years."[79] Using human methods to do her work indicates Sarah must bear the consequences of her efforts to give God a helping hand. She must endure the scorn of her servant girl Hagar (Gen 16:4) and the scoffing of her stepson Ishmael (Gen 21:9). Her solution to her infertility problem was culturally acceptable, but with Abram she was called to come out of this culture. What seemed the right thing to do actually made all three parties feel guilty and their mutual recriminations caused badly strained relationships.[80] Scullion suggested Sarai's treatment of Hagar connects her behavior with the unacceptable performance of the antediluvians and Babel.[81] Her harsh treatment of her slave was not God's way, and there was no blessing in it.

As Hagar's employer, there was no justification for Sarai's anger towards her servant who was merely exulting (in classic Babel fashion) in a job well done. Sarai even blamed Abram for doing as she had suggested! (Gen 16:5). Abram in his anger repudiates any relationship he had with Hagar, denoting her once more as Sarai's maid (Gen 16:3).[82] Notably, the mistreated Hagar is helped by God himself (Gen 16:7–14), and his interaction with her is in marked contrast to his brief exchange with her mistress.[83]

This pericope clearly shows that attempting to work in human knowledge and power does not result in blessing. Sarah's story shows a do-it-yourself fulfillment of divine promises is not God's plan. The suffering that results from rushing ahead of God, no matter how reasonable or socially acceptable, is clearly demonstrated in Sarah's story.

God Chose Sarah to do Unique Work

Sarah is clearly chosen by God for her task, which no one else could perform. It is possible that it was precisely because of her infertility, and not in spite of, that she was chosen by God to demonstrate human incapability and God's creative capability. What God accomplished in Sarah's life was a unique creative act.

Her story illustrates the important principle that each person has a unique contribution to the work of a group, a position no one else can fill, a principle overlooked in a society focused on results. Despite Sarah's

---

79. Wenham, *Genesis 16–50*, 13.
80. Arnold, *Genesis*, 163.
81. Scullion, *Genesis: A Commentary*, 237.
82. Thompson, "Abram, Sarai, Hagar."
83. Humphries, *Character of God*, 119.

awareness of her own incapacity, she was not to be cast aside, either by herself or others.

Sarah was exceptionally old at the time she conceived Isaac, too old from a human perspective to be any further use for the fulfillment of providing the promised heir (Gen 18:11). Denigration of the value of older people is a significant contemporary issue, one repudiated in the story of Sarah. However, Sarah herself, instead of recognizing her helplessness as being an opportunity for God to demonstrate his power, like so many, blamed God, found her own solution, and caused a great deal of trouble. Her solution to the problem is reminiscent of the disastrous results when Eve enticed her husband to listen.[84]

Sarah's predicament indicates that humans cannot assume that any promise made by God will automatically be fulfilled for them in accordance with their own understanding of how it should be fulfilled. The Edenic promise of fertility was delayed twenty-five years for Sarah, and it was delayed till its fulfillment seemed impossible. Her handicap was God's chosen tool to re-teach dependence on him.

But God's blessing Sarah with a son in her old age not only removed her sense of inferiority, but made her loved (Gen 24:67) and esteemed (Gen 23:2).

Lot: The Opportunistic Nephew

Lot, Abraham's nephew, serves as a constant reminder of both the danger and subtlety of the self-serving Babel approach to life. He enters the Genesis narrative as the significant only grandson of Terah (Gen 11:27–31),[85] and thus likely to be deeply imbued with the Babel culture. Although there is no record that Lot is blessed, he is the focus of Abraham's interest (Gen 13:8, 14:13–17, 18:16–33). Abram may have once regarded Lot as his heir, because it is after Abram's return from rescuing Lot from the battle of the Chedorlaomer confederacy that he expresses his concern that there is only a servant as his heir (Gen 15:2).

---

84. Reno, *Genesis*, 165.
85. Hamilton, *Book of Genesis Chapters 1–17*, 376.

Lot Worked for Personal Advantage

When Lot makes personal economic advantage his goal (Gen 13:10-11), he is very much the average man.[86] His noticing the desirability of the Jordon Plain, calling it the garden of the Lord, echoes Eve beside the forbidden tree.[87] Thus in contrast to Abraham, Lot, like the Tower-builders, made personal advantage his goal, and in doing so lost everything. Without Abram's help he would have lost all his material possessions to the Chedorlaomer confederacy, and he eventually lost everything except his two daughters in the fiery destruction of Sodom (Gen 19:26). It is only because of Abraham's intercession that his life was saved (Gen 18:22-33, 19:29). He disappears from the Genesis narrative in a fog of incestuous disgrace with his two rescued daughters (Gen 19:30-38). Two godless nations that descended from him were a curse to Abraham's offspring (Gen 19:36-38).

Lot Blessed because of Abraham

Because of Abraham, Lot is the recipient of God's concern, as two angels in human disguise rescue him from the anger of the Sodomite mob and the destruction of the city (Gen 19:1-22). Although "God remembered Abraham" (Gen 19:29) echoes Gen 8:1, "God remembered Noah," it is Lot, not Abraham, who is actually saved. This substitution of Abraham's name for Lot's makes an important point: Lot was not physically saved because of his own merits or connection with God, but through Abraham's intercession.[88] Yet there is no record of his demonstrating any gratitude towards his uncle or God for his benefits. Although Abraham's working life was sometimes checkered, the tragic contemporary story of Lot invites comparison. The disastrous results of a God-knowing person living life with a focus on material benefit are clearly shown. Lot set out to gain, but ended up losing everything. He serves as a tragic warning against working to make personal advantage the priority.

The Work of the Oldest Servant

The work of Abraham's trusted oldest servant is a beautiful codicil to Abraham's life, and particularly his work training his household (Gen 18:19).

---

86. Plaut, *Torah: Modern Commentary; Genesis*, 186.
87. Hamilton, *Book of Genesis Chapters 1-17*, 392.
88. Wenham, *Genesis 16-50*, 39.

This servant showed remarkable faith in God, and impeccable planning for a work assignment. He is a faultless example of human work.

Table 9: The Oldest Servant's Work

Work Activity	Suggested Modern Equivalent	Strategy	Outcome	Reference
Ruler of Abraham's household	CEO	Faithful in all tasks required	Trusted	Gen 24:2
Find wife for Isaac	Sensitive diplomatic mission	Honest appraisal of difficulties with supervisor, careful preparation, prayer, honest presentation of request, compelling persuasion	Mission successful Grateful thanksgiving Acknowledgement of God's blessing	Overall Gen 24:1–67 Gen 24:1–9 Gen 24:10 Gen 24:12–14 (rep v. 42–44) Gen 24:26–27 (rep v. 48)

Genesis chapter 24 is the longest pericope in the patriarchal story, and noted as a "guidance narrative" attesting to God's hand in the success of Abraham's life.[89] It is carefully composed,[90] and some see it as the center of the Genesis narrative.[91] In the manner of inclusion,[92] it connects the beginning and ending of Abraham's life with blessing and highlights the effectiveness of God's plan for human work. It shows how successful someone who relies totally on God's leading and blessing can be, illustrating divine guidance.[93] The chiastic structure of Genesis demonstrates that the miracles of this pericope complement the miraculous blessing of the birth of Isaac.

---

89. Westermann, *Genesis 12–36*, 382; Wenham, *Genesis 16–50*, 154.
90. Scullion, *Genesis: A Commentary*, 185.
91. Brodie, *Genesis as Dialogue*, 281.
92. Waltke, *Genesis: A Commentary*, 326.
93. Arnold, *Genesis*, 217.

The Servant trusts God in his Work

The oldest servant (nameless, but possibly Eliezer of Damascus, Abraham's one-time intended heir, Gen 15:2) epitomizes God's trust in Abraham's ability to train his household (Gen 18:19). The way the servant carries out his difficult, apparently almost impossible task to find a wife for the heir is presented as without fault. Most noteworthy is his repeated reliance on God for the success of his undertaking (Gen 24:12–14) and his ascribing all his achieved success to God (Gen 24:48).

Trusting God no Substitute for Careful Preparation in Work

However, the servant's reliance on God does not nullify the importance of recognizing the difficulties of his specific task, nor his making careful preparation for it. He does not shrink from presenting Abraham with the decided possibility that even if he does find a suitable woman she may not be willing to make the long and arduous journey from her homeland (Gen 24:5). He also ensured he had ample provisions to demonstrate to prospective women and their families evidence of Abraham's material wealth, and his son Isaac's suitability as a potential groom (Gen 24:10, 22, 53). Although Waltke suggested, "The scene wrestles with the interplay of human responsibility (faith in action) and divine initiative (perfectly coordinated circumstances),"[94] there is no incongruity.

The servant acts in faith, leaving results to God. The first thing he does when he arrives at the well is ask God for assistance (Gen 24:12–14). When he finds he has met a young woman who belongs to Abraham's relatives, he bows in thankful prayer (Gen 24:26–27). He recognizes God in all that he does; he does not run ahead in self-determined eagerness, or lag behind in his duty. The criteria used by the servant to choose a suitable bride are not her looks but her ability to work hard (Gen 24:14), indicating the character qualties behind this display of service, such as diligence and kindness.

The servant remained focused on his task, and refused to be delayed by the suggestions of Rebekah's family (Gen 24:55–57). He gently insisted that because God has prospered him, he must continue his journey back to his master: either Rebekah is willing to go now, or she is not. His firmness of purpose is matched by Rebekah's willingness to go, a willingness that reflects the call of Abram.[95]

---

94. Waltke, *Genesis: A Commentary*, 326.
95. Reno, *Genesis*, 215.

The servant must have felt due pride when he was able to point out Isaac to Rebekah, and later tell the story of his successful trip (Gen 24:64–66). But he must also have felt a sense of blessing himself as he observed the loving relationship that developed between the couple (Gen 24:67).

The Servant's Work Echoes the Call of Abram

The work of the oldest servant, nameless yet whose exploits have been carefully recorded for posterity, displays the power of Abraham's blessed working relationship with God most clearly. It is noteworthy that Genesis 24 contains many allusions to the call of Abraham,[96] both in the personal and communal blessings involved with it. In the longest Genesis pericope, the author suggests both the value of routine work performed carefully and faithfully and the importance of recognizing that all success comes from God. The manner of the servant's working results in blessing on all: blessing for Abraham, blessing for Isaac, blessing for Rebekah, and even blessing for Rebekah's family. It clearly demonstrates the blessed nature of working with God, and shows appreciative sensitivity towards human relationship.

Summary

The call of Abraham may be the thematic center of the Pentateuch, but it is the life of Abraham that demonstrates most clearly how God desires humanity to work with him. The doctrine of Calling (or Vocation) is the heart of the Protestant contribution to ideas about work. The call of Abraham illuminates the concept of "vocation" in two conspicuous ways. First is the call's remarkable requirement for obedience and separation from cultural norms, and the second, its noticeable emphasis on blessing. The special significance of blessing in the call of Abraham is its call to "return to God's original plan of blessing all peoples of the earth," and thus it draws attention to the original creation work mandate (Gen 1:28).

Recognizing that the original blessing was connected with the dominion given humanity over the creatures God had made (the work of caring for them)[97] suggests the essential quality of *imago Dei* is willingness to work to share the blessings of God with others. It has been aptly observed that Abraham's call expands his perspective on blessings from himself to the

---

96. Waltke, *Genesis: A Commentary*, 326.
97. Moltmann, *God in Creation*, 224.

whole world.[98] The blessing of Genesis is an active principle that always originates from God. It includes intimate relationship with God and beneficial relationships with other humans and animals.

Abraham and most of his work associates struggled to understand their need to rely on God. Abraham's struggles to believe that God would preserve and protect him or heal his wife's infertility are similar to the struggles of all contemporary humans. The life of his nephew Lot represents the majority who place personal benefit over all other considerations, but also the resulting tragic degenerative decline of such a life.

---

98. Waltke, *Genesis: A Commentary*, 203.

10

Jacob the Worker, Genesis 25:19—50:14

THE STORY OF JACOB spans half the book of Genesis, from his birth (Gen 25:24–26) to his funeral (Gen 50:1–14). His narrative covers one arm of the chiastic structure, and provides a thought-provoking mix of both primeval sin issues and patriarchal blessing. The theme of work is especially conspicuous in the Jacob pericopes. The incompatibility between a self-serving "Babel" approach to work and God's call to work under his blessing is clearly exposed. A prominent characteristic of Jacob's narrative is his relentless search for blessing. The Jacob pericopes indicate blessing cannot be obtained by using Babel-type methods.

Jacob's Parents

Jacob's story begins with his parents, Isaac and Rebekah. Although there is no mention of Abraham pronouncing any blessing upon Isaac, after Abraham's death the text records that God himself blessed him (Gen 25:11). Jacob would have been fifteen years old when his grandfather Abraham died (compare Gen 21:5, 25:26 and 25:7).

Isaac is Blessed

There is less drama in the life of Isaac than in that of his father Abraham,[1] but it is noteworthy that Gen 26:12–13 describes Isaac as *gādôl*, great, emphasizing both his wealth and his social standing with the surrounding nations. Furthermore, Isaac, the narrator, and Abimelech the Philistine all say,

---

1. Plaut, *Torah: Modern Commentary; Genesis*, 251.

adding to a total of five times, that God blessed him (Gen 25:11, 26:3, 12, 23, 29). This compares with the four times others note Abraham is blessed.

Table 10: Isaac's Work

Work Activity	Suggested Modern Equivalent	Strategy	Outcome	Reference
Submission to father's instructions	Co-operation with superiors		Revelation of God's Plan	Gen 22:7-19
Herdsman	Rancher	Continue father's work	Success	Gen 25:5, 26:14
Produce child	Self-actualization, achieve dream	Pray to God	Child conceived	Gen 25:20-21
Cope with famine conditions	Unemployment	Obeys God's directions, but hides wife's identity (like his father)	Host neighbors reprimand him for the deceit	Gen 26:1-11
Crop-growing	Farmer	Innovative undertaking for a herdsman.	Massive crops that produced envy in neighbors	Gen 26:12-16
Dig wells, despite these repeatedly being taken over by locals	Irrigation development. Persistence despite opposition	Move on and keep digging new wells	Eventually neighbors see God is with him	Gen 26:15, 18-22, note v. 28
Built altar	Church-building	Response to God's appearance	Neighbors ask for a treaty	Gen 26:23-33

Two of these blessings are from God, when Isaac was told not to go to Egypt (Gen 26:2-5) and when the wells his herdsmen dug were being filled by envious Philistines (Gen 26:13-15). Twice the narrator reports God blessed him: after his father's death (Gen 25:11) and when his crops are extremely bountiful (Gen 26:12). The envious Philistines also admit that Isaac's success is because God is with him and has blessed him (Gen 26:28–29). When Abimelech, with his advisor Ahuzzah and army commander Phicol, come to meet Isaac to request a peace treaty they make the remarkable declaration that Isaac is blessed, *brk*, of *Yahweh* (Gen 26:29). Despite their envy, these people know both the name, and the power, of the God this altar-building, spectacular crop-growing sojourner in their midst worshipped.

To the work of cattle-breeder, like his father (Gen 12:16, 13:2), Isaac added crop-growing, suggesting a more settled existence (Gen 26:14, 26:12). This also indicates Isaac's innovative approach to work, and his willingness to try new activities. He was signally successful in this crop growing, reaping hundredfold crops (Gen 26:12). The text is emphatic, repeating *gādôl*, "greatness or prosperity," three times: "The man began to prosper (be great), and continued prospering (being great) until he became very prosperous (very great)" (Gen 26:13). Arnold noted that in his acquisition of great wealth, altar-building, well-digging, and covenant-making, Isaac is his father's son.[2]

Isaac Prays

Isaac demonstrated he had learned from his father's experience. When his own wife, Rebekah, remained childless for twenty years he turned to God and prayed to solve the difficulty (Gen 25:21–26). His prayer was answered with twins, a doubling of blessing. When famine struck, he showed a willingness to listen to God and go where he directs (Gen 26:2–6). This is quite different from Abraham's behavior under similar situations.

Fearful for Personal Safety

However, Isaac showed the same anxiety for personal safety as did his father Abraham. He denied the true identify of his wife, Rebekah, thus endangering her and bringing disapproval on himself from his neighbors (Gen 26:7–11). In his crop-growing, however, Isaac demonstrated to those same disapproving and envious neighbors that God was blessing him, and, as with his father, they came and asked for a treaty of peace (Gen 26:26–33). Isaac's experience with his neighbors introduces a complication to the concept of blessing: his success in crop-growing and animal husbandry provoked dangerous envy in his neighbors (Gen 26:14).

---

2. Arnold, *Genesis*, 239.

Comparison of Abraham's and Isaac's Concerns regarding Blessing

A major difference between Abraham's concept of blessing and his son's was that whereas Abraham was the frequent recipient of God's promised blessing, Isaac not only received blessing but was also anxious to ensure that he himself delivered blessing to his offspring. Isaac did not horde the blessing for himself, but he appears mistaken in deeming it his responsibility to ensure blessing will be experienced by his chosen son. Much of the Isaac story is given to the pericope of his attempt to bless his firstborn son (Gen 27:1–46). The Hebrew noun for blessing, *bĕrākā*, occurs seven times, and the verb no less than twenty-one times in this story,[3] indicating the intensity of desire in the minds of all concerned.

Isaac Consults his Taste, not his God

Waltke pointed out that the account of Isaac's attempt to pass on blessing is framed by the two negative reports of Esau's marriages to "foreign" women (Gen 26:34–35, 28:6–9).[4] This overt focus on the undesirability of Esau's independent behavior in a core patriarchal function, obtaining a godly wife to produce offspring to pass on the blessing of God, hints that Isaac's plans to give blessing to this son may not be sanctioned by God.[5] Isaac was driven by culture and custom to pass the birthright to the firstborn; he did not consult God. His own experience of being an especially blessed younger son may have also influenced him.

Kidner noted that the textual focus on Isaac making his taste buds the prerequisite for the blessing procedure hints at disapproval (Gen 27:4).[6] It echoes the last time there was a focus on taste in the Genesis narrative: beside the tree of knowledge of good and evil. Kidner also suggested Isaac failed because of this reliance on his senses, the classic human means of gaining knowledge and evidence, rather than relying on God's direction.[7] The text indicates Isaac does not consult God in his attempts to bless Esau. The Genesis author rarely passes judgment on the characters described, but the negative implication from the suffering that came to his family from

3. Waltke, *Genesis: A Commentary*, 375.
4. Ibid.
5. Ibid.
6. Kidner, *Genesis*, 156.
7. Ibid.

Isaac's determined seizure of the role of blesser, as also occurred when Sarah presented her maid to Abram, suggests his action was neither good nor part of God's plan.

Isaac Handicapped with Blindness

The narrative identifies Isaac's sense of inadequacy, his blindness, was the cause of his precipitous attempt to bless Esau (Gen 27:1). This reminds the reader of the same sense of personal inadequacy that prompted Sarah into unwise action (Gen 16:1–2). By focusing on their limitations, two well-intentioned people, Sarah and Isaac, usurped the role of God in attempting to achieve the goals they believed God desired. In both situations the result of this seizure of divine role was broken relationship, and the opposite of the blessing intended. This same sense of powerlessness, combined with personal preference, goaded Rebekah to resort to the outrageous deceit she perpetrated to achieve the blessing for Jacob.

Rebekah the Mother of Jacob

Jacob's mother is presented as a well-developed character, an energetic and decisive woman who made things happen. But her life ends in a tragic shadow of uncertainty. Again the failure of human initiative to achieve the divine plan is highlighted by the tragic situations resulting from Rebekah's well-intentioned intervention in Isaac's plan to bless his firstborn son. God had told her the elder was to serve the younger (Gen 25:23), but she took it upon herself to ensure the divine pronouncement was fulfilled.

Rebekah is presented as a blessed answer to prayer (Gen 24:12–15). The criterion for Rebekah's selection was her willingness to work hard. The narrator highlights her quickness, *mihar*, three times (Gen 24:18–20, 46). Apparently, she regularly did the fetching and carrying of water for her family (Gen 24:15), but watering ten camels single-handedly was a major undertaking for a young woman. Although her hard work was the sign that set her apart as chosen by God for Isaac's wife, it is indicates she was accustomed to working hard. There is no specific textual indication that she is blessed by anyone, but Isaac loved her (Gen 24:67). Further, Isaac's plea for her to have a child after waiting twenty years (Gen 25:20–24) was doubly blessed and she was granted a twin pregnancy.

"Rebekah's hospitality [and work] sharply contrast with [her brother] Laban who rushes to the servant 'as soon as he had seen the nose ring,' Gen 24:56."[8] Rebekah's focus was on service, not personal gain, but Laban's focus was on the gold, the opportunity for gain.

Table 11: Rebekah's Varied Work

Work Activity	Suggested Modern Equivalent	Strategy	Outcome	Reference
Water stranger's camels	Diligence in doing the routine task opens way for extracurricular opportunity	Assess need, Act vigorously	Further job offer	Gen 24:15–20, 44
Invitation to be Isaac's wife	Challenging job offer	Get facts, relocate	Success: beloved wife	Gen 24:34–58, 67
Obtaining blessing for Jacob (favorite son)	Threat to ambition fulfillment/ competition	Use skills to preempt opposition/ competition	Success, but shattered relationships	Gen 27:5–17
Protect Jacob from threat	Look after self-interest	Use contact and diplomacy	Success, but lost contact with son	Gen 27:42–46

Rebekah takes over God's Role

Rebekah misused her quickness and rushed to prevent her husband going against what she believed was the will of God (Gen 25:23). Although she knew God's will for her sons by personal divine revelation, she did not rely on God for the fulfillment of this plan. Perhaps, as suggested, her sense of powerlessness to prevent Isaac from carrying out his plan to bless Esau was a significant factor in her behavior.

Although her deception was successful in obtaining blessing for Jacob, her attempt to make things work out according to her own knowledge and

---

8. Waltke, *Genesis: A Commentary*, 325.

understanding resulted in potentially lethally broken relationships between her sons Jacob and Esau (Gen 27:41), and the permanent loss of Jacob to herself. By sending Jacob back to Padan Aram instead of sending for a wife as Abraham had done for Isaac, she may also have contributed to the relationship difficulties in Jacob's family. The text thus suggests that even when prophecy has shown God's plan, working to force its fulfillment does not meet with success.

Jacob: The Man who Wrestled with Man and with God

Work is the dominant theme in Jacob's story, intimated by its commencing with the lentil pericope (and even his name, "grabber"). The lentil story deals with the occupations of Jacob and Esau,[9] and reveals the motivations and foci of the twins. It echoes the Cain-Abel pericope where occupation also began the narrative (Gen 4:2). Clearly Jacob was willing to exploit any situation for his own gain, even robbing his hungry brother to obtain the birthright. He is a frightened but willing accomplice when his mother suggests deceiving his father Isaac to obtain the patriarchal blessing (Gen 27:5-19).

Jacob's Focus: Gaining Blessing by his Own Effort

Although Jacob was materially successful, and later when talking with his wives and Laban he was able to attribute this to the blessing of God, he spent the entire first part of his life struggling to obtain blessing by his own efforts, and much of the last part wallowing in misery at his losses (Gen 33–35, 37, 47:9).

The Jacob-Esau story is a power struggle (echoes of antediluvian violence) where the focus of concern is the same as the contemporary one of self-interest, gain, and possession.[10] Jacob's focus is on gaining the blessing, but not on the terms of the blessing.

Jacob's unhappiness is shown in the unfolding pericopes as due to his efforts to work things out in his own way, without reliance on God. Although in the patriarchal narratives "it is due to God's blessing that children

---

9. Westermann, *Genesis 12–36*, 416–17.
10. Ibid., 574.

are born and grow up, that work is crowned with productive growth,"[11] Jacob's focus is on his own efforts and not on his God. It could be said that God blessed Jacob in spite of himself, and not because of himself.

Jacob is a failure in his family life. Because of his tendency to display partiality between both his wives and children, bitterly quarreling wives and disagreeably hostile children surround him (Gen 29:31—30:2, 37:3-4). There is a strong sense that there is no blessing for Jacob anywhere within the family, and this serves to heighten his longing for it.

Jacob is Faithless

At no point in the narrative is there any doubt about Jacob's allegiance to Yahweh. But Jacob is conspicuous for his lack of faith and poor communion with God. Even in the pericope of the ladder with angels, the vision of God's promised blessing corresponding to the call of Abram, Jacob appears as a self-centered deal-maker, focused on bargaining for the promised blessing by his own efforts (Gen 28:20-22).[12] "Jacob's offer to pay tithe [Gen 28:22] implies his hope of obtaining riches through his work."[13] He gives no indication that he sees himself directed by God,[14] in contrast to his unquestioningly obedient grandfather Abraham.

Jacob's arrival in Haran contrasts sharply with that of the devoutly prayerful oldest servant. There is no prayer for help as Jacob arrives at the well, nor word of appreciation that he has found his family. His poverty of both spiritual strength and personal fortune contrasts dramatically with the faithful servant of Abraham.[15] "Jacob is ever trying to secure God's blessing through his own efforts . . . he continues prayerless . . . He stumbles into a providential marriage with neither petition nor praise . . . As his wives struggle for God's blessing in children to validate their marriages, Jacob is reduced to a stud."[16] Not until twenty years later, when he is ready to leave his time of service with Laban, does Jacob finally, for the first time, acknowledge God's blessing in his life (Gen 30:30). Not until he acknowledged that it was God who was blessing him did he gain the strength to defy Laban's cruel servitude and have the power to take leadership of his family and leave.[17]

11. Ibid., 575.
12. Cotter, *Genesis*, xxxiv.
13. Westermann, *Genesis 12-36*, 438.
14. Humphries, *Character of God*, 165.
15. Sarna, *Understanding Genesis*, 201; Waltke, *Genesis: A Commentary*, 398.
16. Waltke, *Genesis: A Commentary*, 408.
17. Ibid., 422-23.

Table 12: Jacob's Work

Work Activity	Suggested Modern Equivalent	Strategy	Outcome	Reference
Cook, possibly gardener, tough dealer	Chef, market gardener, entrepreneur	Exploit brother's need	Won birthright	Gen 25:29–34
Relocate to Padan Aram	Find employment out of town, even overseas	Go alone	God blessed him, Jacob offers a bargaining allegiance	Gen 28:1–22
Remove stone covering well	Brute strength, opportunistic attitude	Impress Rachel	She invited him home	Gen 29:1–14
Working as shepherd seven years for Rachel	Apprenticeship, exploited labor	Focus on the dream (his love for Rachel)	Passed over	Gen 29:7, 15–20, 29–30
Working as shepherd seven years more for Rachel	Exploited labor, retraining to keep job, trapped in boring job	Stick to dream doggedly	Made it!	Gen 29:30 Gen 31:38–41
Sire son for favorite but infertile wife	Impossible job	Get angry, accept human suggestions, delegate	Sons, but apparently unappreciated, and not from Rachel. Bitter family relationships	Gen 30:1–8
Continue working for Laban for wages	Share farmer, employer/employee issues. Big business versus small business	Use folklore, science, and business principles	Became prosperous, but Laban's sons jealous	Gen 30:43—31:3

Work Activity	Suggested Modern Equivalent	Strategy	Outcome	Reference
Selective animal breeder	Scientist / animal breeder	Use best known scientific method	Circumvents damaging company policies	Gen 30:37–43
Built house	Real estate ownership	Unknown	More settled?	Gen 33:17
Bought land for 100 pieces of money	Expanding real estate	Unknown	More settled?	Gen 33:19
Erected altar	Built church	Because he came safely to Shechem		Gen 33:18, 20
Sends Joseph to check brothers' work	Company Director	Favoritism	Disastrous loss of favored son	Gen 37:12–14, 15–26
Buys food from Egypt	Import/export	Offers good price plus bonus, agrees to terms	Successful	Gen 43:11–13
Blesses family and Pharaoh	Government official allocating public awards		Words recorded for posterity	Gen 47:10, 48:8–20, 49:1–28

Jacob the Workaholic

Jacob's vigorous work ethic is demonstrated when he arrived in the ancestral country. He rushed to remove the stone from the mouth of the well (Gen 29:1–10). This contrasts strongly, in positive light, with the shirking and lazy shepherds,[18] indicating the importance of a job well done in either Jacob's or the narrator's thinking. It gives a clear picture of Jacob as "a man full of thrust and enterprise."[19] No wonder Laban was keen to procure

---

18. Ibid., 401.
19. Kidner, *Genesis*, 160.

his services (Gen 20:15). Jacob appeared to Laban as a benefactor, a real asset to the family business.[20] Further, Jacob's confidence that by his own hard work he could achieve his goals is suggested by his offer to work seven years for Rachel: the offer was so extreme Laban was bound to accept.[21] Thus, although Jacob was penniless with nothing to offer for the customary bride price, his obvious willingness to work hard convinced even the tough-minded Laban that he was an asset.

Jacob's life is dominated by work, and in the Laban-Jacob pericope (Gen 29:14–30), the Hebrew *'bd*, "to work or to serve," occurs frequently.[22] Work is clearly the central theme in this narrative,[23] "represent[ing] Jacob's exile in Haran . . . Jacob has entered the dark night of *slavery* [emphasis supplied]."[24] That Jacob was indeed virtually a slave to Laban is poignantly shown when he fled from his uncle, and, challenging the pursuing Laban (Gen 31:38–42), rehearsed the difficulties of his twenty-year struggle caring for the flocks.

Jacob's do-it-yourself approach to life extended to his own funeral. At the end of his life he was struggling to recognize God's part in his success. In contrast to the funeral of Sarah, he gave minute directions about his burial, which his sons carried out (Gen 49:29–33, 50:12). Unlike Joseph's simple trusting request, "God will surely visit you, and you shall carry my bones from here" (Gen 50:25), Jacob makes no mention of God, nor does he express significant hope for the future.

Wages and Commercial Deals Dominate the Jacob Narrative

The issue of wages and commercial deals looms prominently in the Jacob story. Laban, as his employer, is shown in a poor light for exploiting his penniless nephew Jacob (also a refugee from his murderous brother, Gen 27:41) with sharp dealing, deceit, hard labor, and uncertain wages (Gen 29:15–30, 30:25–43). Even in his marriage Jacob was hired by wage, Hebrew *sākar*, by his wives (Gen 30:16). "In the story of the mandrakes his marriage to Leah is reduced to a commercial contract."[25] This is the fifth of many commercial

---

20. Ibid.
21. Plaut, *Torah: Modern Commentary; Genesis*, 289.
22. Waltke, *Genesis: A Commentary*, 403.
23. Mathews, *Genesis 11:27—50:26*, 456.
24. Waltke, *Genesis: A Commentary*, 403.
25. Ibid., 413.

exchanges highlighted in the Jacob cycle[26] (see Table 13 below). Yet the story of the mandrakes, showing that this family trades in things that should be above trade, has a surprising twist.[27] The mandrakes do nothing for Rachel, but Leah gains another son by parting with them.[28]

The inventory of commercial activity in Jacobs's household indicates just how much business activity dominated their lives. They used their assets to obtain the good things in life, and even the not-so-good pleasures available in the surrounding culture (Gen 38:17). The shrewd and dishonest bargaining of Laban did not go unnoticed by his grandsons, who, teenagers when the family left, had learned all too well from him (see Gen 34 and 38). Laban's treatment of Jacob probably contradicted ancient shepherding contracts, where shepherds normally received as much as twenty percent of new births,[29] and no doubt there was discussion about this situation in the family.

26. Ibid.

27. Kidner, *Genesis*, 162.

28. Ibid. Although Mathews considers that Joseph was conceived because of their use. Mathews, *Genesis 11:27—50:26*, 487.

29. Finkelstein, "Old Bablyonian Herding Contract," 30–36, quoted in Arnold, *Genesis*, 272.

Table 13: Commercial Transactions in the Jacob Narrative

Goods/Service	Exchanged for	Reference
Pot lentils	Birthright from Esau	Gen 25:29–34
Identity and food	Blessing from Isaac	Gen 27:5–29
Tithe	Blessing from God	Gen 28:20–22
Farm work / shepherd	Wives from Laban	Gen 29:15–30
Mandrakes	Sex with wife	Gen 30:14–16
Farm work / shepherd	Stock from Laban	Gen 30:25–36
Lavish gifts	Esau's friendship	Gen 32:3–21
100 pieces of silver	Land from Hamor, Shechem's father	Gen 33:17–19
Shechem's bride price and Hamor's offer of trade in the land	Offered for Dinah	Gen 34:11
Massacre of Shechemites	Sister's honor and a rich plunder of goods	Gen 34:2, 25–31
Separation from Esau	Land	Gen 36:6–8
Joseph sold by brothers	20 pieces of silver	Gen 37:28
Goat	Sex with Tamar	Gen 38:16–17
Trading in wool (Judah and possibly Jacob)	Presumably food and other goods	Gen 38:12
Money	Food from Egypt	Gen 42:2–3
Money and goods	Food from Egypt	Gen 42:11–13

Blessing in Jacob's Life

Blessing, or more accurately a search for blessing, dominates the Jacob story. Jacob's passionate search for blessing for himself begins his story (Gen 25:29–34), and the last thing he does is pass on blessing (Gen 49:22–26).

Six times, not quite the perfect number and possibly symbolizing his focus on work, yet one more than those recorded for his father, Jacob is noted by others as being blessed, or spoken to in blessing, by God (Gen 28:13–15, 31:3, 32:26–29, 35:1, 35:9–12, 46:2–4). Many of these times were associated with the difficulties and obstacles in his life: at Bethel after his banishment from home when he stole the blessing from Esau; after the struggle at the brook Jabbok; after the massacre of the city of Shechem and Hamor; and when he was obviously in great doubt about the propriety of going down to Egypt.

Only twice do other people either bless Jacob, or note he is blessed. Although his desire for blessing is dramatically revealed when he attempts to seize his brother's blessing, his father Isaac only unintentionally blessed him at that time (Gen 27:26–29). The deep yearning for blessing continued, and Jacob was still searching for blessing twenty years later when he was accosted at the brook Jabbok, pled for blessing, and received it from his unknown assailant (Gen 32:24–30). This time the blessing was no accident. The second time Jacob is described as being blessed was when he tried to leave Laban, and his uncle finally testified he had been blessed as a result of his association with Jacob (Gen 30:27). However, Laban, at this time as in all others, was more focused on his own advantage than his nephew's value.

Three times Jacob, somewhat belatedly, recognized that God blessed him: first, when he encouraged his wives to flee with him from their father's grueling service (Gen 31:4–13); second, when he encountered the irate Laban after the family had successfully fled (Gen 31:42); third, when he met Esau after twenty years' absence (Gen 33:5, 11). Each of these times is fraught with considerable anxiety and it appears Jacob needed to reassure himself that God had been with him, rather than expressing a confident appreciation of the blessing of God in his life.

Jacob's passionate desire for blessing is eventually matched by his willingness to pronounce blessing on others. Four times, the globally significant number, the text records that he blessed other people. Significantly, the first person upon whom he pronounced blessing was Esau, his estranged brother (Gen 33:10–11). After the reconciliation of his children and his own safe arrival in Egypt, he was in strong blessing mode, and blessed Pharaoh (Gen 47:7, 10). He blessed the two sons of Joseph (Gen 48:1–20), and reversed the blessing order on these boys so that the younger was placed ahead of the elder. Despite Joseph's protest, Jacob insisted on the younger being given precedence, reflecting his own father's insistently preferential behavior more than one hundred years earlier (there is no indication of any direction from God on this matter). Finally, he pronounced prophetic words on all his twelve sons (Gen 49:1–28), but it was only Joseph who actually received clear words of blessing (Gen 49:22–26).

Jacob's No-Work Blessing

When Jacob finally had his lifelong search for blessing granted (Gen 32:26–29), it was accompanied by a very disabling injury. "Jacob was left alone; and a man wrestled with him until the breaking of the day. Now when he saw that he could not prevail against him, he touched the socket of his hip, and the socket of Jacob's hip was out of joint as he wrestled with him" (Gen 32:24–25). The text highlights his aloneness: "Jacob was left alone," and his struggle. Jacob had been struggling to do things alone and in his own way for a long time. Surprisingly, even shockingly, the first blessing action of the assailant is to cripple Jacob. Only after this no-work injury was Jacob blessed with a name change that signified his relationship with God.

Jacob's hip injury meant it was no longer possible for him to work as he had been doing. From this point there is no reference in the narrative to any physical activity from Jacob. He directs activities, but there are no physical exploits like removing the stone cover from the well, or caring for sheep. The carts sent by Joseph to help the move to Egypt, which clinched Jacob's recognition that it was Joseph who had summoned him (Gen 45:21, 27), indicate that Jacob was no longer capable of walking any significant distance. Furthermore, soon after the Jabbok encounter, Jacob bought land, perhaps signifying that a nomadic existence was now difficult for him (Gen 33:19). The importance of this injury is that an enforced rest accompanied blessing in Jacob's life. Perhaps Jacob did not realize it, but this enforced inactivity, this rest, was no doubt the special blessing he needed from God. Blessing is a gift from God, and not the result of a human struggle. This forced cessation of work was a mere shadow of the blessed rest God envisioned when he instituted the Sabbath rest.

Jacob's Science and the Beginning of his Understanding

Laban's unfair changes of wage policy, potentially very damaging to Jacob's prosperity, were apparently circumvented by Jacob's use of folklore science (Gen 30:37–43). Jacob's methods, though amusing to contemporary readers, appeared to get results. Through his shrewdness with breeding animals he became wealthy via honest, though cunning means.[30] Significantly, this description of folklore science involves a striking display of word play: when Jacob made his sticks white, in Hebrew he made them *lbn*. Even more striking and meaningful is that the verb *lbn* in the qal refers to brick-making, and is used in the Genesis narrative for the activity of the Tower-builders (Gen 11:3), and later in the Pentateuch for the gruelling brick-making of the Israelite slaves prior to their liberation (Exod 5:7, 14).[31] English translations mask the Hebrew's significant hint that Laban the man represents the rejected Babel-style brick-making work ethic, and Jacob's work with him was in the manner of Babel.

Jacob appears successful with his folk-science. Only at the end of twenty years of servitude, when facing the jealousy of Laban's sons and encouraging his wives to return with him to Canaan, is Jacob finally able to face the realization, and even more importantly admit it, that it was not his "science" and hard work that achieved good results, but the blessing of God that gave him wealth (Gen 31:4-9). This is the first time Jacob verbally recognized God's blessing in his life, and admitted that it was not his own hard work that won him success. The three times Jacob recognized that God blessed him seemed more to reassure himself rather than the free expression of appreciation for God's blessing in his life. Jacob seemed blind to the numerous times God intervened in his life. His birth was an answer to the prayer of his father (Gen 25:21). His mother received prophetic messages about his life (Gen 25:23). God appeared to him in a special dream on the road to Haran (Gen 28:12-15), but although awed by this experience, his response was simply a bargain: "If God will . . . then Yahweh will be my God" (Gen 28:20-21). There is no indication he recognized God led him safely to the family home in Haran. When his favorite wife proved to have the family problem of infertility, he simply got angry with her distress (Gen 30:1-2). There is no prayer on her behalf as his father had done for his mother. He certainly showed no pleasure in the blessing of Leah's fecundity. But, terrified of his brother's attack, he remembered God and pled with him for his deliverance (Gen 32:9-12).

Yet despite his blindness to God's numerous interventions, God did not give up on Jacob. He personally told him to leave Laban (Gen 31:3). The angels of God met him on his way to Esau (Gen 32:1). A God-man met him and wrestled with him at the brook Jabbok, the beginning of change. After this, Jacob calls what he originally had denoted as an appeasement offering for his brother (Gen 32:20) a "blessing" that indicated God's gracious

---

30. Scullion, *Genesis: A Commentary*, 219.
31. Clines, *Concise Dictionary*, 190.

dealing with him (Gen 33:11). After the Shechem massacre God told to him to leave the area (Gen 35:1), and spoke to him again as they travelled through the country (Gen 35:9–12). God sent specific encouragement when Jacob anxiously journeyed towards Egypt (Gen 46:1–5).

The meager three times Jacob expresses recognition for his blessings reflect his approach to life: "Jacob is ever trying to secure God's blessing through his own efforts."[32] He is so focused on his own performance, his own work, that he is blind to the work of God in his life. He is a very contemporary human.

"Children of Israel" rather than *"Children of Abraham"*

It is perhaps significant that the nation that fulfilled God's promise in the call of Abraham (Gen 12:1–3) should be called the "Children of Israel" and not the "Children of Abraham." Although Jacob was blessed, and began to change after his Jabbok experience, a name change does not guarantee an immediate character change. Abraham was still lying about his wife's identity after his name change (compare Gen 17:5 and 20:1–17). Jacob's unwise preferential treatment of his sons occurred after his name-change and blessing.

In many ways the nation Abraham's descendants became reflected the attitudes and behavior of Jacob much more than it did those of their primary ancestor Abraham, as shown by the prophetic pronouncements on the nation. God's people Israel showed a marked tendency to try to work things out for themselves, to obtain the blessing by their own effort, instead of relying on the blessing of God.

Jacob's Work Associates

Like Abraham, there were significant others who were an important part of Jacob's work. For Jacob they were his sharp-dealing uncle Laban, his two wives, his poorly influenced children, and (in the next chapter) his favorite son Joseph.

---

32. Waltke, *Genesis: A Commentary*, 408.

Laban the Whitened Man

Both Laban and Lot are significant Genesis characters who demonstrate the futility of focusing on personal gain to the detriment of the needs of others. Laban's apparently well-mannered approach highlights how dangerously deceptive inappropriate work principles and ethics can be. As already noted, his name *lbn*, "to whiten," offers an interesting word play. Was he an albino? Was it a nickname because he attempted to whiten what was really black? Or did his focus on work and profit indicate "brick-making" slavery? Laban corresponds to the Tower culture that Abraham was asked to leave. At the end of his long association with his nephew, he speaks of "the God of your father," but does not claim this God as his own, and is primarily concerned about the theft of his own gods (Gen 32:29–30).

Profit his Aim

Laban's focus is on material and financial benefit.[33] He enters the narrative noticing his sister wearing the golden gifts of Abraham's servant (Gen 24:30), and that the servant is standing by the rare and costly camels.[34] He wastes no time (the text says ran) to achieve his goal of personal benefit from Abraham's servant (Gen 24:29, 29:13). This interest in personal gain continues to the very end.[35] Even his daughters are seen as sources of personal gain (Gen 31:14–15) and they see no future for themselves with him.

---

33. Wenham, *Genesis 16–50*, 268.
34. Ibid., 146.
35. Ibid., 268.

Table 14: Laban's Work

Work Activity	Suggested Modern Equivalent	Strategy	Outcome	Reference
Observed sister's bracelets and the camels	Seize business opportunity	"Run" to source of supply	Further business opportunity	Gen 24:29–32
Hospitality to Jacob, pastoralist	Seize business opportunity	"Run" to Jacob	Further business opportunity	Gen 29:13–14
Employ Jacob	Employer	Promise worker their goals can be achieved	Obtained services of good worker for seven years	Gen 29:18–20
Give Leah instead of Rachel	Change contract, change policies,	Excuse sharp dealing as cultural norm	Gain good worker for another seven years	Gen 29:23–30
Offer percentage of profit for work done	Partnership Share farmer	Change bureaucratic rules and legal terms Change policies	Lose partner	Gen 30:25—31:21
Threaten, attempt to get Jacob to return to his service	Lawsuits, coerced labor	Took his brethren (witnesses and "the board") and pursued Jacob	God intervenes	Gen 31:22–43
Make a covenant with Jacob	Union negotiation	Use religious forms to own advantage, Empty promises	Permanent separation of parties	Gen 31:44–55

Laban's Apparently Good Manners

Laban's fiscal interest is hidden behind a genial façade and impeccably good manners. His suggestion that his sister Rebekah "stay a while" (Gen 24:55) may have been due to concern about his sister, but there is the lurking suspicion that he hoped for more of the gold jewelry. He sounds magnanimous and fatherly when he says, after the benefit of a month's free labor from Jacob, "Because you are my relative should you serve me for nothing? Tell me, what should your wages be?" (Gen 29:15). When caught despicably deceiving his nephew by exchanging the bride, he suavely points out local custom mysteriously ignored for the seven years of Jacob's servitude, and calmly suggests another seven years' work for the right bride! (Gen 29:26-27). Laban appears to have exploited the broken relationships in Jacob's family to retain his nephew's service. When Jacob tried to leave after fourteen years' of work, Laban is in beguiling and pleading mode: "Please stay, if I have found favor in your eyes, for I have learned by experience that the Lord has blessed me for your sake" (Gen 30:27). Finally, faced with the inevitable that Jacob has gone and will not return, he becomes the injured daddy-uncle, bewailing his lack of opportunity to offer a farewell party to his family (Gen 31:26-28). His offer of organizing a party is not in character (Gen 31:27), and the operative word for this party is indeed "might": it seems unlikely it would ever have happened.

Self-Interest his Focus

Perhaps Laban's concern to achieve the covenant between himself and Jacob is his fear that Jacob might use his privileged relationship with God to harm him, just as he, Laban, had intended to harm Jacob (Gen 31:29). The request for a covenant indicates fear more than good will. His final strategy of turning blame on Jacob for stealing the gods (Gen 31:30) is typical of his lifelong policy of preserving his own interests at the expense of others. Thus, a selfish, godless approach to work can be hidden behind a very pleasant façade. It was probably this agreeable aspect of Laban's dealings that beguiled Jacob into continuing to work with his uncle for twenty years.

God Intervened on Jacob's Behalf

God intervened on behalf of the faithless Jacob. Not only did God directly tell Jacob to leave (Gen 31:3), but Laban also received a dream warning him to desist in his plan to harm Jacob, his employee (Gen 31:29). Less dramatically, but like Lot, he disappears from the narrative in a fog of self-seeking.

Jacob's Wives: Bargaining rules their Lives

The lives of Jacob's wives are dominated by commercial exchange. They each gain a husband from a business contract (Gen 29:18, 27), and this continues even with their acquisition of children. While all the names of Leah's children reflect her intense bargaining for Jacob's affection, one, Issachar, is even called "hire, wages" (Gen 30:18).[36] Leah and Rachel are both truly daughters of their wheeling-dealing father, Laban.

Table 15: Rachel and Leah's Work (with Bilhah and Zilpah)

Work Activity	Suggested Modern Equivalent	Strategy	Outcome	Reference
Rachel	Shepherdess	Do job required	Attract further work	Gen 29:6, 9
Leah—get husband	Overcoming competition	Get in favor with father and apply local customs	Unloved	Gen 29:15–30
Rachel—produce children	Any target setting, achieving the dream	1. Try anger, then delegate 2. Trade mandrakes for love	No children and angry husband	Gen 30:1–21
Bargaining with sister to use mandrakes	Smart advertising	Offer what one sister has for what the other sister needs	God ignored the bargain and listened to Leah	Gen 30:14–17

---

36. Scullion, *Genesis: A Commentary*, 217.

Work Activity	Suggested Modern Equivalent	Strategy	Outcome	Reference
Rachel tries to secure inheritance by stealing Laban's gods.	Look after self interest	Hide father's gods	Risked her own life	Gen 31:14-16, 26-35

Whereas Rebekah entered the patriarchal lives caring for the animals of Abraham's servant, Jacob is the willing servant of the woman he wishes to marry. This foreshadows the role Jacob will play in Laban's household.[37] It subtly hints that the women of this household are not an unmitigated blessing. However, like her aunt Rebekah, Rachel was used to hard work, and was the shepherdess in the family. There is no indication what role Leah played in the family economy.

The lives of these sisters demonstrate the tragic results of competition and a truncated, purely financial approach to life. The commercial transaction is so characteristic of these sisters that they even trade with each other for sex with their husband (Gen 30:14–18). Leah must have been a willing party to the marriage deception, and although her strategy procured a husband (and a job) it produced no joy. Her deception may have been poetic justice for Jacob the deceiver of his brother and father, but it intensified the family disease. Her sons grew up to be weak (Reuben, Gen 35:22), cruel (Simeon and Levi, Gen 34:25–29, Judah, Gen 37:26–27), or indifferent to the suffering of others (Issachar and Zebulun, Gen 37:19–20, 25). Whilst both these women were eventually successful in having children, and enjoyed the material benefits of an energetic husband, business activity dominated their existence (Gen 30:14–18). However, their strategy of giving their servant girls as concubines for Jacob to produce more children on their behalf does not seem to have added further misery to the household (Gen 30:39). Perhaps the family was so miserable it was not possible to make it more so.

The only time the sister-wives are recorded as agreeing is when they leave their father, and predictably their only concern at this time is once again a commercial one: their lack of inheritance from their father (Gen 31:14–16). Note in the table above, Rachel's action in stealing the images of her father's household gods may indicate the commercial objective to eventually lay

---

37. Mathews, *Genesis 11:27—50:26*, 455.

claim to his inheritance.[38] She unwittingly risked her life in this futile attempt to gain further wealth (Gen 31:30–35). Her action also suggests she may not have been fully committed to the God of her husband Jacob.

Children's Names Indicate no Love just Competition

The life of this family cannot be described as blessed. The narrator attributes Leah's fertility to God's activity, and Leah recognized this, but her concern was the lack of her husband's love, not appreciation of God's blessing (Gen 29:31–35). Not until the birth of her fourth son, Judah, does she thank God, saying, "*This time* [emphasis supplied] I will praise the Lord" (Gen 29:35). With the exception of Judah, none of the names she gave her sons reflect gratitude to God. They are called "See a son" (Reuben), "Heard" (Simeon), "Attached" (Levi), "Praise" (Judah), "Wages" (Issachar), and "Dwelling or honor" (Zebulon),[39] all the cries of an unloved and commercially minded woman, but hardly a God-trusting one. Strangely, it is only with the birth of her maid Zilpah's children that Leah starts to think of blessing in her life. Asher is so named because, Leah, not his birth mother Zilpah, says, "Women will call me blessed, or happy" (Gen 30:13). There is a significant lack of reference to her husband. Leah called Zilpah's first son Gad, a troop (Gen 30:11), with clearly triumphant, enumerative commercial connotations.

The children born to Rachel's maid Bilhah also reflect the intense rivalry between the sisters. They are called "Judged" and "Wrestled" (Gen 30:5–7). But finally "God remembers and God hears" Rachel (Gen 30:22), and she too conceived a son. She recognized God's hand in her conception, naming him Joseph, "God adds" (Gen 30:22–24), as she announced triumphantly (no doubt with the sisterly rivalry still in her mind) "The Lord shall *add* to me another son!" But there is no mention of God in her mortal agony at the birth of Benjamin (Gen 35:16–20), and Jacob, by renaming the baby, brusquely overturns her pathetic name for this son, from Benoni to Benjamin (Gen 35:18). Whilst Rachel's death giving birth to Benjamin is recorded (Gen 35:16–20) and Jacob later describes with pathos his loss of her (Gen 48:7), Leah merely appears to disappear from the record. Not until Jacob faces his own death does he casually mention that she happens to be buried with the rest of the ancestors (Gen 49:29–31).

---

38. The Nuzi tablets suggest possession of these gods strengthened claim to inheritance, Kidner, *Genesis*, 165.

39. Mathews, *Genesis 11:27—50:26*, 480–85.

Although Rachel and Leah formed an important part in producing heirs for the patriarchal family, their lives were made bitter by the competitive attitude they each had. This bore tragic fruit in the lives of their children. There is nothing to indicate that their lives moved beyond this raw rivalry and focus on financial interest, and they serve primarily as examples of the misery caused by lack of trust, and the destroyed relationship that results from deceit and competition in any home and work situation. They, with their father Laban, displayed a Tower culture mentality, and this is supported by reference to the chiastic structure of the Genesis story.

Jacob's Children

As the Genesis story moves towards its conclusion, violent episodes and ungodly behavior are encountered. This is no surpise given the misery in the family. The chiastic structure of Genesis illuminates the god-expelled aspect of this situation. The sons of Leah are the leaders in this behavior. Their conduct echoes the violence of the antediluvians, yet they are the "seed" of Abraham, and ostensibly under the covenant of blessing promised their great-grandfather. They were either totally ignorant or rebellious, or mistaken in their understanding of their role in carrying out the command to be a blessing.

Massacre of the City of Hamor and Shechem

Dinah's visit to the women of the land appears innocent (Gen 34:1), but its results were dire. Shechem, one of the local lads saw her, seized her, and raped her[40] (Gen 34:2). But if his methods were rough and violent, his intention became worthy and he decided to marry her. Her brothers were furious (Gen 34:7), but they bided their time while the wedding negotiations were underway, even offering (deviously) the apparently legitimizing demand to have Shechem and the males of his city circumcised so he could be accepted as a prospective groom (Gen 34:13–15).

Shechem and his father Hamor agreed, but on the third day when the men were still recovering from their surgery, Simeon and Levi massacred and looted the entire city (Gen 34:25–29). "Their moral indignation

---

40. Some have labeled this pericope, "The Rape of Shechem," see Coats, *Genesis with an Introduction*, 233. Quoted in Gonzalez, *Where Sin Abounds*, 207. However, there is sound exegetical evidence that Dinah was raped, see Davidson, R., *Flame of Yahweh*, 512–18.

turns to Lamech-like [antediluvian] revenge."[41] Throughout this dreadful violence Jacob is passive, apparently afraid of consequences (Gen 34:5, 30). The brothers however, clearly think they are doing the right thing, and are upholding "virtuous" behavior. They respond to their frightened father's remonstrance with, "Should he treat our sister like a prostitute?" (Gen 34:31). Like Abraham with Abimelech, reliance on their own perceptions of the attitudes of the people of the land caused their dreadfully wrong response.

Reuben's Incest

Reuben, the eldest, had sexual intercourse with Bilhah his stepmother, but remarkably, Jacob did nothing (Gen 35:22). Reuben's offense occurred after the death of Rachel, and may have been Reuben's way of striking back at his father for favoritism against his mother.[42] More likely it could be regarded as a power play against his father's leadership.[43] Whatever the reasons, the family was losing all sense of decency and moving towards antediluvian-style violence and anarchy.

Violent Envy

Joseph, the second-youngest son, was singled out for special favor by his unwise father (Gen 37:3-4). Joseph, equally unwise, and possibly a spoilt teenager,[44] shares some dreams, and caused the hatred in the family to escalate (Gen 37:5-11). Sibling rivalry is not new in Genesis, but nine of the brothers, led by Judah, revenge themselves in a spectacularly horrific way. Only Reuben seemed to have pity (Gen 37:21-22). After planning murder, Judah proposed a profitable plan (echoes of Uncle Laban and certainly the family *modus operandi*) and, in one of the most violently appalling tales in the whole Bible, the brothers sold Joseph as a slave (Gen 37:18-28).

Perhaps the land was not filled with violence (Gen 6:11), but the family of Jacob certainly was. These men, born during the fractious years of sojourn with their greedy, conniving uncle Laban (Gen 29:31—30:1), and miserably fighting mothers (Gen 30:1, 14-15), one of whom was clearly unloved (Gen 29:31), had only self-serving role models. They were Laban's relatives, but without any pretense of his charm, or veneer of concern.

---

41. Waltke, *Genesis: A Commentary*, 460.
42. Gonzalez, *Where Sin Abounds*, 209.
43. Ibid., 209-10.
44. Cotter, *Genesis*, 290.

Judah

Despite his mother's praising God for his birth, Judah's first action in the narrative is to cruelly initiate the sale of his brother Joseph. This portrays him as a ruthless profiteer (Gen 37:26). His disregard for the fate of his younger brother is chilling in its brutality.

Following this pericope, the focus of Judah's attention becomes his Adullamite friend Hirah, their sheep-shearing and trading business, and the easing of his own lustful sensations (Gen 38:1, 12–18). He married the (significantly unnamed) daughter of the Canaanite Shua (Gen 38:1), echoing the primordial narrative's disregard for the worth of women.[45] The simple comment that his Canaanite wife named both their second and third sons, and "he was in Chezib[46] when she bore" their third child Shelah (Gen 38:4–5), suggests considerable lack of both husbandly and fatherly concern.

Alter showed how the Judah-Tamar episode contributes to the Joseph narrative,[47] but this does not help appreciate Judah as a character. Turner pointed out the temptation aspect of the verbs used in Gen 38:2—*r'h*, "saw," and *lqḥ*, "took"—are the same as those earlier used to describe the woman's taking the fruit (Gen 3:6), the sons of God cohabiting with the daughters of humans (6:2), Pharaoh taking Sarai into his harem (12:15), and Shechem's rape of Dinah (34:2).[48] Scullion suggested that Judah may have visited a temple prostitute (Gen 38:21–22), believing it would increase flock fertility.[49] Notably, the price Judah paid Tamar in exchange for sex, a goat, was not a good bargain and far in excess of the usual price, a loaf of bread.[50]

But as the sin and violence in the family reaches a peak, Judah confronted himself.

Tamar: Judah's Forgotten Woman

Tamar, chosen by Judah as a bride for his firstborn son Er, despite her being a Canaanite, was left a widow because of her husband's wickedness (Gen 38:6–7). The text gives no indication what that wickedness was. She was then passed like a commodity to Judah's second son Onan in the hope that

---

45. See section "the contribution of women" in the previous chapter.
46. Chezib has been identified with "lie and deceit," raising a question as to what Judah was actually doing there, Turner, *Genesis*, 165.
47. Alter, *Art of Biblical Literature*, 3–12.
48. Turner, *Genesis*, 2nd ed., 168.
49. Scullion, *Genesis: A Commentary*, 300.
50. See Proverbs 2:26, as noted in Turner, *Genesis*, 167.

with his help she would "raise up an heir" for her dead husband (Gen 38:8). True to grandfather Laban's values, and his father Judah's, Onan was not interested in anything not personally of benefit to himself, and was uncooperative in the "make an heir for brother" project that would deprive him, Onan, of the inheritance. For this selfishness he too died (Gen 38:9–10). Judah, now afraid that he would lose his only remaining son, Shelah, decided Tamar must be sent back to her family, and stay there till this third son Shelah reached maturity. But it is doubtful he intended further contact with her (Gen 38:11). By telling Tamar to wait for the third son, Judah did not give her permission to remarry, and condemned her to a bleak future.

Table 16: Judah's Work (with Tamar)

Work Activity	Suggested Modern Equivalent	Strategy	Outcome	Reference
Selling Joseph	Profitable but exploiting business, e.g., tobacco industry	Ruthless utilization of available market, the Midianites	20 shekels' profit (between 10 men!)	Gen 37:26–28
Producing sons and grandsons	Maintaining family business	Protect own interests, deny Tamar rights	Exposed, recognizes his own failings	Gen 38:1–26
Sheep breeder and shearer with Hiram	Business partnerships	Mix with crowd	Loss of moral standards	Gen 38:1–2, 12–13
Persuade father to allow Benjamin to go	Employment contract negotiation	Offer self as guarantor	Benjamin allowed to go	Gen 43:8–10, 13
Persuade Joseph to release Benjamin	International contract negotiation	Persuasive appeal	Benjamin released, family reunited and provided for	Gen 44:14–34
Leader in charge Egypt venture	Leader of any new venture	Utilize previous knowledge	Arrive safely in Egypt	Gen 46:28

On Judah's nameless wife who is left to bear and name children on her own, and on his callous disregard for his daughter-in-law Tamar's needs, a spotlight is focused on the situation of women in the patriarchal times. As noted in the previous chapter, although they could be desired for their good looks (Gen 12:11, 24:16), they were often valued simply for their ability to work hard.[51] Tamar, already twice-married, with limited chances of remarrying, was doomed to a life of hard work in her family, with no chance of the joy and social esteem a child could bring. The desperate measures she took to achieve a pregnancy strongly indicate her bleak future.

Tamar the widow is apparently trapped, without a future. Then she learned her father-in-law was to shear his sheep. Perhaps she knew any prostitute could attract Judah. Perhaps she knew he had been seduced by Canaanite idolatry, and would be interested in the services of a temple prostitute to enhance the fertility of his flock.[52] What is certain is her simple plan to change her clothes and sit in an open place looking like a harlot quickly attracted Judah's attention and gave her what she most wanted, a pregnancy. But she was smart enough to get evidence of the identity of the father of her illegitimate child (Gen 38:12–19).

Discovery of her illicit pregnancy appeared to give Judah a chance to rid himself of an unwanted responsibility, and in righteous indignation he ruthlessly ordered her to be burned (Gen 38:24). His shock must have been great when he discovered the cause of his daughter-in-law's pregnancy, and he was forced to admit, "She has been more righteous than I" (Gen 38:26). Zornberg suggested that when Judah recognized the pledges, it was "not simply his pledge to Tamar—the seal, the cord and staff that symbolized his authority. He recognized, in effect, himself."[53] Tamar's action confronted Judah with the reality of his own behavior, and the truth about himself. There is also the suggestion that Tamar is actually given a "double blessing," as she, like Rebekah, had not just one child, but twins (Gen 38:27–30).

The Transformation of Judah

If the Genesis narrative ended with the birth of Perez and Zerah (Gen 38:27–30), it would be reasonable to conclude that little had been gained by the dramatic call of Abraham. Judah was right, other people were indeed more righteous than he (Gen 38:26). The double *tôlēdôt* of the rejected Esau (Gen 36) suggests his descendants were living in stable community long

---

51. Bachmann, *Women at Work*.
52. Scullion, *Genesis: A Commentary*, 300.
53. Zornberg, *Beginning of Desire*, 277.

before the descendants of Jacob were. The Tamar-Judah narrative is not interpolated awkwardly into the Joseph story, but it is the culmination of the series of pericopes that reveal the patriarchs were no more successful in achieving blessing by their own knowledge and efforts than were the cursed people in the primordial narrative, as Gonzalez asserts.[54]

But Genesis ends with two more powerful narratives: the remarkable character transformation of Judah (and his brothers), and the totally unexpected social transformation of Joseph, from slave to chief minister of Egypt. When Judah next enters the narrative, his focused energy and attention were directed towards the good of others, especially his family. No longer is his focus personal gain.[55] His efforts to persuade first his father to let Benjamin go to Egypt, and then Joseph to let Benjamin return home, are models of diplomatic endeavor. His plea to Joseph to release Benjamin, in which he mentions his father a significant fourteen times, is the longest speech in Genesis, and "the finest specimen of dignified and persuasive eloquence in the Old Testament."[56]

Perhaps most significantly, as Reno noted, Judah, unlike Cain, finally shows he is willing to be his brother's keeper, even to the giving of himself.[57] The only other character in the Genesis narrative portrayed as making such a selfless sacrifice is his great-grandfather Abraham who was willing to give up his beloved Isaac (Gen 22:1–18). In revealing the heights of selflessness that Judah attained, the Genesis author justifies the inclusion of the sordid tales of his callous disinterest in his wife and children, and his moral failure with his daughter-in-law Tamar. The depths from which he had come underscore the magnitude of his development. The story of Judah "buttresses the central theme of the Joseph novel—God turns good from evil."[58]

Whilst Judah's contribution to the Genesis narrative is very great, it is important not to make Judah and Joseph compete for the principal role. Competition has no place in the concept of work being portrayed in the Genesis narratives. Both brothers were highly significant, but all brothers were important. Whilst Judah's life demonstrates blessing in action, Joseph's story clearly enunciates the principles involved.

---

54. Gonzalez, *Where Sin Abounds*, 2–8.

55. Cotter, *Genesis*, 316.

56. Skinner, *Critical and Exegetial Commentary*, quoted in Wenham, *Genesis 16–50*, 425.

57. Reno, *Genesis*, 281.

58. Arnold, *Genesis*, 329.

Summary

The narrative of Jacob is characterized by hard work, commercial contracts, and severely disrupted relationships. Although his father was the result of special blessing, and his parents' marriage founded on blessing, Jacob struggled to find blessing in his own life. His efforts to cheat his brother of blessing and then obtain blessing by his own hard work resulted in virtual slavery for himself and a family riddled with disrupted relationships. Despite little evidence of his trust in God, God did not abandon him, and he was eventually able to acknowledge that his material blessings came from God, and break away from his uncle's slavery.

His lifelong quest for blessing was granted with a work-reducing injury, suggesting the importance of respite from work. His unwise favoritism of his son Joseph continued the strife in his family, although this favoritism may have had some basis, given the immoral and cruel behavior of his other sons, and their unseemly concern for easy money when they sold Joseph into slavery. Jacob's life ended in comparative comfort when, under the specific blessing of God, he was the recipient of the blessings Joseph was able to offer in Egypt.

Other characters in the Jacob story illuminate important aspects of the Genesis portrayal of work. The acceptability of Laban's focus on personal profit at the expense of others is repudiated by direct intervention of God. God speaks to Laban and warns him not to harm Jacob (Gen 31:24). Laban's quarrelling and commercially minded daughters do not produce noble children for Jacob, but the narrative indicates that God overruled the work of their lives, and brought about good.

11

The Epiphany of Joseph, Genesis 37:1—50:26

ALTHOUGH THE STORY OF Jacob covers half the book of Genesis, the Joseph novella[1] that concludes it is the longest continuous narrative block.[2] The chiastic structure gives weight to the assertion that the novella demonstrates God's work to prosper humans in their work (Gen 39:2–5) and to overrule situations so as to bring blessing into their lives, and into the lives of those around them (Gen 45:5b). In the chiastic structure it has correspondence to opening chapters of Genesis, balancing the work of God performed in Creation, the importance of relationship, and demonstrating God's power to bless the least promising of situations. The focus is not on the skills and achievements of Joseph.

Codicil or Climax?

Like the Tower pericope, the Joseph narrative is carefully written. Some regard it as the best-constructed story in Hebrew literature.[3] Others claim it is the finest narrative in the Bible, and should be considered among the best literature ever written.[4] It is a dramatic rags-to-riches thriller, the ultimate success tale of someone overcoming horrifying intrigue. The elegant use of motifs connects the various parts of the story: dreams, of Joseph, of the prisoners, and of Pharaoh himself, and finally a dream for Jacob; clothing, whose

---

1. From a literary perspective the Joseph narrative is regarded as a novella, a stand-alone, tightly-constructed collection of episodes that make up a longer story, but this does not presuppose the work is fictional.

2. Brodie, *Genesis as Dialogue*, 5–11.

3. Reynaud, *Reading with New Eyes*, 94.

4. Arnold, *Genesis*, 351.

changes mark the highs and lows of the roller coaster story; pits, whether an empty cistern, a gaol, or even despair; deception and recognition; and money, the reward of work. Money is mentioned twenty times in the narrative, and Joseph was sold for twenty pieces of silver.[5] This intense use of motif suggests the author's intention was to impart a significant message. It is said the key to understanding the novella, and thus its message, is to recognize its construction.[6] The key to its meaning lies in recognizing the chiastic structure of the entire book of Genesis. Brodie suggested: "The Joseph story is not a special pearl, different from the rest of Genesis. Rather, it is of a piece with the book as a whole. It is Genesis breaking into full bloom, a blossoming that builds on all that precedes."[7]

God: The Lead Character in the Joseph Novella

Turner, noting the literary achievement of the novella, expressed concern about its apparent central character. "With the Joseph story, or more accurately the story of Joseph's family, we reach the most sustained, almost seamlessly constructed narrative block in Genesis. It is human activity, rather than the divine, that is the center of attention. God is present, though more often than not he is invoked by characters rather than being explicitly active. Yet, as if to underline the nature of the book, Joseph might be the most finely portrayed character in Genesis, but he is also the most enigmatic of all, more so even than Jacob."[8] This puzzle can be elucidated if it is recognized that Joseph is not the central character of the story. Despite the apparent focus on human activity, that is work, the narrative points steadily to the activity of God in a way that is highly enlightening for developing a theology of work.

Westermann considered Joseph was a "man of achievement,"[9] but noted another important aspect to this story: "Time and again, one is struck by the fact that most of the circumstances in this story could just as easily have taken place in our own modern day."[10] Because of this, the narrative has often been invested with contemporary work ethics and theology, those that focus on success and achievement. However, this popular

5. Waltke, *Genesis: A Commentary*, 541.
6. Reynaud, *Reading with New Eyes*, 95.
7. Brodie, *Genesis as Dialogue*, 351.
8. Turner, *Genesis*, 6.
9. Westermann, *Genesis 37–50*, 62.
10. Westermann, *Joseph: Studies*, vii.

rags-to-riches, prison-to-power image of the story can distort its theological concept of work and obscure its full import. Westermann also noted, "the Joseph narrative has found remarkably faint echo in the writings of the OT and the NT,"[11] suggesting its import may not have been fully appreciated even by Hebrew writers.

The Joseph story is not about human success, but about what God achieved working through a willing human whose life was blessed and who was used by God to bless others. In the chiastic structure it becomes the counterpart of the first four chapters of Genesis. While God is not reported as speaking directly to Joseph, there are numerous times when the narrator reports that God is with him, that it is God who enables him to succeed. In the Potiphar pericope, five times, within two verses, it is noted that God was with Joseph (Gen 39:2–3). Significantly, the text notes that "the Lord blessed the Egyptian's house for Joseph's sake" (Gen 39:5): the purpose of blessing Joseph was to spread blessing to others. Three times during his time in the prison the presence of God in his life is noted (Gen 39:21, 23), and Joseph blessed the butler and baker, and no doubt others, with his kindly attention.

Lest this success is the result of God's favoring Joseph, as his father Jacob had done, the text indicates Joseph centered his life on God and cared about others. Joseph was willing to go to any length, even risking the white-hot displeasure of his Egyptian master's wife, rather than "sin against God" (Gen 39:9). God is with Joseph because Joseph has chosen God, not because God was playing favorites. Joseph displays his commitment to God even in unfavorable circumstances, when he is a slave in the Egyptian dungeon and he informs two troubled fellow prisoners that it is only God who can interpret dreams (Gen 40:7–8).

Joseph the Outstanding Worker

The Joseph novella begins with work. "Joseph, being seventeen years old, was pasturing the flock with his brothers" (Gen 37:2), and notes the quality of work performed. "He was a boy with the sons of Bilhah and Zilpah, his father's wives. And Joseph brought a bad report of them to their father" (Gen 37:2). Cotter suggested that the pre-Egypt Joseph was a spoilt teenager,[12] and Turner noted the term used for the report, *dibbāh*, could mean a false or slanderous report (cf. Num 13:32, the report of the spies), indicating Joseph was slandering his brothers.[13] However, the report of the spies was true, although it emphasized the pessimistic aspects of the conquest of Canaan.

11. Westermann, *Genesis 37–50*, 252. The passages that mention Joseph are Ps 105:16–22; Acts 7:9–14; Heb 11:21–22.

12. Cotter, *Genesis*, 290.

13. Turner, *Genesis*, 159.

Moreover, the animosity of the brothers to Joseph was not triggered by this report, but rather by their father's favoritism and bestowal of the special coat (Gen 37:2-4). Thus from the beginning of the story, Joseph's work is favorably contrasted with the work of at least four of his brothers (Gen 30:3-13, 37:2). But he was also a member of the same severely flawed family that produced the sexually corrupt Reuben and Judah, and the cruel Simeon, Levi, and Judah.

As the story progresses, the other brothers are portrayed as focused on easy money rather than diligent work. The idea of making quick money by the sale of their brother to the Ishmaelites motivated them to send Joseph to slavery, although twenty pieces of silver divided between ten does not seem a very good bargain (Gen 37:26-28).

Joseph: Performance gives Credibility to his Favored Position.

Joseph's subsequent behavior gives credibility to Jacob's favoritism of his second youngest son. Whilst Jacob's partiality was a disastrous quality in a father, his ability to recognize the potential of this son shows considerable prescience. Joseph's response to Potiphar's wife contrasts favorably with the sexual behavior of two of his brothers, Reuben (Gen 35:22) and Judah (Gen 38).

Brodie noted with humor that Joseph cares for sheep, but Judah shears them (Gen 38:13).[14] Whilst not presupposing any superiority of one type of work over the other, this implies that Joseph was willing to do the basic shepherding and not just the profitable shearing. Thus Joseph the worker is contrasted favorably against the majority of his brothers, recognizing that Benjamin was not involved.

The situation the brothers used to remove Joseph from their lives was a work setting. Joseph seems cast in the role of supervisor or overseer (he is presented wearing his special coat which may have precluded physical work, Gen 37:23, and asked by his father to go and check what his brothers are doing). Jacob's words, "Go now, see if it is well with your brothers and with the flock and bring me word" (Gen 37:14), mean either concern for their personal safety, or for their work, or both. Shechem, the scene of the massacre of its inhabitants by Simeon and Levi (Gen 34:25-28), would give Jacob ample reason to be concerned for their physical welfare. The reader should also note the introduction of this place of violent deeds hints at violence to come.

---

14. Brodie, *Genesis as Dialogue*, 363.

Table 17: Joseph's Work

Work Activity	Suggested Modern Equivalent	Strategy	Outcome	Reference
Shepherd with brothers	Farm work	Report bearer ? Boasts about dreams	Brothers hate him	Gen 37:2–4
Sent to report on brothers	Inspector	Gather information	Sold to Egypt	Gen 37:12–28
Slave for Potiphar	Menial, low paid work,	Trust God and do best	Promotion	Gen 39:1
Overseer for Potiphar	CEO of corporation[15]	Continue to do best	Falsely accused	Gen 39:2–6
Prisoner	Unfair dismissal	Keep doing best	Promotion	Gen 39:20–23
Dream interpreter	Advisor/ Consultant	Acknowledged wisdom from God alone	Promotion	Gen 40:5–23, 41:1–43
Pharaoh's chief minister	Government administrator	Utilize all skills	Prevented national and international starvation crisis	Gen 41:37–57
Interrogate brothers	Police, judge, or magistrate	Use shock, scare, buddy, and bargaining tactics	All information needed obtained	Gen 42:1—44:17
Provide for father's family	Social service	Win official favor Ask family to relocate Utilize their skills	Family survives. Work as Pharaoh's chief herdsmen	Gen 45:17–20, 46:31–36

---

15. Cotter, *Genesis*, 291.

Joseph's Dreams Involve Work

Joseph's first dream includes work. All the brothers were in the field: "we were binding sheaves in the field" (Gen 37:5–8). Both this and the following dream about the sun, moon, and stars indicate the brothers would become subordinate to Joseph, but importantly, Joseph is portrayed as a worker.

The dreams Joseph interpreted in the prison were the dreams of workers about their work, their dreams hinting that their work may have been of questionable quality. Joseph's interpretations were simply about restoring (or otherwise) these men to their given work.

The dreams of Pharaoh that Joseph interpreted with dramatic results for his own working life involved the daily work situations of the Egyptian people. The implied divine involvement in the repetitious human work motif of all these dreams seems to be more than accidental.

Joseph the Successful Worker: The Narrator's Seven Declarations

When the narrative takes up Joseph's plight in Egypt he is a slave (worker). Given his previous portrayal as a "superior" worker it is no surprise that he is described as "a successful man" (Gen 39:2f.). What is surprising is that this success is not attributed to his hard, capable, or faithful work. Four times the reason for his success in Potiphar's house is stated as "the Lord was with Joseph," and seven times in the chapter (Gen 39:2, 3, 5, 21, 23). God was the cause of his success. It was the "Lord who caused all that he did to succeed in his hands" (Gen 39:3); moreover, Potiphar, blessed because of this, took note, and made Joseph overseer (Gen 39:6).

The family picture of Joseph may have been that of a superior but boastful worker, unwisely favored by his father. But the Egyptian picture of Joseph is clearly that of a man who enjoys the benefits of God's presence in his work. His success in Egypt is attributed entirely to God, nothing more, nothing less. Joseph is successful, but he is not a self-made man.[16]

God gave Joseph Success

Turner noted that much space is devoted to underlining that Yahweh was with Joseph.[17] It is only in chapter 39 of the Joseph novella that deity is

---

16. Reno, *Genesis*, 269.
17. Turner, *Genesis*, 172.

given the name of Yahweh.[18] This frequent mention of Yahweh God as the cause of Joseph's success clearly portrays God as the lead character of the novella. God was with Joseph in the particularly discouraging situations of his enslavement and later imprisonment, although this did not prevent apparent disaster. Somewhere, between the terror of being sold as a slave and becoming a slave, Joseph became a man so committed to God he could be blessed by God in everything. The preceding Genesis narrative indicates this is no accident. To be a person blessed by God requires commitment to God's way. The numerous examples of others who lost the blessing (Adam and Eve, Cain, Lot, Ishmael, Esau) or who suffered from erroneous choices (Abraham in Egypt, Sarai with Hagar, Isaac with Rebekah and Jacob and the birthright blessing) make the all-inclusive assessment of Potiphar regarding Joseph remarkable. His master saw that God made *everything* he did prosper (Gen 39:3). "He has only one resource to help him—the God of his fathers is with him . . . God's assistance has its effect on Joseph's bearing. He prospers his work. From this springs loyalty and responsibility . . . Joseph acquires a high degree of responsibility because of the success God confers on him."[19]

God's Success not Synonymous with Prosperity

The surprise of the narrative is that life does not continue straightforward for Joseph. The heady ascent from slave to overseer would underscore the statement that "God was with him" was true. At the height of this apparent success, Joseph publicly takes his stand on God's side (Gen 39:9), refuses the suggestions of his master's wife, and, losing everything, is sent to prison.

The text thus indicates that being blessed by God and prospering God's way is not synonymous with contemporary concepts of success. What makes Joseph successful is that God is with him even in prison (Gen 39:21), not that he is an achiever. The statements regarding the source of Joseph's success are made by the narrator, but when tempted by Potiphar's wife Joseph shows he recognized God was the source of his success, refusing her overtures on the ground that he would not sin against his God. This declaration brought him no reward, only demotion from slave to prisoner. Yet even in prison the narrator thrice reports: "the Lord was with him and whatever he did the Lord made it succeed" (Gen 39:21–23). This word succeed, *ṣlḥ*,

---

18. Humphries, *Joseph and His Family*, 131. This excludes the Judah pericope of ch. 38, where Yahweh is recorded as being responsible for the premature deaths of the two wicked sons of Judah.

19. Westermann, *Genesis 37–50*, 69.

was also used for the successful work of the faithful oldest servant of Abraham (Gen 24:42, 56).

God shows Loyalty

Humphries' translation of Gen 39:21 offers valuable insights into Joseph's relationship with God when Joseph is unjustifiably imprisoned: "Yahweh was with Joseph, and he extended to him loyalty, *ḥesed*, and he insured his favor in the eyes of the officer of the house of confinement." "Rarely in the entire Genesis narrative, is the very particular covenantal term *ḥesed* used . . . the term speaks of upholding one's end of a relationship."[20] The narrator thus indicates Joseph and God are working partners. Westermann suggested that the *ḥesed*, "grace, loyalty," that God extends to Joseph is not presented as an attribute of God, but, significantly, as a "description of God's activity."[21] "Because the Lord was with him; and whatever he did the Lord made it (*ṣlḥ*) prosper" (Gen 39:23). Prosper is the last word of this passage in both Hebrew and English.[22] God prospers Joseph because Joseph has chosen to work with God.

Joseph Acknowledges the Power of God

Josephs' own appreciation of God's help is apparent when he has opportunity to claim recognition in his own right. His chance comes from his own attention to detail: he noticed the butler and baker were troubled (Gen 40:6). Westermann regarded this interest in others as an important indicator of Joseph's general caring attitude.[23] However, it is not clear whether this is due to his being a generally kindly person, or to the presence of God being with him. Later events might suggest it was primarily due to God's presence with him. However, an appreciation of this innate or God-given kindliness of Joseph is important when trying to comprehend the extraordinary events that later occur between him and his brothers.

When asked to interpret dreams, whether for two prisoners in gaol or for the Pharaoh of the land, Joseph declares he can do this only by the power of God (Gen 40:8, 41:16). The first people whose dreams Joseph interprets

---

20. Humphries, *Character of God*, 210–11. The term *ḥesed* is found in the request for a covenant between Abraham and Abimelech (Gen 21:23), Clines, *Concise Dictionary*, 126.
21. Westermann, *Joseph: Studies*, 30.
22. Arnold, *Genesis*, 333.
23. Westermann, *Joseph: Studies*, 37.

are workers, ordinary palace staff, and their presence in the prison is a reference to the quality of their work. The unfortunate baker would have been a highly skilled man. Plaut noted that Egyptian cuisine had fifty-seven varieties of bread and thirty-eight known cakes.[24] But lest the arrival of the butler and unfortunate baker be seen as opportunities for human action, the narrative has an important detail. Only once does Joseph try to "make" something happen for his own benefit, and in this he is signally unsuccessful. He asks the butler to remember him when he is released, but the butler does not (Gen 40:14–15, 23). Joseph spends two more years in jail. This is the nadir of Joseph's experience.[25] This simple detail serves to emphasize that humans do not make things happen, not even good and justifiable things. Joseph's longing to leave the prison was clearly appropriate, but it was not his personal efforts that achieved this.

Kidner pointed out that Joseph's first word to Pharaoh, an exclamation, "It is not in me!" is one word in the Hebrew.[26] "I can't do it!" "Not I!" (Gen 41:16) is his blunt response to the most powerful of kings, but he adds, God, *'Elohim*, can. The king is impressed and tells his dreams. These dreams involve the ordinary farming work of Egypt, grain growing and animal husbandry. Following his interpretation, Joseph offers a workable solution to the threatened disaster. Pharaoh, impressed with his astuteness, appoints Joseph on the spot. Whether Pharaoh and his servants recognized exactly which god gave the interpretation and the advice is not clear, but he certainly considered both divinely inspired (Gen 41:37–38), and the term they use, *ruaḥ 'Elohim*, indicates it is Joseph's God to whom they attribute his success in both interpretation and advice. Joseph clearly stated that dream interpretation came only from God (Gen 40:8, 41:16, 25). Although he did not state the practical political suggestions also came from God, at least Pharaoh seems to think so:[27] "Inasmuch as God has shown you all this" (Gen 41:39). Thus Joseph's dramatic rise to a senior position in Egyptian civil service is attributed entirely to the presence of God being with him.

Joseph the Contemporary-type Worker

For the next nine (and no doubt fourteen) years Joseph was very busy. The text bristles with the verbs of Joseph's activity, as highlighted. "Joseph was thirty years old when he *entered the service* of Pharaoh king of Egypt. And

24. Plaut, *Torah: Modern Commentary; Genesis*, 384.
25. Turner, *Genesis*, 174.
26. Kidner, *Genesis*, 195.
27. Turner, *Genesis*, 176.

Joseph *went out* from the presence of Pharaoh and *went through* all the land of Egypt. During the seven plentiful years the earth produced abundantly, and he *gathered up* all the food of those years, which occurred in the land of Egypt, and *put* the food in the cities. He *put in* every city food from the fields around it. And Joseph *stored up* grain in great abundance, like the sand of the sea, until he *ceased to measure* it, for it *could not be measured*" (Gen 41:46–49). Joseph did not sit in his palace office and give orders; he went through all the land collecting the grain (without modern transport), or at least ensuring it was collected. He was a very busy man.

Westermann observed "This [chap 41] is a peculiarly modern chapter . . . stating clearly that in certain situations the gift of blessing must be supplemented by a well-thought-out policy which can only be administered by a central authority . . ."[28] This statement affirms Joseph's activity, but it reflects a dubious contemporary appreciation of policies, strategies, guidelines, and procedures which block out a perceived need for God to give success. There is no reason to doubt the policy Joseph applied was an astute one, and Joseph's work most worthwhile. But the absence of any affirmation that God was giving him success at this time of his life is disquieting, although it reflects contemporary thinking to attribute success to personal human effort.

God Acknowledged only Twice

In all this busyness after Joseph is installed as governor, God is mentioned only twice in chapter 41.[29] Both those occasions refer to his private life, to the birth of his boys, and significantly not to his successful career. Although Judah's Canaanite wife was unnamed in the manner of the inconsequential primordial women, Joseph's Egyptian wife Asenath is named twice, and her noble connections with the Egyptian priesthood identified (Gen 41:45, 50). The name of one son expresses Joseph's relief at being able to forget his unhappy family connections, which amnesis Joseph attributes to God (Gen 41:51). Turner noted Joseph made no attempt to contact his family of origin, even though as a successful courtier he could probably easily have done so.[30] The other son's name expresses gratitude that his family is growing. Perhaps

---

28. Westermann, *Genesis 37–50*, 98.

29. This is clear in the Hebrew and is reflected in all translations, but especially clear in the very literal translation of Alter, *Genesis: Translation and Commentary*, 241–43.

30. Turner, *Genesis*, 178.

this reference to God in the family setting reinforces the importance of family making.

However, nothing is said about God being with him or making him successful as an Egyptian official. Although Westermann suggested, "In this entire narrative there is not even the faintest reflection of the Egyptian cult,"[31] this silence regarding the presence of God in his working life during these years is disquieting. The contrast between the frequent assertions that God was with him during his years of slavery and imprisonment is stark. Joseph may still believe in God, but his awareness of the presence of God seems to have retreated to the background.

Enslaving the Egyptians: Joseph's Flaws

As the famine progressed in Egypt, there was the issue of Joseph's enslaving the Egyptians in exchange for their buying food (Gen 47:13–26). Plaut suggested that Joseph was very fair in the demands he made on the Egyptians, and that a rental payment of one fifth to the king was very modest, for under Syrian rule the Jews paid the king no less than one third of their seed, and one half of their fruits.[32] It appears that although Pharaoh took Joseph's interpretation of the dreams seriously, and made provision for the famine, the people of Egypt did not. But to agree to enslave them in perpetuity seems severe, because these people had been free citizens of the country prior to the famine, paying no rental at all. It is possible this action attributed to Joseph was simply the application of a general Egyptian policy, but it may have planted seeds for the future resentment of Hebrews and their own ultimate enslavement. Westermann's recognition that Joseph does not seem to have been idolized by the Hebrew people suggests they may have been suspicious that he paved the way for their slavery.[33]

Whatever the reason, the application of this policy, together with the suggestion of his youthful boasting, and his natural but failed attempt to get out of the prison, offer enough evidence to indicate Joseph was a normal, flawed human, an important consideration when he is unexpectedly confronted with his brothers. It also emphasizes that Joseph's achievements were not due to his inate ability, or that everything he did was working with God.

---

31. Westermann, *Joseph: Studies*, 39.
32. Plaut, *Torah: Modern Commentary; Genesis*, 452, f.n.
33. Westermann, *Genesis 37–50*, 252.

Joseph takes Center Stage

When Joseph was salvaged from the prison to appear before Pharaoh, he was quick to restrain any attempt to attribute his ability to interpret dreams to personal talent, and acknowledged God as the sole agent capable of doing this (Gen 41:16). But now, as he rushes around collecting grain, events are attributed to Joseph. As the predicted famine takes effect, they are known as "the seven years of famine . . . as *Joseph* [emphasis supplied] had said" (Gen 41:53). The solution to these disastrous events is Joseph: "When all the land of Egypt was famished, the people cried to Pharaoh for bread. Pharaoh said to all the Egyptians, '*Go to Joseph*. What *he* says to you, do'" (Gen 41:55). "Moreover, *all the earth came to Egypt* to *Joseph* to buy grain [all emphases supplied]" (Gen 41:57).

Joseph, it seems, is now the central character. And God is forgotten.

Joseph the Governor of the Land

But as this national champion struts around his appreciative kingdom, there enter from the sidelines ten specters from his past, bowing to the ground. The ancient dreams are about to be spectacularly fulfilled (Gen 42:6). The narrator stresses at this point Joseph's position of power and control: "Now Joseph was governor over the land. He was the one who sold to all the people of the land" (Gen 42:6). Joseph was in charge. Joseph was busy. Yet there is some contradiction in this statement. How could Joseph be both governor of the land, and the servant shopkeeper selling bushels of grain? Earlier, we are told that Joseph put grain in every city (Gen 41:48b). Obviously he could not personally be in every place at once. Joyce Baldwin observed pertinently: "Though there was grain to be bought in every part of Egypt, and Joseph could not have superintended every sale, *it so happened* [emphasis supplied] that these foreigners arrived at the main supply base, where Joseph was in charge."[34] Perhaps all foreigners coming to Egypt to buy grain were sent to the head office. Even so, it seems unlikely that Joseph was superintending all sales. This apparent chance meeting must be seen as more than coincidental.

Immediately Joseph recognized his brothers, but "he treated them like strangers and spoke roughly to them" (Gen 42:7a). The next verse repeats the fact that Joseph recognized his brothers, but adds they did not recognize him. Repetitions are always significant in Hebrew literature, establishing an important fact. Joseph knew, but they did not. The man who was kind to a

---

34. Baldwin, *Message of Genesis 12–50*, 179.

pair of despondent prisoners now speaks anything but kindly to the men he knows are his brothers. Moreover, he remembered his dreams (Gen 42:9).

The Tortured Joseph

Although recognizing that most commentators interpret Joseph's behavior towards his brothers as testing them, Turner noted the text records that his behavior is connected with his remembering his dreams.[35] Certainly, these men bowing before Joseph with their faces to the ground (Gen 42:6) must have brought him powerful reminders of those ridiculed dreams of long ago. But whereas Turner saw Joseph's subsequent behavior resulting from his desire to see the dreams fulfilled (including obtaining parental obeisance), and he regarded Joseph as being as vindictive as his former mistress, the wife of Potiphar, it is plausible that the memory of the dreams catapulted him back to his gladly forgotten past (note the name of his first born son) and caused a severe identity crisis. He was shocked, and had great inner uncertainty[36] and inner conflict.[37] Plaut suggested, agreeing with Turner, that he may want revenge more than he desired love.[38]

What is certain is that Joseph now has it within his power to make those youthful dreams come true in a chillingly dreadful reality. All the power and grandeur of his Egyptian position would be as nothing if only he could get these grovelling brothers to not only acknowledge who he is, but pay for what they had done to him.

So, it must be asked, why did he not reveal himself to them immediately? This seems to be what the memory of the dream would call for. Certainly the brothers were being tested by Joseph, and tested where their weakness had previously lain. It is of significance that between Gen 42:25 and 45:22, silver is mentioned twenty times.[39] The brothers had previously put more value on money than on life itself,[40] and Joseph had been sold for twenty pieces of silver, so this repetition of money highlights the commercial interest of the family in general and the brothers in particular. The testing strongly focuses on the commercial interest of the brothers.

---

35. Turner, *Genesis*, 187.
36. Reno, *Genesis*, 275.
37. Plaut, *Torah: Modern Commentary; Genesis*, 407.
38. Ibid.
39. Waltke, *Genesis: A Commentary*, 541.
40. Sternberg, *Poetics of Biblical Narrative*, 293–94. Noted also in Waltke, *Genesis: A Commentary*, 548.

However, it could also be suggested that Joseph is going through a severe struggle. His original dreams spoke of his own coming to power, of his own achievement, but offered nothing to suggest by what means this would be achieved. Now he must acknowledge that actually nothing he has done caused those dreams to come true, and nothing his cruel brothers did stopped the dreams from being fulfilled.

Perhaps the most revealing incident is one Turner pointed out. Joseph swears, twice, by the life of Pharaoh (Gen 42:15–16), something no other Hebrew ever does.[41] This is the equivalent of a denial of both himself and *Yahweh Elohim*, the God who gave him success. At this point Joseph is a very troubled and divided person.

Joseph's Temptation

The situation is reminiscent of the Genesis 3 temptation. Recognizing the chiastic structure of the Genesis narrative, a situation of significant testing becomes likely as the book nears its conclusion. The test has generally been seen as Joseph testing his brothers. However, the contemplated fratricide of Genesis 37 is reminiscent of the Cain-Abel tragedy, and therefore an Eden-style temptation episode is more likely after this point in the narrative. Genesis 38 offered a sexual "temptation" situation, but here the protagonist Judah did not come through favorably. Joseph was tempted sexually by his mistress, and passes that test (Gen 39:6–10). The literary structure of Genesis is too sophisticated for the narrative line to be suppressed for technique, but, as has been asserted, Genesis concludes in a manner that reflects its opening. Thus a testing not merely of moral integrity or fraternal love is likely, but most important of all, a test of commitment and loyalty to God.

Earlier in the narrative, Joseph is shown capable of impressive levelheaded thinking. His first encounter with Pharaoh and the advice offered is a masterpiece of wise, logical planning. His encounter with his seductive master's wife shows strong-minded commitment to the path of duty. But his "testing" of his brothers demonstrates completely random and illogical thinking. Although his behavior towards them perhaps becomes more logical (though vindictive) as the narrative progresses, at first it is presented as very jumbled. He says, "Send one of you . . . and bring your brother . . . you remain confined," and then puts them all in custody for three days. Finally he keeps just one brother in custody and sends all the rest back (Gen 42:16–20). His episodes of weeping are further evidence that he is not in good control of himself (Gen 42:24, 43:30).

---

41. Turner, *Genesis*, 180.

Joseph is confronted with a choice: either he will acknowledge God as the source of all his prosperity and power, the one who enabled his work to prosper, even as governor of Egypt, or he will see himself as the deserving recipient of this power to be used how he, Joseph, best thinks fit. He can either accept the groveling subservience of his brothers as his rightful due (remembering his dreams), or he can recognize God's sovereignty in overruling all that has happened to him. He gives himself a long time to think about it, several months at least, between the two visits of his brothers.

Judah: The Witness of a Transformed Life

Judah, as noted in the last chapter, is an unlikely protagonist for good. As the fourth son of the unloved Leah, his was hardly a favorable beginning, even if his name does mean praise (Gen 29:31–35). He entered the Joseph novella as the cruel instigator of the sale of his brother for a few paltry pieces of silver (Gen 37:26). His part in the Tamar pericope indicates that whereas Joseph passed a severe sexual temptation when he encountered his lascivious mistress, Judah did not come through with flying colors when he was sexually tested. Judah is portrayed as being firmly in the wrong camp.

But Judah made one revealing comment. Confronted with the truth about his own role in the sordid mess concerning his daughter-in-law turned prostitute, after self-righteously threatening to burn her for her promiscuous behavior, he exclaims, "She is more righteous than I" (Gen 38:26). This intimates the beginning of a new way of thinking.

Now, when the whole family is under the threats of the demanding governor of Egypt, Judah offers himself to his father as surety for Benjamin's safety (Gen 43:9). Reuben's offer for his own sons to be killed if he failed to provide for Benjamin's safety is both rash and unjust (Gen 42:37). Judah's selfless offer is presented with such rational conviction that even Jacob is persuaded to let Benjamin go (Gen 43:11). Judah has moved beyond focusing on his own needs, and recognizes "others." From his previously totally self-serving life he now indicates he understands the implications of the command "be a blessing."

When confronted with the belligerent governor of the land, Judah continued to be persuasive and convincing. Whilst he offered himself as a surety, he did not focus on his own needs. Judah remembered the father who shook with fear after his headstrong sons massacred the Shechemites

(Gen 34:30); who sank into comfortless grief at the loss of his son Joseph, for which they were all responsible (Gen 37:35); and no doubt the shame he himself caused by his behavior with his daughter-in-law Tamar (Gen 38). With everything he had, making the longest speech in Genesis, Judah pled for mercy towards this aging father, ending, "For how can I go back to my father if the boy is not with me? I fear to see the evil that would find my father" (Gen 44:34).

"Then," the Genesis text says, "Joseph could not control himself" (Gen 45:1).

Joseph's God Epiphany

Judah's speech successfully refocused Joseph's thinking from his personal suffering at the hands of his cruel brothers to his father's pain. Gone now were any further thoughts he may have had of revenge and injury to his brothers.[42] He is back to a God-focused and blessing-others mode. As he made himself known to his brothers, four times in rapid succession he averred that it was not them, nor himself, but God who brought events to pass.[43] "God sent me before you to preserve life . . . God sent me before you to preserve a posterity . . . God . . . has made me a father to Pharaoh . . . God has made me lord over all Egypt" (Gen 45:5-9).

There is no doubt that Judah played an important part in helping consolidate his brother's understanding and decision. But as Joseph stood, no doubt shocked at the change in this once cruel brother, he was reduced to tears by the realization of just how amazingly God had led in the lives of his family. Thus when Joseph finally revealed himself to his frightened brothers, the focus is not on Judah's speech, although Joseph first talks about his father (Gen 45:3). Joseph's words reflect thoughts that may have been slowly gathering in his brain for many months, perhaps since his first meeting with his siblings, but which finally have clarity. They tumble out in rapid succession. "God sent me before you . . . God sent me before you . . . it was not you who sent me here but God . . . God has made me lord of all Egypt" (Gen 45:5-9). Establishing the fact beyond all possible doubt, Joseph acknowledges God's activity in all the events of his life, including the painful times, and not merely the times of success.

Although Turner suggested that Joseph's assertion that God was involved in all the events of his life has all the hallmarks of an idea that has

---

42. Plaut, *Torah: Modern Commentary; Genesis*, 407.
43. Ibid., 423.

only now dawned on him,[44] and it is often asserted that Judah's speech reveals that the brothers have changed (which they certainly have), it is also likely the speech catalyzed Joseph's understanding.[45] Nowhere in the narrative is Joseph's behavior with his brothers explained. What is clear is that Joseph's approach to them changed; suddenly he stopped harassing them.

If Joseph had not had the insight that God had been working for the good of both himself and his family there would have been no reconciliation. There may have been no food for the family, had he allowed natural revengeful feelings to dictate his actions. Without Joseph's personal recognition of the centrality of the working of God in the family situation, the story would have had a very different outcome.

Joseph's Relationship Epiphany

When Joseph recognized that it was God who had overruled in all the events of his own and his family's lives, his response was more than merely to declare this. He immediately began to rebuild relationships with his brothers and the rest of his family (Gen 45:3). The importance of restored relationship is clearly a major theme of the Joseph narrative. Significantly however, relationships could not be restored until God was recognized as the chief performer in all their activities. This restoration of family relationship echoes the introduction of the marriage relationship in the creation pericope, and the "oneness" portrayed there. The rebuilding of these relationships took many years. It was not a single event. Seventeen years after the brothers first met again in Egypt there was still anxiety in their relationship. The brothers apparently attributed Joseph's kindness to them as due to their father who had favored him decades earlier (Gen 50:15–18). Perhaps because of his obvious political power the brothers did not trust Joseph. In spite of all he had done for the family, he was still just "the governor of the land." They were too afraid to even speak directly to him, and send a message purporting to be from their dead father (very manipulative), begging for forgiveness of their past wrongdoing (Gen 50:15–17). This time once again it was Joseph's understanding of the place of God in his life that enabled the family relationships to grow and develop (Gen 50:19–21).

When he received this message from his brothers Joseph again wept. He said, "Do not be afraid, for am I in the place of God?" (Gen 50:19). Moreover, he assured them that he was willing to be "his brother's keeper." "'Now therefore, do not be afraid; I will provide for you and your little ones.'

44. Turner, *Genesis*, 197.
45. Ibid.

And he comforted them and spoke kindly to them" (Gen 50:21). Whereas he had once spoken harshly to his brothers (Gen 42:7), now he spoke words of comfort. Joseph was a blessing not only to the hungry Egyptians, but also to his own family.

Unwavering Allegiance: Joseph's Seven Declarations

The last chapters of Genesis record that the family was brought safely to "the best of the land of Egypt" (Gen 45:18). Perhaps it is not *the* Promised Land, as Gonzalez complains,[46] but it was *a* promised land.[47]

The final dream of the narrative is given to Jacob to assure him that going to Egypt was the right thing to do. In this dream, God speaks directly for the first and only time in the Joseph novella, and has the final say in dreams (Gen 46:2–4). The message endorses the family is "walking" where God wants them to go.

In the last chapters of Genesis, Jacob, who had been searching for blessing all his life, now started dispensing blessing to others, first to Pharaoh (Gen 47:7), then to Joseph's sons (Gen 48), and finally to all his sons (Gen 49). The narrative has moved back to the blessing mode of the opening chapters of Genesis. Joseph is not presented as a plaster saint. His actions regarding the virtual enslavement of all the Egyptians in order for them to pay for food can be questioned. But his declarations recognizing God's sovereignty bring the Genesis narrative to a coherent conclusion.

Am I in the Place of God?

In the closing chapter of Genesis, Joseph reiterates that he attributes to God all his success and looks forward to the future with the same confidence. Importantly, he does not change his position from his former dramatic recognition that God was the great worker, the great planner and master of circumstances. Joseph declaims his own outstanding achievements and recognizes his power is limited when he says, "Am I in the place of God?" He reiterates three times his enduring conviction that God is working for his family, and will continue to do so in the future. "God meant it for good,"

---

46. Gonzalez, *Where Sin Abounds*, 256.

47. The Genesis text does not offer the fulfillment of God's blessing to Abram. This fulfillment even lies outside the Pentateuch Torah, and it is found only partially within the hexateuch.

he confidently states, later declaring, "God will visit you." Then to reinforce the concept he makes his brothers swear at his deathbed, "God will surely visit you, and you shall carry up my bones from here" (Gen 50:19–25). It is noticeable that Joseph is no longer swearing by Pharaoh.

When Joseph revealed himself to his brothers, four times he declared God had been responsible for working out an impressive plan for their salvation. Now he adds another three declarations that bring to seven his confidently stated assurance that God has and will work on behalf of his chosen family (Gen 45:5–9, 50:20, 24–26).

Genesis begins with a seven-part announcement of the creative work of God (Gen 1:1–31), and it ends with Joseph's seven-part declaration of his redeeming work in the life of Joseph and his family (Gen 44:5–9, 50:20, 24–26). There are seven declarations by the narrator that God is with Joseph when he began his career in Egypt (Gen 39:2–5, 21–23), and there are another seven by Joseph himself as the narrative comes to a close. God is clearly the lead character, the Master Worker, of the Joseph novella, and indeed of the entire book of Genesis.

Summary: Back to the Beginning

Genesis begins with a declaration that God worked on behalf of humans. The Joseph novella ends the Genesis narrative with a declaration that God still works in the lives of people. It indicates God works with anyone who will let him, whether a hard working Joseph or a dubious Judah.

But the Genesis narrative repeatedly demonstrates Turner's observation, that consistently throughout the book, when humans insist that they bring about promised blessings by their own efforts, the results end only in suffering and disaster.[48] Looking at it from another perspective, Baldwin states: "From the start the impetus towards salvation [in Genesis] comes, not from man, but from God."[49]

The Joseph narrative is a story of great contemporary relevance, especially chapter 41.[50] Joseph, the hard worker who achieves a rages-to-riches-and-power success story, is appealing to the contemporary psyche. The omission of God from the busy life of Joseph as he administered Egypt (Gen 41:41–57) also subtly reflects modern society. The power of the novella is that its successful protagonist finally recognizes not only his personal utter

---

48. Turner, *Genesis*, 201.
49. Baldwin, *Message of Genesis 12–50*, 222.
50. Westermann, *Genesis 37–50*, 98.

dependence on God, but that it is only through God that he has been instrumental in obtaining great blessing for his family.

Gonzalez's concern that the family is not in the Promised Land, and Joseph is left languishing in a coffin is reasonable, but he failed to understand that whilst the lesson may be over, the story is not. God still has work to do, of that Joseph is confident. "God will visit you and bring you out of this land to the land that he swore to Abraham, to Isaac, and to Jacob" (Gen 50:24). Creating good out of bad, of overruling the affairs of humanity, remains as much the prerogative of God as it was to create a world from chaos, which Genesis declares God alone did in the beginning (Gen 1:1). And Joseph endorses this with his powerful rejoinder, "Am I in the place of God?" The answer is clearly, "no."

12

Conclusions

A STUDY OF THE whole Genesis text offers a sound basis on which to develop a practical biblical theology of everyday human work. This theology can be called a "blessed relationship" theology of work; it asserts God is the source of all human benefit, and recipients of this benefit can share it with others. With God's blessing humans can relate beneficially to all God's creation, from the ground from which they were originally made, to the plants given for food, and the animals they were to enjoy and care for. Mutual benefit and blessing, not individual profit or achievement, should govern all work, and the relationships work always involves.

The Genesis narrative portrays at least five foundational aspects of a theology of work: God's pivotal creational and salvific work; work as part of human ontology; the inadequacy of human work without divine guidance; the dangerous potential for work to be the focus of hubris and thus the greatest source of human sin; and the need for humans to acknowledge God's blessing in their lives and relinquish claims to their own achievements.

The Chiastic Structure of Genesis

The theology of work emerging from Genesis is supported by the demonstrated chiastic structure of the book. This structure elucidates the theme of work in the narrative and indicates the focus of the book is on the work of God. But the center of the chiasm indicates how humans should respond to their own work, and to the relationships they encounter in their workplaces. The chiastic structure reveals the five pivotal aspects of work.

The Work of God

Genesis begins with God's work in creating the world, and ends with God rescuing, that is, saving, Jacob's family. In the first creation pericope, the prominence of speaking and pronouncement verbs gives a picture of God effortlessly speaking into existence whatever he chooses. This pericope portrays God's power, sovereignty, and infinite ability to achieve whatever plans he has, and ends with the institution of the Sabbath. The second creation pericope suggests God's application of effort, emphasizes relationship, and ends with the institution of marriage.

The third chapter indicates that God did not abandon the human couple after their rejection of his sovereignty, but continued to work actively on their behalf. The concluding Joseph novella of the Genesis story, with its dramatic slave-to-senior-civil-servant success plot, appeals to the contemporary work psyche. Yet both the narrator and Joseph attribute this success entirely to the intervention of God, each no less than seven times, refuting any assertion that Joseph's success can be attributed to his superior work performance.

God is revealed as the champion of the Joseph account as well as the central character of the creation pericopes. The story of Joseph does not highlight his personal achievement, but rather the power and blessing of God. Joseph's final words look forward to the continuing work of God on the behalf of his people: "God will surely visit you." The focus is entirely on trusting the work God will ultimately do for his people. At the heart of the Joseph story is relationship development, echoing the second creation pericope. When Joseph recognized his success was due to God's blessing he was able to rebuild the broken relationships in his family.

Work: Part of Original Human Ontology

Three passages in the first two chapters of Genesis indicate God intended to share the opportunities of work with humans (Gen 1:26–28, 2:5, 15–17). The gift of dominion, the term used to embrace the work lovingly given humanity, depended on, and was restrained by, the human choice for right relationship with their Sovereign God. God's instructions for human work (Gen 2:15–17) contain the basis for this relationship between God and the human race and indicates their dominion had limits.

The work given humans is described in terms of service, *'ābad* and *šāmar*, and by establishing one small restriction, humans were made aware that they were answerable to God for the use they made of the gift of dominion. Humans were made to relate to God (Gen 2:5, 3:8–9); to the ground and its plants (Gen 1:29, 2:15); to each other (Gen 1:26–28, 2:18, 21–24); and to the other creatures made by God (Gen 1:26–28, 2:19).

Despite their failure at the tree, humans were sent from the garden to work (Gen 3:23). Noah was given work to do (Gen 6:14–22). Abraham was called to be a blessing (Gen 12:1–3). God blessed the wide variety of Joseph's work.

The call of Abraham acts as a prototype for total commitment to God, and denotes that blessing is the manner in which God intends a called person to work. Abram's call promised abundant blessings from God, but Abram was also commanded to *be a blessing*. The Genesis text shows that Abraham and his immediate descendants struggled to understand this concept. They all tried to bring about promised blessings by pre-empting the revealed plans of God. Their efforts to do so invariably caused the blessing to be delayed and relationships to become distressed. Awareness of this can bring both encouragement and warning to followers of God. Importantly, Abraham's call brings a distinct change in the Genesis narrative, from the primordial narrative demonstrating curse on inadequate human work, to the blessing of working with God.

The Inadequacy of God-expelled Work

After the Fall, before the pronouncement of any curses, unaided human effort is shown as seriously inadequate. The choice of material, fig leaves, and style, a *ḥăgōrâ* (a belt or loincloth), were ineffective for clothing nakedness. God had to intervene to provide a *kutōnet* (a long shirt-like garment) for them (Gen 3:21), indicating that human work is not effective without the blessing of God. The subsequently pronounced curse, that both the man and the woman will experience *'iṣābôn*, "pain and toil," in their work confirms their struggle to work effectively. The work of humans has thus undergone significant change, from the initial co-operative partnership envisioned in Gen 2:5, to one of painful struggle.

All five curse situations in the primordial narrative impact human working conditions, and show the inadequacy of unaided human endeavor. The first curse was on the ground that humans needed to work to gain their food. The second curse was again on working the ground, following Cain's refusal to cooperate with God. The third curse was the Flood, caused by the violence of human activity. God considered human work was so bad that it was fit only for destruction. The enigmatic fourth curse unequivocally involves work, the slavery of unrelenting work that characterized the family of Ham. The Tower of Babel pericope recounts the fifth curse situation, and unambiguously presents hubris in work as the major sin issue.

Work's Dangerous Sin Potential

Perhaps God-expelled work's capability to cause hubris is the most sobering aspect of the study's findings: the primordial narrative's portrayal of work as potentially the source of humanity's greatest sin. Originally, sin was giving into the temptation that knowledge and ability could be obtained apart from the Creator God. A series of increasing sin situations, all of which involve working conditions, culminates in the Tower of Babel story, which clearly shows that humanity's hubris from its own work capability is self-worship, that is idolatry, the first sin defined in the Decalogue.

The people of Babel arrogantly believed that they could defy God and by their own work accomplish anything they chose. The pericope warns that to work in defiance of God is the most serious error. By destroying effective communication, God halted their ambitious work plans. The Tower narrative is the capstone of the primeval narrative, and it represents the human attitude that seeks to elevate itself above the authority of God, following the fatal train of Eve's desire for all knowledge, Cain's defiance, the antediluvian's corruption and violence, and the slavish work of Ham's descendants. It is no doubt because of this tendency for humans to take dangerous pride in their work that the fourth commandment asks them to refrain from work, and to remember and reflect on who is the source of their life, their power and their ability.

But the patriarchal narrative also carries a warning. Patriarchal efforts to bring about promised blessing by pre-empting the revealed plans of God invariably caused the blessing to be delayed and relationships to be distressed. Even when there is a sincere desire to be a blessing, God's people should not attempt to usurp his activity.

Acknowledging God: Relinquishing Achievement

The call of Abraham not only acts as a prototype of the call to total commitment to God, but also denotes that blessing is the manner in which God intends a called person to work. Abraham's call promised abundant blessing from God, but he was also commanded to *be a blessing*.

Yet the center of the chiastic structure of Genesis, Abraham's call to sacrifice Isaac, suggests the appropriate response of humans to their work. They must give up claims to personal achievement and self-actualization and recognize that all their achievements are due to the blessing of God. God asked Abraham to give up ownership of Isaac, who was clearly Abraham's greatest achievement. Once Abraham was willing to recognize who "owned" his son, then he was able to be the assured recipient of all the blessings promised him when he was first called to follow God.

Also highlighted at the center of the chiasm is the crucial importance of appreciating relationship in work. When humans were created they were intended to work in relationship, in loving interdependence, the husband and wife as *helpmeets*. Although Abraham did not initially appreciate the importance of Sarah's role in achieving the promised beginning of a great nation, ultimately, as he made preparations for her funeral, her value is clearly demonstrated. Sarah's funeral preparations are entirely the result of Abraham's appreciation of her. The Genesis theology of work is not only about God's people working to bless others, but also about recognizing the mutually beneficial nature of all work.

Corollaries to the Genesis Theology of Work

There are three important corollaries that emerge from the Genesis theology of work.

Co-laborers with God

Semantics can be difficult, but there is a significant difference between the biblical concept of being God's co-laborer, and the concept of being a co-creationist. The Bible presents *bārā'*, "to create," as an activity belonging to God alone. However, the contemporary English term "create" usually simply means make, with the aspect of initiation, the equivalent of the Hebrew *'āśâ*. It cannot be regarded as wrong to "create" a symphony, a piece of artwork, a productive garden or farm or a fine piece of machinery that will be a blessing to others. Humans know good and evil, and are capable of producing good. But what is essential is to recognize God as the source of all ability.

Being co-laborers with God however, has the important, indeed essential, aspect that presupposes work will be done in accordance with divine intention, and will result in the transmission of divine blessing. Only by performing work that is in accordance with God's plan and blessing can a person be said to be a co-laborer with God. Thus not all human work fulfills the divine plan.

Worship

Genesis shows the important connection between a person's work and what a person worships. The worship issues of sovereignty and allegiance became significant factors in the confrontation with the serpent, who suggested that doing things God's way restricted the potential of human ability. The relationship between work and idolization is shown in the pericope of the brothers Cain and Abel. Both come to worship and bring an offering, but one is accepted and the other not. The subsequent curse pronounced indicates Cain's approach to work was a significant factor in making his worship unacceptable. The sin pericopes of the primordial narrative culminate in a work situation that was intimately connected to a worship strategy: to reach heaven.

To walk with God (an ongoing activity) is the preferred Genesis portrayal of true worship. Enoch walked with God, Noah the same, Abraham is commanded to do so, and his call *lek ləkā*, "Go! Walk!" (repeated twice, Gen 12:1, 22:2), encapsulates this concept. Worship is a prominent feature of the patriarchal narratives, with the building of altars that witnessed to the patriarchs' allegiance to Yahweh God. The Genesis narrative indicates that the right approach to daily work is essential if an acceptable approach to worship is to be attained, and illuminates the reason why work and worship are coupled in the Decalogue.

Blessing and Eschatology

Miller and Bosch both suggest that mainstream Christian theologies of work presuppose a postmillennial or amillennial view of eschatology, with nothing to offer a premillennial eschatology. The blessing theology of work has no such difficulties. Confidant that God will perform his end-time work in his time, humans can focus on the Great Commission of sharing the Good News of Jesus, and work towards developing blessing in their communities.

The Great Commission of Jesus, to be witnesses to his saving power, is the greatest blessing that can be shared with others. But the God-ordained physical nature of humanity means that people need housing and clothing and feeding, and all activity in this physical area of life is valuable and a blessing to others. All efforts to bring physical blessing into the lives of family and fellow workers is appropriate groundwork to prepare people to receive the full blessing of acceptance of God's leadership in their lives, and to prepare themselves for the return of Jesus.

To work in blessing recognizes all blessing originates from God. Genesis presents human work as an invited opportunity from God for humans to join him to bring blessing to his created world while they wait for God to effect the ultimate salvation and transformation of the world.

Changing Christian Theologies of Work

However, throughout the two-thousand-year history of Christianity, theologies of work have undergone change. Although Christians have always been concerned that their theologies of work have a biblical base, the changes have primarily been driven by sociological and historical factors, with limited reference to biblical foundations.

Early Christian ideas on work were Jewish (which appreciated the physical world and ordinary work), but these were soon influenced by the dualism of Greek philosophy. This led to the penitential theology of work, considered to have a biblical base in the curses placed on humanity after their Fall in the Garden of Eden. At the Reformation, both Luther and Calvin recognized work was part of the original unfallen ontology of humans (Gen 2:15). Emphasis was placed on the idea of God's call to humans, but the concept of call, "vocation," became the basis for the so-called Protestant work ethic that led to an increasing emphasis on the material rewards of ordinary work. Contemporary Protestant theologies of work are exemplified by Volf's enunciation of a world transformed by work performed under the guidance of the Holy Spirit. The Roman Catholic theology of work has also undergone change, initiated by the 1891 encyclical, *Rerum Novarum*, of Pope Leo XIII, and now is the co-creational theology of work.

The Co-creation Theology of Human Work

The exposition of the doctrine of co-creation in Pope John Paul's *Laborem Exercens* is regarded by many as one of the most remarkable documents on human work. Its sensitivity to the needs of ordinary workers is commendable, and its attempt to establish its teachings from biblical material laudable. Its recognition of the importance of inter-human relationship in work situations means the encyclical has much to offer Christian theology.

But several concepts of the doctrine present difficulties. Of special concern is Hauerwas' allegation that the co-creation theology of work is potentially idolatrous. Furthermore, its biblical base has been recognized as inadequate, primarily three verses (Gen 1:26–28). Goosen, although sympathetic towards the doctrine, recognized it does not offer appreciation of maintenance activity such as that of a repair mechanic or street-sweeper. The implication in *Laborens Exercens* that God's declaration that the created world was very good and finished was, in fact, not true, implies that God's declarations cannot be trusted, which is worrying. The idea that human work will perfect the world is disquieting, as is the concept that *all* human work is co-creative. This study of Genesis refutes the conclusions of the doctrine of co-creation.

Transformational Theology of Work

Volf rejects a Genesis "protological" base for his theology of work because he rejects a "mere" maintenance concept of work, and considers that to work under the Holy Spirit allows new things. However, the transformational doctrine of human work also has difficulties: its denigration of maintenance work; the idea that human endeavor is essential to bring the world to a state of readiness before God can return; and the hint (probably unintentional) that the Holy Spirit is relegated to the role of human tool to accomplish human tasks.

Genesis clearly portrays the current human situation that this world is presently not in the very good state achieved at creation, and it indicates that God himself, and not human effort, will restore the human situation to the original state of perfect blessing. Significantly, Genesis portrays all human attempts to prematurely procure, achieve, or pass on blessing as doomed to delay the desired blessing and cause relational distress. However, while waiting for God to restore creation to its original state, humans, by working with God, are able to share blessing, but always from and under the oversight of God.

Practical Applications of the Blessing Model of Work

The blessing theology of work is radical. Its advocacy to return towards God's original plan for human work does not readily harmonize with contemporary approaches to work. But, the concepts are workable, and have the important advantage of eliminating the anxiety from work by removing the focus on achievement.

The significant aspect of work in blessing is its joyous God-and-others focused quality. To work in blessing invokes the important choice factor of attitude, and challenges current notions of reward and incentive. The world currently is far from its original "very good," and the Genesis account notes that unpleasant occupation can be forced upon a person: Joseph had no choice about being sold as a slave, or being sent to prison. But he did have a choice about his attitude, and his choices proved to be a blessing to himself and others.

Christian Attitudes and Organizations

Recognizing that not all current work situations are in accordance with God's plans means not all workplaces will apply the principles of blessing. But all Christians can apply them to their own lives and work situations. However, these approaches could be applied to Christian organizations, with useful implications. Attempts to implement these changes are likely to reveal how much these institutions have been following the norms of society rather than being shaped by Christian ideals and a biblical Christian theology of work.

A significant consequence would be a return to the Reformation principle of the value of all work roles, although not necessarily the static roles envisioned by Luther. The essential purpose of work is to be a blessing, which means there can be no hierarchy based on any other criteria. The blue-collar/white-collar workforce dichotomy is immediately shattered. The Reformation insight that all work is a vocation from God would be appreciated. The Genesis text notes that Joseph was given success, that is, he was a blessing, as an Egyptian slave and prisoner as well as when serving as chief minister in the land.

Current approaches to education would require major reassessment, with destructive competition being reduced, and students encouraged to discover their own abilities and to use them to benefit society. The goal of education would not be achievement and the attainment of financially beneficial employment, but rather to recognize and develop each person's potential to bless others.

Christian attitudes to retirement and unemployment would change. The increasing tendency for industrialized cultures to regard older people as a burden leads to anxiety about coping with an aging population. But when people are appreciated simply for their blessing, their worth is appreciated. Older people would not be measured as production units, but appreciated for the wisdom, support, and knowledge of history they offer their friends and families. These friends and families in return would regard it as an opportunity for blessing to allow older people to carry a lighter work burden in the community. Unemployed people would recognize that God calls everyone to be a blessing, and they have unique opportunities for exploring ways to bring blessing to their society. They would thus be encouraged to have better self-appreciation. The employed would realize that the idea of unemployment is unthinkable for it is not possible that a person has nothing to offer others. Society would be actively seeking to find ways to accept and appreciate the blessing all people can offer.

These suggestions are not a modified version of the current transformational theology. The world is recognized as being far from perfect, and the theology of blessing requires that God be recognized as the source and instigator of all change towards social perfection. Humans would work in blessing not to make something happen that they desire to achieve, but simply because God has blessed them and they desire to share that blessing with others.

A significant consequence of working in blessing is that it removes anxiety. There is no dogged resignation and blind submission to distressing situations, but every situation offers opportunity to demonstrate God's promise that he will bless, and that he can bring blessing out of the most discouraging circumstances.

Bibliography

Abate, Frank R., and Elizabeth Jewell. *The New Oxford American Dictionary*. New York: Oxford University Press, 2001.
Agrell, Göran. *Work, Toil and Sustenance*. Translated by Stephen Westerholm. Lund, SWE: Verbum-Håkan Ohlssons, 1976.
Aitken, James K. *The Semantics of Blessing and Cursing in Ancient Hebrew*. Ancient Near Eastern Studies. Louvain, BEL: Peeters, 2007.
Alexander, Philip S. "Pre-Emptive Exegesis: Genesis Rabba's Reading of the Story of Creation." *Journal of Jewish Studies* 43 (1992) 230–45.
Alter, Robert. *The Art of Biblical Narrative*. New York: Basic, 1981.
———. *Genesis: Translation and Commentary*. New York: W. W. Norton, 1996.
Aquinas, Thomas. *Summa Theologiae*. New York: Christian Classics, 1981.
Arendt, Hannah. *The Human Condition*. Chicago: University of Chicago Press, 1958.
Armstrong, Karen. *In the Beginning: A New Interpretation of Genesis*. New York: Ballantine, 1996.
Arnold, Bill T. *Genesis*. New Cambridge Bible Commentary. Edited by Ben Witherington III. Cambridge: Cambridge University Press, 2009.
Augustine. *The City of God*. Translated by Marcus Dodd. Peabody, MA: Henrickson, 2009.
———. *Confessions*. Translated by Albert C. Outler, edited by Tom Gill. Gainesville, FL: Bridge-Logos, 2003.
Bachmann, Mercedes L. Garcia. *Women at Work in the Deuteronomistic History*. Atlanta, GA: Scholars, 2013.
Baldwin, Joyce G. *The Message of Genesis 12–50: From Abraham to Joseph*. Edited by J. A. Motyer. Leicester, ENG: InterVarsity, 1986.
Barth, Karl. *Church Dogmatics*. Vol. 3, *The Doctrine of Creation, Part 1*. Translated by J. W. Edwards et al. Edinburgh: T & T Clark, 1958.
———. *Church Dogmatics*. Vol. 3, *The Doctrine of Creation, Part 4*. Edited by G. W. Bromley and T. F. Torrance. Edinburgh: T & T Clark, 1961.
Beal, Timothy. "Reception History and Beyond: Toward the Cultural History of Scriptures." *Biblical Interpretation* 19 (2011) 357–72.
Beckmann, David M. *Where Faith and Economics Meet: A Christian Critique*. Minneapolis, MN: Augsburg, 1982.
Ben Zvi, Ehud, et al. *Readings in Biblical Hebrew: An Intermediate Textbook*. New Haven, CT: Yale University Press, 1993.

Benedict. *The Rule of St Benedict*. Translated by Anthony C. Meisel and M. L. del Mastro. New York: Image, 1975.

———. "The Rule of St Benedict." In *Callings*, edited by William C. Placher, 128–32. Grand Rapids, MI: Eerdmans, 2005.

Bergsma, John Sietze, and Scott Walker Hahn. "Noah's Nakedness and the Curse on Canaan." *JBL* 124 (2005) 25–40.

Bernis, Jonathan. *A Rabbi Looks at Jesus of Nazareth*. Bloomington, IN: Chosen, 2011.

Blocher, Henri. *In the Beginning: The Opening Chapters of Genesis*. Translated by David G. Preston. Downers Grove, IL: InterVarsity, 1984.

Blustein, David L. *The Psychology of Working: A New Perspective for Career Development, Counseling, and Public Policy*. Mahwah, NJ: Lawrence Erlbaum Associates, 2006.

Borgman, Paul. *Genesis: The Story We haven't Heard*. Downers Grove, IL: InterVarsity, 2001.

Bosch, David J. *Transforming Mission: Paradigm Shifts in Theology of Mission*. Maryknoll, NY: Orbis, 1991.

Botterweck, G., and H. Ringgren, eds. *Theological Dictionary of the Old Testament*. Vol. 2. Grand Rapids, MI: Eerdmans, 1975.

Brichto, H. C. *The Names of God: Poetic Readings in Biblical Beginnings*. New York: Oxford University Press, 1998.

Brock, Brian. Review of *A Theology of Work: Work and the New Creation* and *The Heavenly Good of Earthly Work*, by Darrell Cosden. *EJT* 17 (2008) 93–94.

Brodie, Thomas L. *Genesis as Dialogue*. New York: Oxford University Press, 2001.

Brown, Raymond E., et al., eds. *Jerome Biblical Commentary*. London: Geoffery Chapman, 1969.

Brueggemann, Walter. *Genesis: A Biblical Commentary for Teaching and Preaching*. Atlanta, GA: John Knox, 1982.

———. Review of *The Curse of Cain: The Violent Legacy of Monotheism*, by Regina Schwartz. *Theology Today* 54 (1998) 534–36.

Brunner, Emil. *The Christian Doctrine of Creation and Redemption*. Translated by Olive Wyon. London: Lutterworth, 1952.

Calvin, John. *Genesis*. Edited by A. McGrath and J. I. Packer. Wheaton, IL: Crossway, 2001.

———. *Institutes of the Christian Religion*. 2 vols. Translated by L. Battles. Philadelphia, PA: Westminster, 1960.

Cannadine, David. *The Undivided Past: Humanity Beyond Our Differences*. New York: Alfred Knopf, 2013.

Carlyle, Thomas. *Past and Present*. Boston: Riverside, 1965.

Cassuto, Umberto. *A Commentary on the Book of Genesis (Part One): From Adam to Noah*. Translated by Israel Abrahams. Jerusalem: Magnes, 1961.

———. *A Commentary on the Book of Genesis (Part Two): From Noah to Abraham*. Translated by Israel Abrahams. Jerusalem: Magnes, 1964.

Chenu, M. D. *The Theology of Work: An Exploration*. Translated by Lillian Soiron. Dublin: Gill & Son, 1963.

Childs, Brevard S. *Biblical Theology of the Old and New Testaments*. Minneapolis, MN: Fortress, 1993.

Chisholm, Robert B. *From Exegesis to Exposition: A Practical Guide to Using Biblical Hebrew*. Grand Rapids, MI: Baker, 1998.

Chittick, William C. *The Sufi Doctrine of Rumi*. Bloomington, IN: World Wisdom, 2005.

Churchill, Winston S. *A History of the English-Speaking Peoples*. Vol. 2, *The New World*. London: Cassell, 1956.
Clements, K. W. *Faith on the Frontier: A Life of J. H. Oldham*. Edinburgh: T & T Clark, 1999.
Clines, David J. A., ed. *The Concise Dictionary of Classical Hebrew*. Sheffield, ENG: Sheffield Phoenix, 2009.
———. *The Theme of the Pentateuch*. Sheffield, ENG: JSOT, 1978.
Coats, George W. *Genesis with an Introduction to Narrative Literature*. Forms of the Old Testament Literature 1. Grand Rapids, MI: Eerdmens, 1983.
Collins, C. John. *Genesis 1–4: A Linguistic, Literary, and Theological Commentary*. Phillipsburg, NJ: P & R, 2006.
Cosden, Darrell. *The Heavenly Good of Earthly Work*. Milton Keynes, ENG: Paternoster, 2006.
———. *A Theology of Work: Work and the New Creation*. Carlisle, ENG: Paternoster, 2004.
———. "A Theology of Work." Unpublished notes. 2012.
Cotter, David W. *Genesis*. Berit Olam: Studies in Hebrew Narrative & Poetry. Collegeville, MN: Liturgical, 2003.
Dalley, Stephanie. *Myths from Mesopotamia*. New York: Oxford University Press, 1989. Reprint, 2008.
Davidsen, Ole. "The Mythical Foundation of History: A Religio-Semiotic Analysis of the Story of the Fall." *Zeichen und Realität* 51. Edited by Erhardt Guttgemanns. Bonn, DEU: Linguista Biblica Bonn, 1982.
Davidson, Ian. *Voltaire: A Life*. London: Profile, 2010.
Davidson, JoAnn. "Eschatology and Genesis 22." *JATS* 11 (2000) 232–47.
Davidson, Richard M. *The Flame of Yahweh: Sexuality in the Old Testament*. Peabody, MA: Hendrickson, 2007.
Davies, Gwyn. "Under Seige: The Roman Field Works at Masada." *Bulletin of the American Schools of Oriental Research* 362 (2011) 65–83.
Dorr, Luther M. *The Bivocational Pastor*. Nashville, TN: Broadman, 1988.
Doukhan, Jacques. "The Center of the Aqedah: A Study of the Literary Structure of Genesis 22:1–19." *Andrews University Seminary Studies* 31 (1993) 17–28.
———. *Ecclesiastes: All is Vanity*. Nampa, ID: Pacific, 2006.
Dover, Kenneth J. *Greek Popular Morality in the Time of Plato and Aristotle*. Berkeley, CA: University of California Press, 1974.
Dumbrell, W. J. *Covenant and Creation: A Theology of Old Testament Covenants*. Eugene, OR: Wipf & Stock, 2009.
———. *Search for Order: Biblical Eschatology in Focus*. Grand Rapids, MI: Baker, 1994.
Dunn, James D. G. "The Problem of Biblical Theology." In *Out of Egypt: Biblical Theology and Biblical Interpretation*, edited by Craig Bartholomew et al., 172–83. Milton Keynes, ENG: Paternoster, 2004.
Dybdahl, Jon L., ed. *Andrews Study Bible*. Berrien Springs, MI: Andrews University Press, 2010.
Ellis, Peter E. *The Yahwist: The Bible's First Theologian*. Notre Dame, IN: Fides, 1968.
Ellul, Jacques. *The Technological Society*. Translated by John Wilkinson. New York: Alfred A. Knopf, 1964.
Engels, Friedrich. "On the History of Early Christianity." In *Basic Writings on Politics and Philosophy*, edited by Lewis S. Feuer, 209–35. London: Collins, 1969.

Ferguson, Niall. *The Ascent of Money: A Financial History of the World.* London: Penguin, 2009.
Finkelstein, Jacob J. "An Old Babylonian Herding Contract and Genesis 31:38f." *JAOS* 88 (1968) 30–36.
Fishbane, M. *Biblical Interpretation in Ancient Israel.* Oxford: Clarendon, 1988.
———. "Composition and Structure in the Jacob Cycle (Gen 25:19—35:22)." *Journal of Jewish Studies* 26 (1975) 15–38.
Fretheim, Terence E. *God and World in the Old Testament: A Relational Theology of Creation.* Nashville, TN: Abingdon, 2005.
Garrett, D. A. *Rethinking Genesis: The Sources and Authorship of the First Book of the Pentateuch.* Grand Rapids, MI: Baker, 1991.
Gibson, John C. L. *Genesis.* Vol. 2. Philadelphia, PA: Westminster, 1982.
Giogetti, Andrew. "The 'Mock Building Account' of Genesis 11:1–9: Polemic against Mesopotamian Royal Ideology." *Vetus Testamentum* 64 (2014) 1–20.
Goldingay, John. *Old Testament Theology.* Vol. 1, *Israel's Gospel.* Downers Grove, IL: InterVarsity, 2003.
———. *Old Testament Theology.* Vol. 2, *Israel's Faith.* Downers Grove, IL: InterVarsity 2006.
———. *Old Testament Theology.* Vol. 3, *Israel's Life.* Downers Grove, IL: InterVarsity, 2009.
Goldingay, John, and Robert Innes. *God at Work.* Nottingham, ENG: Grove, 1994.
Gonzalez, Robert R. *Where Sin Abounds: The Spread of Sin and the Curse in Genesis with Special Focus on the Patriarchal Narratives.* Eugene, OR: Wipf & Stock, 2009.
Goosen, Gideon. *The Theology of Work.* Theology Today 22. Edited by Edward Yarnold. Hales Corner, WI: Clergy Service, 1974.
Goossen, Richard J., and R. Paul Stevens. *Entrepreneurial Leadership: Discovering Your Calling, Making a Difference.* Downers Grove, IL: InterVarsity, 2013.
Hafemann, Scott J. "The Covenant Relationship." In *Central Themes in Biblical Theology*, edited by S. J. Hafeman and P. R. House, 20–65. Nottingham, ENG: InterVarsity, 2007.
Hagner, Donald H. Review of *Matthew 8–20*, by Ulrich Luz. *JBL* 121 (2002) 766–69.
Hamilton, Victor P. *The Book of Genesis Chapters 1–17.* New International Commentary on the Old Testament. Grand Rapids, MI: Eerdmans, 1990.
Hardy, Lee. *The Fabric of This World: Inquiries into Calling, Career Choice, and the Design of Human Work.* Grand Rapids, MI: Eerdmans, 1990.
Harland, P. J. "Vertical or Horizontal: The Sin of Babel." *Vetus Testamentum* 48 (1998) 515–33.
Harrison, Peter. "Fill the Earth and Subdue it: Biblical Warrants for Colonization in Seventeenth Century England." *Journal of Religious History* 29 (2005) 3–24.
Hart, Ian. "Genesis 1:1—2:3 as a Prologue to the Book of Genesis." *Tyndale Bulletin* 46 (1995) 315–36.
———. "The Teaching of Luther and Calvin About Ordinary Work: 1. Martin Luther (1483-1546)." *The Evangelical Quarterly* 67 (1995) 35–52.
———. "The Teaching of Luther and Calvin About Ordinary Work: 2. John Calvin (1509–64)." *The Evangelical Quarterly* 67 (1995) 121–35.
———. "The Teaching of the Puritans About Ordinary Work." *The Evangelical Quarterly* 67 (1995) 195–209.
———. "A Theology of Every Day Work." Unpublished PhD thesis notes.

Hasel, Gerhard F. *Old Testament Theology: Basic Issues in the Curent Debate.* 4th ed. Grand Rapids, MI: Eerdmans, 1991.
Hauerwas, Stanley. "Work as Co-Creationism: A Critique of a Remarkably Bad Idea." In *Co-Creationism and Capitalism*, edited by J. W. Houck and O. F. Williams, 42–58. Lanham, MD: University Press of America, 1983.
Heatley, William G. *The Gift of Work: Spiritual Disciplines for the Workplace.* Colorado Springs, CO: NavPress, 2008.
Hegel, Georg. *Elements of the Philosophy of Right.* Cambridge Texts in the History of Political Thought. Edited by Allen W. Wood. Cambridge: Cambridge University Press, 1991.
Heiges, Donald. *The Christian's Calling.* Philadelphia, PA: Fortress, 1984.
Helyer, Larry R. "The Separation of Abram and Lot: Its Significance in the Patriarchal Narratives." *JSOT* 26 (1983) 77–88.
Heschel, Abraham Joshua. *The Sabbath.* New York: Farrar, Strauss & Giroux, 1951.
Hesiod. *Works and Days.* Translated by M. L. West. New York: Oxford University Press, 1998.
Hiebert, Theodore. "The Tower of Babel and the Origin of the World's Cultures." *JBL* 126 (2007) 29–58.
Holl, Karl. "History of the Word Vocation (Beruf)." *Review and Expositor* 55 (1958) 127–54.
Hollenbach, David. "Human Work and the Story of Creation: Theology and Ethics in Laborem Exerens." In *Co-Creation and Capitalism*, edited by J. W. Houck and O. F. Williams, 59–77. Lanham, MD: University Press of America, 1983.
Holmes, Arthur. *Building the Christian Academy.* Grand Rapids, MI: Eerdmans, 2001.
Homer. *The Iliad.* Translated by Martin Hammond. London: Penguin, 1987.
Horsley, Richard. "The Zealots: Their Origin, Relationships and Importance in Jewish Revolt." *Novum Testamentum* 28 (1986) 159–92.
Houck, John W., and Oliver F. Williams. *Co-Creation and Capitalism: John Paul II's Laborem Exercens.* Lanham, MD: University Press of America, 1983.
House, Paul R. "Examining the Narratives of Old Testament Narrative: An Exploration in Biblical Theology." *WTJ* 67 (2005) 229–45.
Humphries, W. Lee. *The Character of God in the Book of Genesis.* Louisville, KY: Westminster John Knox, 2001.
———. *Joseph and His Family: A Literary Study.* Columbia, SC: University of South Carolina Press, 1988.
Jensen, David H. *Responsive Labor: A Theology of Work.* Louisville, KY: Westminster John Knox, 2006.
John Paul II, Pope. *Dies Domini.* Strathfield, AUS: St Paul's, 1998.
———. *Laborem Exercens.* London: Catholic Truth Society, 1984.
Josephus, Flavius. *Wars of the Jews.* Translated by William Whiston. Grand Rapids, MI: Kregel, 1960.
Kaiser, Edwin G. *New Catholic Encyclopedia.* New York: MacGraw Hill, 1967.
———. *Theology of Work.* Westminster, MD: Newman, 1966.
Kaiser, Walter, Jr. *Toward an Old Testament Theology.* Grand Rapids, MI: Zondervan, 1978.
Kass, Leon R. "What's Wrong with Babel?" *American Scholar* 58 (1989) 41–60.
Keller, Timothy. *Every Good Endeavor.* London: Dutton, Penguin, 2012.

Kessler, Martin, and Karel Deurloo. *A Commentary on Genesis: The Book of Beginnings.* Mahwah, NJ: Paulist, 2004.

Kidner, D. *Genesis.* Tyndale Old Testament Commentaries. Downers Grove, IL: InterVarsity, 1967.

Koselleck, Reinhard. *Futures Past: On the Semantics of Historical Time.* Translated by Keith Tribe. Cambridge, MA: MIT Press, 1985.

Langer, Richard. "Niggle's Leaf and Holland's Opus: Reflctions on the Theological Significance of Work." *Evangelical Review of Theology* 33 (2009) 100–117.

Larive, Armand. *After Sunday: A Theology of Work.* New York: Continuum, 2004.

Leo XIII, Pope. "Rerum Novarum." In *The Papal Encyclicals 1878–1903*, edited by Claudia Carlen Ihm, 241–53. Raleigh, NC: McGrath, 1981.

Levine, Nachman. "The Curse and the Blessing: Narrative Discourse Syntax and Literary Form." *JSOT* 27 (2002) 189–99.

Lightfoot, J. B. *The Apostolic Fathers: Revised Texts with Short Introductions and English Translations.* London: Macmillan, 1893.

Linafelt, Tod. "Prolegomena to Meaning, or, What is 'Literary' About the Torah." *Theological Studies* 69 (2008) 62–79.

Lohfink, Norbert. *Great Themes from the Old Testament.* Translated by Ronald Walls. Edinburgh: T & T Clark, 1982.

Long, V. Phillips. *The Art of Biblical History.* Grand Rapids, MI: Zondervan, 1994.

———. "Historiography of the Old Testament." In *The Face of Old Testament Studies: A Survey of Contemporary Approaches*, edited by D. W. Baker and B. T. Arnold. Grand Rapids, MI: Baker, 1999.

Lunn, Nicholas P. "The Last Words of Jacob and Joseph: A Rhetorical-Structural Analysis of Genesis 49:29–33 and 50:24–26." *Tyndale Bulletin* 59 (2008) 161–80.

Luther, Martin. "Gospel for the Early Christmas Service, Luke 2:15–20." In *Luther's Works*, vol. 52. Philadelphia: Fortress, 1974.

———. *Lectures on Genesis, Chapters 6–14.* Translated by George V. Schick. In *Luther's Works*, vol. 2. Edited by Jaroslav Pelikan. St. Louis, MO: Concordia, 1960.

Macdonald, Nathan. "The Imago Dei and Election: Reading Genesis 1:26–28 and Old Testament Scholarship with Karl Barth." *IJST* 10 (2008) 303–27.

Mackenzie, Alistair. "Faith at Work: Vocation, the Theology of Work and the Pastoral Implications." Masters thesis, University of Otago, 1997.

Mackenzie, Alistair, and Wayne Kirkland. *Where's God on Monday?* Christchurch, NZL: NavPress, 2002.

Mackenzie, Alistair, et al. *Soul Purpose: Making a Differnce in Life and Work.* Christchurch, NZL: NavPress, 2004.

Marguerat, Daniel, and Yvan Bourquin. *How to Read Bible Stories.* Translated by John Bowden. London: SCM, 1999.

Marx, Karl. "Estranged Labor." In *Economic and Philosophic Manuscripts of 1844*, edited by Dirk J. Struik. New York: International, 1964.

Mathews, Kenneth. *Genesis 1—11:26.* New American Commentary 1A. Nashville, TN: Broadman & Holman, 1996.

———. *Genesis 11:27—50:26.* New American Commentary 1B. Nashville, TN: Broadman & Holman, 2005.

McArdle, Patrick. "The Relational Person within a Practical Theology of Healthcare." PhD thesis, Australian Catholic University, 2006.

McLelland, Joseph C. *The Other Six Days: The Christian Meaning of Work and Property.* Toronto: Thorn, 1959.
Mead, James K. *Biblical Theology: Issues, Methods, and Themes.* Louisville, KY: Westminster John Knox, 2007.
Miller, David W. *God at Work: The History and Promise of the Faith at Work Movement.* New York: Oxford University Press, 2007.
Miller, Patrick D. *Genesis 1–11: Studies in Structure and Theme.* JSOT Supplement Series 8. Sheffield, ENG: JSOT, 1984.
———. *Sin and Judgment in the Prophets: A Stylistic and Theological Analysis.* Chico, CA: Scholars, 1982.
Mitchell, Christopher Wright. *The Meaning of BRK "to Bless" in the Old Testament.* SBLDS 95. Atlanta, GA: Scholars, 1987.
Moltmann, Jürgen. *God in Creation.* Translated by Margaret Kohl. London: SCM, 1985.
Moore, Jeffery S. "A Theology of Work for Contemporary Christians." *Sewanee Theological Review* 36 (1993) 520–26.
Naidoff, Bruce D. "A Man to Work the Soil: A New Interpretation of Genesis 2–3." *JSOT* 3 (1978) 2–14.
Neusner, Jacob. "Work in Formative Judaism." In *The Encyclopaedia of Judaism* 4, edited by Jacob Neusner et al., 2829–43. Leiden, NLD: Brill, 2005.
Novak, Michael. "Creation Theology." In *Co-Creationism and Capitalism*, edited by J. W. Houck and O. F. Williams, 17–41. Lanham, MD: University Press of America, 1983.
Oldham, J. H. *Work in Modern Society.* London: SCM, 1950.
Oosterwal, Gottfried. *The Lord's Prayer.* Nampa, ID: Pacific, 2009.
Ouro, Roberto. "The Garden of Eden Account." *Andrews University Seminary Studies* 40 (2002) 219–43.
Pate, C. Marvin, et al. *The Story of Israel: A Biblical Theology.* Downers Grove, IL: InterVarsity, 2004.
Paul VI, Pope. "Gaudium et Spes." In *The Documents of Vatican II*, edited by Walter M. Abott, 199–308. London: Geoffrey Chapman, 1965.
Peterson, Eugene. *Working the Angles: The Shape of Pastoral Integrity.* Grand Rapids, MI: Eerdmans, 1993.
Placher, William C. *Callings: Twenty Centuries of Christian Wisdom on Vocation.* Grand Rapids, MI: Eerdmans, 2005.
Plaut, W. Gunther. *The Torah: A Modern Commentary; Genesis.* New York: Union of American Hebrew Congregations, 1974.
Preece, Gordon. "Callings." In *Theology of Work Project*, 2008. Accessed July 2010 at http://www.theologyofwork.org.
———. *Changing Work Values: A Christian Response.* Melbourne: Acorn, 1995.
———. "The Threefold Call: The Trinitarian Character of Our Everyday Vocations." In *Faith Goes to Work: Reflections from the Marketplace*, edited by Robert J. Banks. Washington, DC: Alban Institute, 1993.
Prewitt, T. J. *The Elusive Covenant: A Structural Semiotic Reading of Genesis.* Bloomington, IN: Indiana University Press, 1990.
Princip, Walter. *Encyclopaedia of Catholicism.* New York: HarperCollins, 1995.
Prothero, Stephen. *God is not One.* Melbourne: Black, 2010.
Purdue, Leo. *Biblical Theology: Introducing the Conversation.* Nashville, TN: Abingdon, 2009.

Rad, Gerhard von. *Genesis: A Commentary*. 2nd ed. The Old Testament Library. Translated by John H. Marks. London: SCM, 1961.
Rauschenbusch, Walter. *Christianity and the Social Crisis*. New York: Macmillan, 1907.
Ravid, Frederick. "Kebash: The Marital Commandment to Subdue the Earth." *Epiphany* 7 (1987) 66-70.
Redekop, Calvin W. "The Promise of Work." *Conrad Grebel Review* 1 (1983) 1-19.
Reno, Russell R. *Genesis*. Grand Rapids, MI: Brazos, 2010.
Reumann, John. *The Promise and Practice of Biblical Theology*. Minneapolis, MN: Fortress, 1991.
Reynaud, Daniel. *Reading with New Eyes: Exploring Scripture through Literary Genre*. Cooranbong, AUS: Avondale Academic, 2000.
Rice, Gene. "The Curse that Never Was." *Journal of Religious Thought* 29 (1972) 5-27.
Richardson, Alan. *The Biblical Doctrine of Work*. Ecumenical Biblical Studies 1. London: SCM, 1952.
———. *Genesis 1-11*. London: SCM, 1971.
Riches, John. "Reception History as a Challenge to Biblical Theology." *JTI* 7 (2013) 171-85.
———. "Why Write a Reception-Historical Commentary?" *JSNT* 2 (2007) 323-32.
Ricoeur, P. *From Text to Action: Essays in Hermeneutics*. London: Athlone, 1991.
Riddlebarger, Kim. *A Case for Amillennialism: Understanding the End Times*. Grand Rapids, MI: Baker, 2003.
Roberts, Jonathan. "Introduction to the Oxford Handbook of the Reception History of the Bible." In *The Oxford Handbook of the Reception History of the Bible*, edited by Michael Lieb et al. Oxford: Oxford Univeristy Press, 2011.
Rogerson, John W., et al. *Genesis and Exodus*. Sheffield, ENG: Sheffield Academic, 2001.
Ross, Allen P. "The Curse of Canaan: Studies in the Book of Genesis, Pt 1." *Bibliotheca Sacra* (1980) 223-40.
Rousseau, Jean-Jacques. *The Discourse and Other Early Political Writings*. Cambridge Texts in the History of Political Thought. Edited by Victor Gourevitch. Cambridge: Cambridge University Press, 1997.
Ryken, Leland. *Work and Leisure in Christian Perspective*. Leicester, ENG: InterVarsity, 1987.
Sailhamer, John H. "Genesis." In *Zondervan NIV Bible Commentary*, edited by K. L. Barker and J. R. Kohlenberger. Vol. 1, *Old Testament*. Grand Rapids, MI: Zondervan, 1994.
Sarna, Nahum. *Understanding Genesis*. New York: Schocken, 1966.
Schwartz, Regina. *The Curse of Cain: The Violent Legacy of Monotheism*. Chicago, IL: University of Chicago Press, 1997.
Scullion, John J. *Genesis: A Commentary for Students, Teachers, and Preachers*. Collegeville, MN: Liturgical, 1992.
———. "Genesis 1-11: An Interpretation." *St Marks Review* 122 (1985) 11-17.
Sheldon, Charles M. *In His Steps: What Would Jesus Do?* Westwood, NJ: Revell, 1967.
Skinner, J. *A Critical and Exegetial Commentary on Genesis*. 2nd ed. Edinburgh: T & T Clark, 1930.
Smith, Adam. *An Inquiry into the Nature and Causes of the Wealth of Nations* (1776). Reprint, Petersfield, ENG: Harriman, 2009.
Smith, Gary V. "Structure and Purpose in Genesis 1-11." *JETS* 20 (1977) 307-19.

Smith, Graeme W. "The Theology of Work in the Postwar Period." Masters thesis, University of Sydney, 1990.
Sommer, Benjamin D. "Old Testament Theology as the Dialectic of Salvation History and Creation: Claus Westermann." In *Biblical Theology: Introducing the Conversation*, edited by Leo Perdue et al. Nashville, TN: Abingdon, 2009.
Stambaugh, John E., and David L. Balch. *The New Testament in its Social Environment.* Library of Early Christianity. Edited by Wayne A. Meeks. Philadelphia, PA: Westminster, 1986.
Stark, Rodney. *The Rise of Christianity: How the Obscure, Marginal Jesus Movement Became the Dominant Religious Force in the Western World in a Few Centuries.* San Francisco, CA: Harper Collins, 1997.
Stefanovic, Ranko. *The Revelation of Jesus Christ: Commentary on the Book of Revelation.* Berrien Springs, MI: Andrews University Press, 2002.
Sternberg, Meir. *The Poetics of Biblical Narrative: Ideological Literature and the Drama of Reading.* Bloomington, IN: Indianna University Press, 1985.
Stevens, R. Paul. *Doing God's Business: Meaning and Motivation for the Marketplace.* Grand Rapids, MI: Eerdmans, 2006.
———. *The Other Six Days.* Grand Rapids, MI: Eerdmans, 1999.
———. *Work Matters: Lessons from Scripture.* Grand Rapids, MI: Eerdmans, 2012.
Stevens, R. Paul, and Alvin Ung. *Taking Your Soul to Work: Discovering the Nine Deadly Sins of the Workplace.* Grand Rapids, MI: Eerdmans, 2010.
Stewart, Claude Y. "Redoing the First Work of Adam: A Creation Conscious Perspective on Naming and Misnaming." *Encounter* 48 (1987) 351–66.
Stordalen, T. *Echoes of Eden: Genesis 2–3 and Symbolism of the Garden in Biblical Hebrew Literature.* Leuven, BEL: Peeters, 2000.
Stott, John R. W. *New Issues Facing Christians Today.* London: Marshall Pickering, 1999.
Tawney, R. H. *Religion and the Rise of Capitalism.* New York: New American Library, 1954.
Tertullian. "Apology." In *The Fathers of the Church* 10. New York: Benziger, 1950.
Thompson, Steven. "Abram, Sarai, Hagar (Genesis 16)." Unpublished manuscript, Avondale College, 2007.
———. "The Boundaries of Christian Hospitality in a Postmodern Setting." In *Exploring the Frontiers of Faith: Festschift in Honour of Dr Jan Paulsen*, edited by B. Schantz and R. Bruisma. Lueneburg, Germany: Advent-Verlag, 2009.
———. "Divine Work." Unpublished manuscript, Avondale College, 2010.
Thompson, Steven, and Elizabeth Ostring. "God's Labor of Love." Unpublished manuscript, Avondale College, 2014.
Tietz, Ryan. Review of *Where Sin Abounds: The Spread of Sin and the Curse in Genesis with Special Focus on the Patriarchal Narratives*, by Robert R. Gonzalez, Jr. *JETS* 54 (2011) 830–32.
Tonstad, Sigve K. *The Lost Meaning of the Seventh Day.* Berrien Springs, MI: Andrews Univeristy Press, 2009.
———. "The Message of the Trees in the Midst of the Garden." *JATS* 19 (2008) 82–97.
Trigg, Roger. *Ideas of Human Nature.* Oxford: Blackwell, 1988.
Troeltsch, Ernst. *Gesammelte Schriften.* Vol. 1, *Die Soziallehren der Christlichen Kirche.* Tübingen, DEU: Mohr, 1977.

Tsevat, Matitiahu. "The Meaning of the Biblical Sabbath." In *The Meaning of the Book of Job and Other Biblical Studies: Essays on the Literature and Religion of the Hebrew Bible*, edited by M. Tsevat. New York: KTAV, 1980.

Turner, Laurence A. *Announcements of Plot in Genesis*. Sheffield, ENG: JSOT, 1990.

———. *Back to the Present: Encountering Genesis in the 21st Century*. Grantham, ENG: Autumn, 2004.

———. *Genesis*. Sheffield, ENG: Sheffield Academic, 2000.

———. *Genesis*. 2nd ed. Sheffield, ENG: Sheffield Phoenix, 2009.

———. "Genesis." In *Dictionary of the Old Testament: Pentateuch*, edited by T. D. Alexander and D. W. Baker, 351. Downers Grove, IL: InterVarsity, 2003.

Vawter, Bruce. *On Genesis: A New Reading*. New York: Doubleday, 1977.

Venema, Cornelius P. Review of *God and Adam: Reformed Theology and the Creation Covenant*, by Rowland S. Ward. *Mid-America Journal of Theology* 14 (2003) 242–48.

Volf, Miroslav. *Work in the Spirit: Toward a Theology of Work*. Eugene, OR: Wipf & Stock, 2001.

Wagner, C. Peter. *The Church in the Workplace: How God's People Can Transform Society*. Ventura, CA: Regal, 2006.

Waltke, Bruce K. *Genesis: A Commentary*. Grand Rapids, MI: Zondervan, 2001.

Walvoord, John F. "Amillennialsm from Augustine to Modern Times." *Bibliotheca Sacra* 106 (1949) 420–31.

Ward, Keith. "Creatio Continua." In *Encyclopedia of Science and Religion*. 2003. Encyclopedia.com. Accessed July 24, 2014. http://www.encyclopedia.com/doc/1G2-3404200119.html.

Ward, Rowland S. *God and Adam: Reformed Theology and the Creation Covenant*. Melbourne: New Melbourne, 2003.

Weber, Max. *The Protestant Ethic and the Spirit of Capitalism*. Translated by Talcott Parsons. New York: Charles Scribner's Sons, 1958.

Wells, M. Jay. "Figural Representation and Canonical Unity." In *Biblical Theology: Retrospect and Prospect*, edited by Scott J. Hafemann. Downers Grove, IL: InterVarsity, 2002.

Wenham, Gordon J. *Genesis 1–15*. Vol. 1. Waco, TX: Word, 1987.

———. *Genesis 16–50*. Vol. 2. Dallas, TX: Word, 1994.

———. *Story as Torah*. Grand Rapids, MI: Baker Academic, 2000.

West, M. L. *The East Face of the Helicon*. New York: Oxford University Press, 1997.

Westermann, C. *Creation*. Philadelphia, PA: Fortress, 1974.

———. *Elements of Old Testament Theology*. Translated by Douglas W. Stott. Atlanta, GA: John Knox, 1982.

———. *Genesis 1–11: A Commentary*. Translated by John J. Scullion. Minneapolis, MN: Augsburg, 1984.

———. *Genesis 12–36: A Commentary*. Translated by John J. Scullion. Minneapolis, MN: Augsburg, 1985.

———. *Genesis 37–50: A Commentary*. Translated by John J. Scullion. Minneapolis, MN: Augsburg, 1986.

———. *Joseph: Studies of the Joseph Stories in Genesis*. Translated by Omar Kaste. Edinburgh: T & T Clark, 1996.

Wheen, Francis. *Karl Marx*. New York: W. W. Norton, 1999.

Wight, Jonathan B. "Introduction." In *An Inquiry into the Nature and Causes of the Wealth of Nations*. Petersfield, ENG: Harriman, 2009.

Williams, David T. "'Fill the Earth and Subdue It' (Gn 1:28): Dominion to Exploit and Pollute?" *Scriptura* 44 (1993) 51–65.

Witherington, Ben, III. *Work: A Kingdom Perspective on Labor*. Grand Rapids, MI: Eerdmans, 2011.

Wright, Christopher J. H. *Walking in the Ways of the Lord: The Ethical Authority of the Old Testament*. Downers Grove, IL: InterVaristy, 1995.

Yamauchi, Edwin M. "The Curse of Ham." *CTR* 6 (2009) 45–60.

Young, Richard Alan. *Is God a Vegetarian? Christianity, Vegetarianism and Animal Rights*. Peru, IL: Open Court, 1999.

Zornberg, Avivah Gottleib. *The Beginning of Desire: Reflections on Genesis*. New York: Doubleday, 1995.

www.ingramcontent.com/pod-product-compliance
Lightning Source LLC
Chambersburg PA
CBHW071244230426
43668CB00011B/1573